Italy and Albania

Italy and Albania: Financial Relations in the Fascist Period

Alessandro Roselli

With a Foreword by *Michael Kaser*

I.B.TAURIS
LONDON · NEW YORK

Published in 2006 by I.B.Tauris & Co. Ltd
6 Salem Road, London W2 4BU
175 Fifth Avenue, New York NY 10010
www.ibtauris.com

In the United States and Canada distributed by Palgrave Macmillan
a division of St Martin's Press
175 Fifth Avenue, New York NY 10010

Translated by Catherine Forner

Library of International Relations 29

ISBN 10: 1 84511 254 7
ISBN 13: 978 1 84511 254 7

A full CIP record for this book is available from the British Library
A full CIP record for this book is available from the Library of Congress

Library of Congress catalog card: available

Typeset in Plantin by Keystroke, Jacaranda Lodge, Wolverhampton
Printed and bound by TJ International Ltd, Padstow, Cornwall

To Daniela and Cesare, again

'. . . timeo Danaos et dona ferentes'
(Virgil, *Aeneid*, II, 49)

Contents

Figures and tables

Figures

Tables

Foreword

Roselli opens this book with a telling comparison: Albania's GDP per capita was a quarter of the Italian in the late 1920s, but is now one-thirteenth. The gap may otherwise be reflected as corresponding, during the inter-war period of which he writes, to the ratio between the two countries being today as India is to the United States, but then as Russia or South Africa is to the US. The decades 1919 to 1943, especially the latter five years when under Italian occupation as '*la Quinta Sponda d'Italia*' (the Fifth Shore of Italy) or part of *L'Italia d'Oltramare* (Overseas Italy), have been termed the 'Golden Age' of its economy, mostly attributable to the resources that Rome provided. On trade, Roselli cites Italian exports to Albania in the three years 1940 to 1942 as nine times the return flow of Italian imports and points out that the real trade balance was still larger because the prices at which Albanian agencies and firms bought in Italy were subsidized to be lower than market prices. Additional profits accrued in Albania, as he notes, because some of those subsidized goods were sold on by Albanian merchants to occupied Greece and Yugoslavia. On capital provision, Roselli shows public works in Albania in those years to have exceeded one billion Albanian francs and investment projects to have been planned which, postponed by hostilities, were implemented by the post-war Communist government – the Elbasan steel mill, the associated exploitation of iron and alloy ores and the country's first railways.

Italian resource flows had been smaller, though still substantial, during Albanian inter-war independence. Roselli cites Italian Foreign Minister Galeazzo Ciano as guaranteeing that expenditure in Albania would be 'borne by the Royal Exchequer' and calculates Italy's financial commitment to Albania to have cumulated by 1938 to 1.8 billion lire, which Roselli equates to 1.8 billion euros in today's money. Such long-run financial support more than offset the persistent trade deficit and allowed the Albanian gold franc to remain stable when world currencies devalued as the gold standard disintegrated in the early 1930s Depression. The currency even appreciated – in real terms the Albanian franc had by 1939 risen by 17 per cent with respect to the stabilized lire of 1927.

Economic dependence on Italy was crystallized in the incorporation in Rome of the new National Bank of Albania in September 1925 and the simultaneous establishment of the Società per lo Sviluppo Economico dell'Albania (SVEA). At the time President Zogu (within a year to designate himself King Zog) declared to the British Minister, Harry Eyres, 'Never will I fall into the hands of Italy.' Roselli records both this and the subsequently expressed objective of the Fascist Italian Foreign Ministry, 'to create potential outlets in Albania for our industrial produce and to get our hands on resources which are of use to us'. For the British reader this book is of particular interest for its exposition of the UK government's unremitting support for Italian penetration of the Albanian economy. As it shows, Italian financial dominance was contrary to the plan for Albanian economic stabilization laid down in a recommendation of September 1923 by the League of Nations Finance Committee (pursuing the League's major study, the Calmès Report of 1922) that an autonomous central bank be established with 75 per cent British, French and Italian equity and the remaining 25 per cent allotted for Belgian, Swedish and Dutch banks and Albanian individuals. The League of Nations Financial Adviser, Jan Hunger, was nevertheless soon dismissed by the Albanian Premier and, instead of replacing him, the League withdrew its interest in the bank's establishment. Roselli's blow-by-blow account of the subsequent Italian takeover is based, as are the many others in this book, on an exhaustive trawl of official and personal papers. Among novel facets is the revelation, in a despatch by the British Chargé d'affaires, Robert Parr, later Sir Robert and Consul-General in Lyons (where the author of this Introduction met him in 1954), that the eventually successful initiative was taken by a Fascist Party functionary, Alessandro Lessona, acting independently of the Palazzo Chigi and without even informing the Italian envoy to Albania, Marchese Durazzo. Another contribution to the real story is about a proposal to create an Albanian Development Corporation (an early use of a title much employed throughout the world after the Second World War) with private British funding. This failed – as Roselli explains – because of what the Foreign Office saw as the 'insufficient standing' of the promoters and 'the strong wish of the British government to appease the Italians'.

Another intermingling of Albanian with British economic history is the Bank of England's custodianship of the gold reserve of the National Bank of Albania, to which Roselli devotes his closing chapter. This must be seen as the definitive academic analysis, previous detailed documentation having all been governmental. Apart from a small stock (64.4 kilograms) held in the Bank's branches in Durrës and Tiranë, the bulk of the gold (2,340.8 kilograms) was deposited in Rome – at its own premises, at the Italian Mint (for coining the Albanian gold franc) and at the Bank of Italy. In September 1943 all the gold was removed by the occupying German army to the vaults of the Reichsbank in Berlin, and later hidden in a potassium mine in Merkers (Thüringia). In April 1945 rumours of it reached Allied officers, who found the hoard of gold, silver, platinum, banknotes and looted valuables. Most of the gold was transferred to the Bank of England, some to the Federal Reserve Bank of New York and its aegis confided to a Tripartite Commission of the British, French and US governments. Roselli's research furnishes the authoritative history of the 'international debates which lasted for the entire Cold War period'. To the study of what was arguably the longest-running 'incident' of the Cold War, the book is an invaluable contribution.

Roselli places his meticulous search of Italian and international archives into the historical context of three significant periods – until around 1925, world expectations were that the League of Nations would apply a new ethos to small states through political protection and economic assistance, as it did to Albania; from then until the Second World War, Fascist/Nazi power strengthened in Europe, drawing Albania into Italy's 'Mare Nostrum'; and on the eve of and during the war, Fascist/Nazi power spread Continent-wide, embodied for Albania in military enforcement of a 'union of the two crowns' and the expulsion of King Zog, Queen Geraldine and the infant Prince Leka (later the Royal Pretender in a failed 1997 coup), who set up court in Britain. If an examination of Albanian archives is absent – Roselli cites a book by the National Bank and a 1984 study by Albanian's leading economic historians, Iljaz Fishta and Veniamin Toci – it could be because little new would be found there, the economic decision power residing in Rome. This book, now available in two major languages, may stimulate further scholarly enquiry in Albania itself.

Michael Kaser,
Emeritus Fellow of St Antony's College,
University of Oxford;
Honorary Professor, University of Birmingham

Preface

It has been authoritatively observed that some of the major challenges facing Albania at the beginning of the new millennium remain the same as those it faced during most of the twentieth century, namely: a level of poverty which places Albania well below most other European countries; a continuous need for external resources; a social framework which is deeply fragmented along geographical and clan lines; and an exceptionally stable currency.[1]

As in the early 1920s, we have recently witnessed a multilateral approach to Albania's financial issues (on the part of the International Monetary Fund recently, and the League of Nations in the 1920s) and the country's subsequent difficulty in servicing its external debt. Then, as now, this financial support was directed towards a substantially new political situation. At that time, the country was emerging from the collapse of the Ottoman Empire; now it is finding stability after the end of the Stalinist regime in 1991.

Albania consistently ranks bottom in the table of European per capita incomes. Its remarkable economic performance of recent years cannot hide the fact that, for example, the gap between Albania's GDP and that of its big neighbour Italy is much higher today than in the late 1920s. At that time, Italy's GDP per capita was four times higher; now it is 13 times the Albanian GDP.[2] The mass migration and pyramid schemes that occurred in the 1990s have their roots in the country's continuing backwardness.

The deeply entrenched north–south divide, symbolized at that time by the fight between Ahmet Zogu, the northern bey, and Fan Noli, the southern bishop, is reflected to some extent nowadays in a party political conflict which sometimes threatens to overstep the boundaries of democratic parliamentary debate.

As in the 1920s, Albania is emerging once again as an important reference point in Italian foreign policy, both because of its geographical proximity (which, among other things, has made Italy a particularly attractive destination for Albanians migrating towards the countries of the

European Union) and because of the new opportunities which the collapse of Communism has opened up to foreign economic initiatives. The fields of banking, oil exploitation and public works are attracting Italy's interest again, and once again Italy is Albania's main trade partner. In the early 1990s, this sort of rediscovery of Albania led an Italian newspaper to argue that Albania could perhaps become Italy's 21st region, or 'the Italian DDR'.[3]

As the present book amply demonstrates, an understanding between the major European powers of the 1920s shifted the responsibility for financial and more general support of the young Albanian state away from the multilateral basis of the League of Nations to a bilateral basis, namely to Italy. This is where any comparison with the past should stop, and the previous unequal relationship between the two countries should remain purely a source of historical interest. The opinion that 'the rapport between Zogu and Italy serves as a paradigm which sheds light on relations between Albanians and Italians even beyond the inter-war period'[4] should be taken with a pinch of salt.

Since 1986, when the Italian version of this book was published, an increasing number of studies on Albanian issues has accumulated, prompted no doubt by the regime change and its consequences. Political, economic and social themes and their connections on the one hand with the wider Balkan crisis and on the other with prospective integration with Western Europe have been amply researched and debated.

This close attention to current issues has not been matched by a corresponding increase of interest in the country's history. For the whole period following Hoxha's death (and, coincidentally, the earlier version of this book), published works focusing specifically on Albania's history have been relatively few, although the Balkan countries in general have received wider attention (within these works dedicated to the Balkan region, Albania remains somewhat peripheral). This is even truer for the economic history of Albania, a somewhat esoteric and relatively unexplored field.

For this reason, the structure of this book has not substantially changed, although I have greatly benefited from certain published sources, as the list of references shows. The main amendments and additions to the book are not particularly related to recent historical literature. They are due to the wider access I have been able to gain to primary sources, particularly British archive records. These have been enlightening from two points of view. Firstly, they have given a better understanding of relations between Britain and Italy in the crucial earlier phase in relations with Zogu. What clearly emerges is the appeasement policy adopted by the British towards Mussolini's ambitions, Britain's gradual disentanglement from Albania, and how financial support for the country was shifted from the League of Nations and channelled into the complicated web of relations between states. Secondly, the archive sources now enable us to fully reconstruct the tangled history of the gold from Albania's reserves over the Cold War period, a topic which lies outside the main body of this research but which can be seen as a follow-up to the history of the inter-war period and again focuses on the conflicting interests of the three countries of Albania, Italy and the United Kingdom.

A *communis opinio* tends to see a close link between the Albanian question and Fascism and to consider Albania as a kind of Fascist trophy, a positive exception to the otherwise disastrous revisionist policies of the Fascists in the Balkan region. On the basis of the documentation I have consulted, however, I find it difficult to share this opinion, especially looking at the question from a financial viewpoint. It is also hard to support the idea that Albania's constitutional, financial and monetary structure, as it stood after the Italian occupation, was the inevitable outcome of foreign and financial policies which were consciously designed by the Fascist regime. The Albanian question had existed well before the advent of Fascism, in fact even before Albania proclaimed itself, shortly after the first decade of the century, as a formally independent state, and had grown primarily from the realization that, amid the evident collapse of the Ottoman Empire, a region strategically situated at the entrance to the Adriatic could not help but become an important focal point for foreign policies, notably that of Italy.

Whilst all aware of the importance of this impoverished region, Italian politicians nonetheless adopted quite varying attitudes towards the Albanian problem, and Italian foreign policy oscillated between two lines. The first took into account the strength and ripeness of Albanian nationalist feeling and supported the country's independence and territorial integrity, except perhaps for keeping possession of certain strategic positions and encouraging an openness to Italian economic influence. The second was in favour of partitioning the country, and in-between the two was the policy supported by those who, whilst wishing Albania to be independent, attempted to procure Italian 'protection' for the young state. Mussolini's foreign policy, grafted as it was on to nationalistic trends, dismissed Giolitti's approach of disengagement, but nonetheless relied for several years on economic penetration into the country, with a view on the one hand to procuring a net benefit for the Italian economy and on the other to keeping King Zog as a faithful and unconditional ally. We can say with certainty that neither of these goals was reached. Leaving aside the second of the two, of which political and diplomatic history have provided ample evidence, this research aims to highlight the fact that, especially in the period immediately preceding the Italian occupation, the huge financial commitment made by Italy in Albania did not produce the results which had been expected. Italy received no benefit, either in terms of its balance of trade, since the funds flowing into Albania were largely used on purchases from third countries, thus financing the large current account deficit in Albania's balance of payments, or in terms of privileged access, in the dual sense of 'exclusive' and 'low-cost', to the land's natural resources, especially its raw materials and agricultural produce.[5] From this last point of view, the hope of seeing Albania functionally integrated into Italy's development process, mainly via the provision of raw materials, especially oil, was certainly disappointed. Furthermore, King Zog was a very bad debtor for Italy. He sucked up massive loans which he essentially failed to repay, partly because of the pressure which servicing the loans would have put on Albania's economy and partly out of a knowledge that his failure to service them was the price Italy was paying to keep him within its own sphere of influence. This unsatisfactory state of financial relations provides an opening for and a partial but important key to understanding the events of the late 1930s, that is, the end of Albania's independence and the creation of a 'lira area' (which, although tiny, is technically interesting from the point of view of financial history), before the turbulent events of the war put a definitive end to the Italian presence.

I would like to say a few words about the method (if this is not too pretentious a word) I have followed throughout this study, which to experts on monetary history will seem to concentrate too much on events and specific actions rather than on working out economic and financial aggregates, and hence be essentially descriptive and institutional, while to readers of 'traditional' history it will seem weighed down by figures and statistics and economic jargon, at the expense of a more in-depth political and diplomatic look at events. What I have actually tried to do is primarily to place in chronological order the material at my disposal and then to give an answer to some thematic issues. I have focused the content of my research more on the individual and the specific than on the collective and the analytical. Though the study may seem to oscillate between these two poles and if the end product is somewhat hybrid, I would like to point out that this was the result of a conscious choice, stemming from an aim to show not just the wood, but also the trees. I would also like to add that, personally, I empathize with the sense of disappointment generated in the reader by historical accounts which rely excessively on economic models and often seem deterministic.

Finally, the study contains numerous references to political and diplomatic aspects of the wider scene, many of which actually pre-date the period on which I have concentrated. These references are aimed at giving the reader, who is not expected to be aware of all the facets of the question, at least some grasp of events which can give a better perspective on and understanding of the individual moments described in this research. Of course, these references lay no claim whatsoever to originality or completeness and should be taken purely in the 'utilitarian' sense I have just described.

The research can be divided into three successive phases. The first deals with the pre-Fascist and, for Albania, the pre-Zogu era (Zogu and Mussolini came to power at almost the same time). It demonstrates Italy's growing interest in the country from the turn of the century onwards, witnessed on an economic level by a marked increase in trade between the two, which was accompanied by a soaring surplus on Italy's side. This phase actually extends to the immediate post-war years, which see Italy under Giolitti going through a period of disengagement from Albania, and the emerging interest of the League of Nations, especially on a financial level, and with it the potential to set the problem of the region's economic development on a multilateral footing.

The second phase covers the years from the Fascists' ascent to power to the Italian occupation. The problem of Albania's economy, which could potentially have been dealt with at an international level under the aegis of the League of Nations,[6] became essentially bilateral. As I emphasized above, this period cannot however be viewed as the fulfilment over time of a conscious political plan of Mussolini's, but rather as the result of a complex series of circumstances, and full of diversity. In the beginning, the relatively moderate approach of the Fascists' foreign policy favoured, as I have said, an essentially economic-based penetration of Albania. The above-mentioned unsatisfactory results of this strategy, combined with a much more aggressive approach to foreign policy in the 1930s and with the need to confront growing German encroachment in the Balkan sector, led to a radical change in the situation.

The third phase, which came into being with the union of the Italian and Albanian crowns, brought Albania definitively into Italy's financial system, within an institutional framework which was totally different from the previous one, to the point where Guarneri, the Minister for Currency and Foreign Exchange, viewed Albanian affairs as being outside his remit.[7] The period of the 'lira area' is too brief to be able to give an exhaustive assessment of its consequences. Partly due to the war, it brought an increase in the exploitation of the country's resources, especially its minerals, to Italy's advantage. In spite of this, even though we are lacking in relevant statistics, we can certainly say that no process of economic integration took place between Albania and Italy, based in any way on complementary aspects of the two economic systems. Even the advantages which Italy gained in the trade relationship with Albania remained lower than the amount of financial resources it had deployed in the country. At the other end, no real development took place in the Albanian economy, which remained in a state of backwardness.

In order to make the figures given in this book less abstract, I have tried to convert some of them into today's money (euros), taking past exchange and inflation rates into account. It goes without saying that the results of this exercise should be viewed with a good deal of caution.

The shift from 'Zogu' to 'Zog' in the text is not casual. I refer to Ahmet bey Zogu before 1928 and to Zog thereafter (this being the name he took in 1928, when he was crowned as King of the Albanians).

The list of acknowledgements should necessarily start with the people who helped me with comments or suggestions regarding the earlier, Italian version of this book: the late professors Renzo De Felice and Enrico Serra; and then Pierluigi Ciocca and Francesco Alfonso of the Bank of Italy, and Pietro Pastorelli of La Sapienza University in Rome.

In connection with this updated version of the book, I am grateful to the following people: Paolo Garofalo of the Bank of Italy for his comments, particularly on the statistical sections; Stuart Allen and Sarah Millard of the Bank of England, Andrew Plummer-Rodriguez of the Foreign and Commonwealth Office, Piet Clement of the Bank for International Settlements and Isabella Cerioni of the Bank of Italy for their archival assistance; Kastriot Robo of the Albanian Embassy, Bejtullah Destani of the Centre for Albanian Studies, in London, and Tanush Frashëri for their support and encouragement; and Flaminia Tamburro, Daniela Lim and Anna Archer of the London office of the Bank of Italy for their involvement in preparing the electronic format of the manuscript. Finally, without the work of Catherine Forner, who had the task of reconciling my Italian 'ornate' phrasing with English conciseness, this version of the book would have never been born.

Chronology

	Political events	Economic/financial events
28 November 1912	Declaration of independence by the National Congress of Albania	
29 July 1913	The Ambassadors' Conference recognises Albania's independence	
1913		First attempt to create an Albanian central bank
22 February 1914	Prince Wilhelm Von Wied accepts the crown of Albania	
3 September 1914	Prince Wilhelm leaves Albania	
2 August 1920	Italo-Albanian protocol: Italy leaves Albania (with the exception of the island of Saseno)	
17 December 1920	Albania's entry into the League of Nations	
9 November 1921	The Ambassadors' Conference recognises a special relationship between Italy and Albania	
September 1922		Publication of the Calmès report
December 1922	Ahmet Zogu becomes Prime Minister	

	Political events	Economic/financial events
April 1923		The League of Nations appoints a Financial Adviser to Albania, J. Hunger
31 August 1923		Hunger report to the League
4 September 1923		League's plan to create an Albanian bank of issue, followed by Wallenberg's (failed) attempts to raise money in London for that purpose
November 1923		Zogu's sale of Mat woods to the Ferrovie dello Stato
20 January–29 February 1924		Trade agreement and settlement convention between Italy and Albania
February 1924		Hunger's dismissal by the Albanian government
27 March 1924		League's 'green light' to Italy for the establishment of a bank of issue in Albania
April 1924		British reluctance to participate in the bank
June 1924	Fan Noli's revolt	
December 1924	Zogu regains power	
January 1925	Albania, born as a principate, becomes a Republic, with Zogu as President	
February 1925		Attempts, by a private British group, to create a bank of issue in Albania (later dismissed by the British government)
24 February 1925		Mario Alberti, head of the Italian financial group, arrives in Albania
2 March 1925		Zogu grants the Anglo-Persian Oil Company an oil concession

12 March 1925		Zogu grants a similar concession to the Ferrovie dello Stato
15 March 1925		Agreement between the Albanian government and the Italian financial group for the creation of the central bank and for granting a loan
23 June–5 July 1925		The Albanian parliament approves the Agreement, and the laws for the National Bank and the Monetary Organisation
2 September 1925		The National Bank of Albania is incorporated in Rome and SVEA is established, as a vehicle for the Italian loan
27 November 1926	Italo-Albanian pact of friendship and security	
22 November 1927	Treaty of Tiranë between Italy and Albania	
21 December 1927		Italian lira stabilisation ('quota novanta')
1 September 1928	Zogu becomes King, as King Zog of the Albanians	
3 May 1930		Albanian land reform law
1931		New Italian loan to Albania
March 1932		Italo-Albanian negotiations for a customs union
1933		Interruption of the 1931 loan. Failure of the customs union negotiations
1935	Reapprochment of Albania to Italy	
28 August 1935		The shares of the National Bank of Albania, following a Royal Decree, are concentrated at INCE (an Italian government agency)
November 1935	Albania doesn't join the League's sanctions to Italy for the Ethiopian war	

	Political events	**Economic/financial events**
19 March 1936		'Package' of new Italian financial assistance to Albania
5 October 1936		Lira devaluation of 40.94%
7–8 April 1939	Italy's occupation of Albania. Flight of Zog	
16 April 1939	King Victor Emmanuel III becomes King of Albania	
20 April 1939		Economic, customs and currency union between Italy and Albania
15 May 1939		Foreign exchange monopoly given to the National Bank of Albania
8 September 1943	Capitulation of Italy and occupation of Albania by Nazi troops	
16 September 1943	Removal of the National Bank of Albania's gold reserve from Rome, by the Nazis	
6 April 1944	Nazi-Albanian agreement on the Albanian gold	
17 November 1944	End of the German occupation of Albania	
13 January 1945		An Albanian law transfers all the assets and liabilities of the National Bank to the new State Bank
14 January 1946	Paris Agreement on German reparations	
27 September 1946	Creation of the Tripartite Gold Commission (TGC) including Britain, France and the United States	
22 October 1946	Corfu Channel incident	
21 May 1947	Italian claim on the Albanian gold presented to the TGC	

15 September 1947	Similar Albanian claim
16 December 1947	Italy admitted to the Gold Pool
14 February–30 June 1948	Two preliminary gold allocations, by the 1948 TGC, to Albania
9 April 1949	The International Court of Justice rules that Albania is responsible for the Corfu Channel incident
11 July 1949	Allocations suspended by the TGC
17 November 1950	Allocations revoked
25 April 1951	Washington Agreement between Britain, France and the United States: the Albanian gold question is submitted to an arbitrator
20 February 1953	According to the arbitrator, the gold belongs to Albania
19 May 1953	Italian appeal
15 June 1954	The International Court of Justice rules on the Italian appeal that it is incompetent to judge
9 June 1958	Further TGC's gold allocation to Albania (gold not delivered)
29 October 1996	Gold delivered to Albania
2–4 December 1997	Nazi Gold Conference in London
13 July 1998	Residual gold distribution to Albania

Albanian Prime Ministers, and Italian and British diplomatic envoys to Albania (1913–1943)

Albania

1912–1913	Ismail Qemal Bey Vlora
1914–1920	Turhan Pasha Përmeti
1920	Sulejman Bey Delvina
1920–1921	Iljas Bey Vrioni
1921	Pandeli Evangjeli
1921	Qazim Koculi
1921	Hasan Bey Prishtina
1921	Idhomene Kosturi
1921–1922	Xhafer Bey Ypi
1922–1924	Ahmet Bey Zogu
1924	Shefqet Bey Vërlaci
1924	Iljas Bey Vrioni
1924	Fan S. Noli
1924–1925	Iljas Bey Vrioni
1925–1928	Ahmet Bey Zogu
1928–1930	Koço (Kostaq) Kota
1930–1935	Pandeli Evangjeli
1935–1936	Mehdi Bey Frashëri
1936–1939	Koço Kota
1939–1942	Shefqet Bey Vërlaci
1942–1943	Mustafa Merlika Kruja
1943	Eqerem Bey Libohova
1943	Maliq Bey Bushati
1943	Eqerem Bey Libohova
1943	Provisional Executive Committee: Ibrahim Bey Biçaku, President, Bedri Bey Pejani, Xhafer Deva, Vehbi Bey Frashëri, Mihal Zallari, Eqrem Telhaj.

Italy

1914	Carlo Aliotti
1922	Marquis Carlo Durazzo
1926	Baron Pompeo Aloisi
1927	Ugo Sola
1930	Antonio Meli Lupi di Soragna
1932	Ottavio A. Koch
1934	Mario Indelli
1936	Francesco Jacomoni di San Savino

United Kingdom

1913–1916	Harry Harling Lamb (British Commissioner on the International Commission of Control in Albania)
1916–1921	vacant
1921	Harry C. A. Eyres
1926	William E. O'Reilly
1926	William Seeds
1928	Sir Robert MacLeod Hodgson
1936	Sir Andrew Ryan

CHAPTER 1

Italy and Albania, 1900–1920

Albania's economic and social situation, and the attitudes of Italy and Austria in the first decade of the century

At the beginning of the last century, Albania was still part of the Ottoman Empire. Its population was fragmented along the various lines of its tribes, dialects, religions and varying degrees of openness to progress.

In particular, the tribal structure of the inhabitants of the mountainous region to the north of the country (the 'Ghegs', who were rough and warlike) had been left almost untouched by the Ottoman presence. They enjoyed considerable autonomy and exemption from taxes, and were only obliged to supply soldiers to the Sublime Porte in times of war. The peoples to the south of the River Shkumbin (the 'Tosks', more sober and refined in nature) were more open and progressive. The population of the area is difficult to assess. The statistics furnished by the Turkish authorities were based on religion (the standard classification used by the Turks being simply that of 'Muslim' and 'non-Muslim') and were misleading, because entire localities failed to register, in order to avoid military conscription. An estimate by the London Conference of 1913, which recognized the country's independence, placed the population figure in the order of nearly 2 million. The huge losses of life during the First World War and especially the devastation of Southern Albania by the Greeks in 1914 lowered that estimate, for the years following the war, to 1.5 million people. According to another estimate, over a territory of 28,748 square kilometres (based on the frontiers defined after the First World War), the population at the end of 1920 was nearly 803,000.

In religious terms, according to estimates relating to the early 1920s, the population was made up of 70 per cent Muslims (as a result of centuries of Turkish domination), around 20 per cent Orthodox, concentrated in the south, around 10 per cent Catholics in the north, and a small minority of other faiths, including Jewish.

The existence of a large Muslim majority was not an obstacle to widespread religious tolerance. This was partly due to the influence of two secondary but influential groups: the Bektashis, or reformed Muslims (whose members constituted a large part of the Muslim population), largely liberal and free-thinkers, with a belief imbued with humanitarian philosophy; and a pseudo-Muslim group in Central Albania, who were both Christians and Muslims at the same time: inwardly Christian, whilst outwardly Muslim, for fear of persecution by the Porte.

It was therefore geographically the smallest region in the Balkans but also the least densely populated (27.9 inhabitants per square kilometre in 1920). Ownership of large estates was widespread and the landowning class of the beys was powerful, often served by their own small armies and frequently in conflict with the Sultan, who attempted to break their power by imposing new taxes and compulsory military service. Next to the beys, the Ottoman state was the largest landowner, owning 36,500 acres in the early twentieth century.[1]

The main economic effect of Turkish domination can be summed up in the word 'stagnation'. The Turks gave Albania neither schools nor roads, nor in fact any benefit whatsoever, and left it essentially in the state in which they had found it in the fifteenth century.[2] However, social conditions differed somewhat between Northern, Central and Southern Albania. In the north, feudalism – introduced there in the Middle Ages by the Normans – blended with the peculiar clan organization of the local people. The Porte constantly played the major families against each other in order to subjugate the area, but there were in fact places which the Turks were never able to enter, such as the Muslim territory of Mat (from which Zogu came) or the Catholic district of Mirditë. Going southward, a more developed environment tended to prevail. Central Albania was characterized by the freehold system of land ownership, the largest lands belonging to the Toptani and Vrioni families.[3] More educated and democratic people were to be found in the area closest to Greece, thanks also to good educational establishments such as Turkish and Greek schools in Korçë, Vlorë and Gjirokastër.[4]

It is outside the scope of this study to discuss the formation of the fervent Albanian nationalist movement and its struggle to assert itself in the face both of the ancient internal divisions outlined above and of the external threats posed not only by the Turkish authorities but also by the expansionist policies of its neighbours Serbia, Montenegro and Greece. I shall also omit the detailed politics of the creeping interest in Albanian affairs shown by Italy on the one hand and Austria-Hungary on the other. The final years of the nineteenth century in fact saw the seeds of a confrontation between these two powers in the Western Balkans, notably in Albania, which 'added fuel to the latent antagonism dating back to Italy's Risorgimento, which was in time to corrode the links, within the Triple Alliance, between Rome and Vienna'.[5]

So, whilst Austria-Hungary saw Albania's acquisition of independence as a barrier to the 'Panslavist' movement and to the expansion into the Balkans of Serbia and Montenegro, Italy saw Albania as a suitable base for expanding its own interests within South-Eastern Europe, given its strategic position at the entrance to the Adriatic but also its potential for economic involvement. The third major power with an interest in Albania was Russia, though its approach was different, as it aimed to extend its own influence in the Balkans by supporting the expansionist policies of the Slavic states.

If we take a closer look from an economic angle at the antagonism between Rome and Vienna over the Balkans at the turn of the century, the most striking fact is that the Italian presence was much more dynamic. The Balkan region was in effect, at least in economic terms, a 'missed opportunity' for Austria-Hungary. As has been noted,[6] with its exports suffering under growing competition from Germany, Austria-Hungary could easily have turned to the less developed Balkan economies as prime candidates for its investments and exports. There are two reasons why this did not happen: on the one hand, the industrial developments in Czechoslovakia and Hungary at the turn of the century were drawing on the dual monarchy's dwindling capital; on the other, the major Viennese banks, hit hard by the stock market collapse of 1873, were still reluctant to invest in new enterprises, preferring to invest more safely in state bonds and ventures, which were traditionally sound.[7]

Italy, however, was starting to look for economic outlets in the Near East. In Webster's opinion, this tendency to turn to the East, that is to the Balkans and Asia Minor, rather than to the South, was a salient feature of Italy's imperialism, and dominated its expansionist plans even before the First World War (the African colonies were of minor importance for the Italian economy). A credible explanation for this tendency can be found not simply in the need to find employment opportunities and commercial outlets, which at the most created a favourable climate and a series of secondary motives, but more in the future of Italian heavy industry itself. In the context of an international field which was at the same time protectionist and highly competitive, the Balkans and the Ottoman Empire offered extraordinary scope as a market both for Italian products and for opportunities in the areas of electrification, transport, port construction, land reclamation and agricultural development.[8]

These general observations certainly seem to be true in the case of Albania, if we consider the Italian initiatives which were already being carried out, or in the main attempted, in Albania before the Ottoman presence began to wane. These initiatives were mainly in the areas of gaining concessions for land exploitation, and building transport infrastructures for rail and sea, as well as in a strengthening of commercial ties, at the expense of Austria's trade with Albania.

Recent historiography on the subject has focused on the enterprises of a group of Italians led by Giacomo Vismara from Bologna, which involved the Banca Commerciale Italiana and then the Bank of Italy itself. This group, with the help of government concessions, aimed to exploit the forests of Central Albania, but also to carry out land reclamation, bridge building and railway projects. The outbreak of war in Libya, however, meant that they did not come to fruition.[9]

Another project which remained dormant was for a railway line across the Balkans to the Adriatic, which would have had to cross Albanian territory, and for which a large share of the funding was to come from Italian capital (a banking syndicate headed by the Credito Mobiliare Italiano was set up for the purpose). This project was one of the many planned by the major powers at the turn of the century as a means of penetrating the Balkan peninsula, economically and otherwise. It never saw daylight, however, as I have mentioned, first because Turkey did not approve of this intervention, and second because the Italian credit institutions had strong doubts about the Italian market being able to cope with the bonds necessary to finance the project.[10]

What did come to fruition was the provision of regular maritime services between the Italian and Albanian ports, operated by the shipping company Puglia, which together with the company Navigazione Generale linked the two shores of the Adriatic, in competition with the Austro-Hungarian lines Lloyd, Adria, Ungaro-Croata and Ragusea.[11]

The clearest picture we can get of Italy's expanding role in the Albanian economy and of its competition with Austria-Hungary comes undoubtedly from the trade statistics. The volume *L'Albania Economica*[12] provides a series of trade data from 1900 onwards which, although extremely fragmented and incomplete, nevertheless provide some useful information on the subject.

The incomplete nature of the data stems primarily from the fact that Albania had not yet gained its independence and the notion of its territory was therefore very hazy and without clearly defined frontiers. The data are also based exclusively on the territory known as 'Lower Albania', the western part of the country, taken to include a part of Epirus, with the city of Janina, which was to become part of Greece under the subsequent drawing of boundaries for the new state.

In spite of its incompleteness, Table 1.1 highlights several points:

(a) Despite still being part of the Ottoman Empire, Albania did not rely on Turkey for the bulk of its imports at the beginning of the 1900s, but on the Austro-Hungarian Empire.

Table 1.1 Imports into Lower Albania, 1900–1910 (in thousands of Italian lire)

	1900	1904	1907	1910
Austria-Hungary	2,035	1,723	1,696	1,739
Turkey	1,581		1,335	
France	953		434	
Great Britain	900		787	
Italy	438	1,709	2,960	3,787
	5,907		7,212	

Source: *L'Albania economica*, based on data from the Italian Commercial Agency in Janina.

(b) In the space of seven years, Italy rose from barely fifth place in the league of exporters to Lower Albania into first place, while all the other countries saw a drop both in their relative quota and in the absolute value of their exports to Albania and, most notably, Austria slipped into second place as commercial partner.

(c) Over a ten-year period, we see a contrast between a reduction in imports from Austria (–14.5 per cent) and a huge increase in Italian imports (+764.6 per cent). If we look only at the first seven years of the century, which are the only years for which we possess more complete statistics, we see that it is precisely the marked increase in Lower Albania's imports from Italy which boosts the total of the imports (+22 per cent) from all the countries in question.

As for exports from Lower Albania, looking only at those into Austria-Hungary and Italy (which are the only ones for which we have relevant data), we see a similar process occurring, that is preferential relations being transferred over the years from Austria to Italy.

As Table 1.2 shows, it is in 1907 again that Italy overtakes Austria as a destination for Albanian goods, while from 1904 onwards exports to Austria steadily decrease. Overall, over a ten-year period, there is a 20.8 per cent decrease in Albanian exports to the Habsburg Empire and a 348.6 per cent increase in exports to Italy.

Table 1.2 Exports from Lower Albania, 1900–1910 (in thousands of Italian lire)

	1900	1904	1907	1910
Austria-Hungary	1,713	2,770	1,473	1,356
Italy	988	1,798	2,210	4,432

Source: See Table 1.1.

Another interesting set of statistics for this period is one that relates to Lower Albania's balance of trade in relation to Italy and Austria-Hungary.

If we assume, as Table 1.1 would suggest, that the two nations of Italy and Austria-Hungary were the most consistent players in Albania's foreign trade, then studying its overall import–export exchanges with these countries can give us a clear enough picture of Lower Albania's balance of trade in the first decade of the century.

If we compare the figures in Table 1.3 with the figures relating to the entire post-war period, and especially those of the Fascist era which is our primary concern here, they are somewhat surprising.

They actually demonstrate a consistent surplus in the balance of trade with Italy (except in 1907). The surplus is even large enough to compensate for the deficit in the balance with Austria-Hungary and thus to keep the overall balance of trade between Lower Albania and the other two countries on the plus side (remembering that these two countries represented a considerable portion of Albania's entire foreign trade). The surplus in Albanian foreign trade – which even a cautious reading of the above figures demonstrates – is in sharp contrast with the chronic deficit which plagues the current account of Albania's balance of payments during the Fascist period.

It is worth stressing again, however, that the figures in Table 1.3 are only partial, covering only certain years and certain countries and referring only to one part of the Albanian territory, and we should therefore be very careful in using them as reliable evidence. Other figures which are set out in Table 1.4 and relate to the territory known as Upper Albania – the higher

Table 1.3 Lower Albania's balance of trade, 1900–1910 (in thousands of Italian lire)

	1900	1904	1907	1910
A) Italy:				
Exports	988	1,798	2,210	4,432
Imports	438	1,709	2,960	3,787
Balance	+550	+89	–750	+645
B) Austria-Hungary:				
Exports	1,713	2,770	1,473	1,356
Imports	2,035	1,723	1,696	1,739
Balance	–322	+1,047	–223	–383
C) A+B:				
Exports	2,701	4,568	3,683	5,788
Imports	2,473	3,432	4,656	5,526
Balance	+228	+1,136	–973	+262

Source: See Table 1.1.

Table 1.4 Imports into Upper Albania, 1910–1911 (in thousands of Italian lire)

	1910	1911
Austria-Hungary	3,592	5,191
Italy	1,952	2,136

Source: See Table 1.1.

region in the interior of the country – do not in fact match up with the previous ones, though being so sparse they cannot lead to any significant conclusions.

These few figures simply highlight a much stronger take-up of Austro-Hungarian exports in this region of the country, but say nothing of any exports out of Albania. Moreover, since they only cover two consecutive years, they are not able to identify any consistent trends in foreign trade in that part of the territory.[13]

Further still, as there are no statistics available on the country's income (which, as we shall see, will pose problems when researching the entire period investigated in the present study), it is not possible to establish how open the Albanian economy was towards other countries and, more precisely, how far, in the decade in question, its peripheral location in the Ottoman Empire, and its proximity to more 'modern' countries such as Italy and the Austro-Hungarian Empire, influenced the volume of the territory's imports and exports, in relation to its own income.

We can, however, make two further observations on the period in question, and they concern the influence which important political events had on the Albanian territory's foreign trade. The first was that the annexing in 1908 of Bosnia-Herzegovina to the Austro-Hungarian Empire (the two territories had been handed over to Austria-Hungary to administer by the Treaty of Berlin of 1878) and the ensuing strong political tension between this empire and the Sublime Porte led to a boycott, even in Albania, of goods from Austria-Hungary, which helps to explain the decline in Austria's position in Albanian foreign trade, at least in Lower Albania. The second was that the outbreak of war between Italy and Turkey in 1911 did not have any major repercussions on trade between Italy and Albania (as shown by Table 1.4, which, however, only covers imports into Upper Albania). This can be explained by the strong resistance put up by the merchants of Vlorë to the boycott against Italy and by the fact that Turkey needed Shkodër for its supply of military provisions.[14] This need would lead us to believe that, in spite of the war, the Sublime Porte was not above obtaining provisions, via Albanian territory, from the country with which it was at war!

The first, turbulent years of Albania's independence: conflicting political and economic interests of foreign powers – enter Britain and the League of Nations

The second decade of the century is teeming with political events of great importance to Albania and to its relations with Italy. In 1912 Albania obtained independence, with Italy and Austria acting as reciprocal counter-balances;[15] it passed through the short-lived governments of Ismail Qemal Bey and Prince Wilhelm Von Wied; it saw its territory occupied by the powers engaged in the First World War; it obtained – thanks to a determined nationalist movement – an end to the Italian occupation; and finally, in 1920, it joined the League of Nations.

It is difficult to see any consistent strategy behind Italian policy during this period as, depending on the different phases and the various protagonists in its foreign policy, it swung between the two extremes of dividing up Albanian territory and recognizing its independence, but always with a high level of interest, be this in maintaining its influence in, or in 'protecting', the new state. Therefore, especially between 1914 and 1920, Italian policy regarding Albania could be charted as 'a line with many curves', which under Sonnino and then Giolitti and Sforza touched 'the level of concrete possibilities and effective interests', in the sense of acknowledging Albania's independence, while in Di San Giuliano, Orlando and Tittoni, and then in Nitti and Scialoja, we had the principal advocates in favour of partitioning the territory.[16]

Austria's position as an antagonist vis-à-vis Italy, in terms of economic initiatives in Albania, continued in the first years of its independence. Furthermore, in the economic field, just as in the political field, the antagonism was often masked by common initiatives in which cooperation between the countries clearly had a strategic motive, being aimed at preventing any exclusive involvement on the part of the rival power. The first attempt to form an Albanian central bank under Ismail Qemal Bey's government,[17] and the loan granted to Prince Von Wied are two typical examples of this tendency which are worth a brief discussion.

The project to create a central bank using foreign capital fitted with the policy of modernization which Ismail Qemal Bey was putting into action.

On this subject, we should start by pointing out that the Albanian government was very anxious that the international commission of the six powers set up by the Ambassadors' Conference, which was engaged in drawing up the boundaries for an independent Albania, should pay particular attention to the south-eastern frontiers of the new state, a region which was a potential source of great friction with Greece. Pressure was brought to bear on the Albanian government, in that the commission would not begin its work until the government itself agreed to the Wienerbankverein and the Banca Commerciale Italiana forming a National Bank of Albania. The government agreed to the plan, therefore, which also included allowing the new bank to operate in the sector of real estate credit. This caused some apprehension in the country as to the consequences of large areas of the territory being mortgaged to foreign capital. The foundation of the bank was also opposed by the Russians – backed by France and Britain – who pointed out that the new credit institution ought to have a broader international base. As a result, the creation of the central bank did not go ahead at that time.[18]

Foreign capital also played a role in Prince Von Wied's accession to power.[19] Once again, the source of the capital was Italy and Austria-Hungary. In his letter of acceptance of the Albanian crown, the prince said:

> The Austro-Hungarian and Italian ambassadors in Berlin inform me . . . that an Austro-Hungarian and an Italian credit institution, on guarantees from their respective governments, are prepared to put at my disposal immediately, for the government of Albania, the sum of 10 million francs, as an advance on a total loan of 75 million, for which the other powers have agreed in principle also to give guarantees.

The prince made this transaction an absolute condition for accepting the throne. The loan was to be administered by the international commission of the six powers. Inevitably, the paying out of the loan was hampered by the political rivalries which plagued the country. The other powers refused to subscribe to it, and even Italy blocked its payments to Albania after only around half of the capital had been paid out, because it failed to obtain any concessions from the Albanian government in the fishing, forestry and telecommunications industries.[20]

As with other loans to Albania, this one also remained unpaid. The subject of the loan was brought up again in 1936 – a sum equal to around 5.5 million lire for Italy – only to be declared irrecoverable by the Italian Finance Ministry, who proceeded to cancel it.[21]

Returning to Italo-Albanian trade, from 1914 onwards an unbroken set of statistics is available, allowing us to trace its development. Table 1.5 reveals that the overall progress of Italo-Albanian foreign trade was very unsteady, lurching backwards and forwards depending on the circumstances at the time, which were obviously connected with the war. The quantitative variations are actually very wide.

Table 1.5 reveals another important factor, however: Albania was building up a considerable deficit in its balance of trade with Italy, which was to remain a permanent feature in the records of economic-financial relations during the period in question in this study.

Table 1.5 Italo-Albanian trade, 1914–1920 (in thousands of Italian lire)

	Exports from Italy to Albania	Imports from Albania to Italy
1914	5,126.6	3,368.8
1915	7,816.6	4,104.7
1916	18,673.2	2,716.4
1917	42,418.7	4,065.3
1918	18,412.4	4,888.4
1919	32,505.2	9,010.9
1920	44,166.5	5,704.0

Source: See Table 1.1.

If we proceed to look at the quota represented by Italy in the overall figures for Albania's foreign trade, it is sufficiently apparent, in spite of the scarcity of available data, that Italy was consolidating its role as principal trade partner with Albania. According to statistics quoted by Calmès, Albanian imports from Italy counted for 63.2 per cent of Albania's total imports in 1920, while Italy in its turn absorbed no less than 93.7 per cent of Albania's exports. The same statistics confirm the emergence of a considerable overall deficit in Albania's foreign trade, as we have already seen to be the case in its trade with Italy: compared with imports totalling 17,533,000 gold francs, exports totalled only 1,522,000 gold francs.[22]

The decade closed with a consolidation of Albanian independence. The policy of partitioning the territory expounded by the Nitti government at the Paris Conference and the parallel tendency for Italy to interpret as direct power of dominion the role of diplomatic representative of the tiny Albanian state entrusted to it by the Treaty of London led to the Albanian nationalist movement taking on a distinctly anti-Italian slant. The new Albanian government which emerged from the Congress of Lushnjë (January 1920), led by Sulejman Bey Delvina, with Ahmet Bey Zogu as Interior Minister, brought about an insurrection against the Italian troops still occupying Vlorë. By the time Giolitti replaced Nitti, Albania had become 'a tooth needing to be pulled'. The 'preliminary protocol' of 2 August 1920, drawn up between Italy and Albania, declared the cessation of all Italian claims and the relinquishment of the whole territory with the exception of the small island of Sazan (Saseno), in the bay of Vlorë.[23]

Meanwhile, another country was showing an interest in Albania and, once again, the economic factor dominated. Britain was drawn to the region by the possibility of exploiting its oil fields, whose existence had been revealed by Italian and Austrian soundings carried out during the war. There is a direct link between Albania's entry into the League of Nations (17 December 1920) and the concession gained by the Anglo-Persian Oil

Company in 1921 to drill for oil in one of these fields.[24] It is a fact that, following Albania's entry into the League of Nations, we see a notable volume of commercial transactions taking place between the British and Albanian governments,[25] and, as we shall see later, when Italian economic penetration into the country began in earnest, British interests did in fact present a major obstacle.

The Yugoslav–Albanian dispute concerning the north-eastern borders, meanwhile, brought Albania closer to Italy. The Ambassadors' Conference, meeting in Paris, approved a protocol on 9 November 1921 (signed by Britain, France, Italy and Japan) which gave an international commission made up of British, French and Italian representatives the task of defining these boundaries. At the same time, Italy obtained recognition from the same conference that a special relationship should exist between itself and Albania, since it was recognized that any alterations to Albania's frontiers could jeopardize Italy's strategic security: hence the authorization for Italy to defend Albania's borders, with the approval of the League of Nations.[26] Thus, while Britain was preparing to build a broader economic base in Albania, the British government did recognize Italy's precedence in political and strategic matters.[27]

On 25 March 1922, the Albanian government – then led by Xhafer Bey Ypi, with Zogu as Interior Minister, but a leader in the Cabinet – turned to the League of Nations for financial assistance, and asked particularly for experts who could put forward proposals for encouraging investments of foreign capital in Albania. The League of Nations gave its Economy and Finance Committee the task of sending experts into the country.

In the May of that year, a report by a commission of the League explained the need to keep any financial support for Albania's economy thoroughly international, or multilateral.[28] In the following September, the previously mentioned Calmès Report was published, which came to be seen as a fundamental text and informed all future analyses of Albania's economic problems, as it brought together and tackled every aspect of the country's economic and financial situation. A detailed look at the report will be necessary for this study.

Meanwhile, in April 1922, the League of Nations turned down a request for a loan from the Albanian government. At the same time, proposals were being considered from foreign banks for forming an Albanian central bank.[29]

In December 1922, Ahmet Zogu, already Minister of the Interior, became Prime Minister. He immediately placed the emphasis on the need for outside expertise and financial help for his country. Marxist Albanian historiography saw in Zogu's rise to power the outcome of a battle between two groups: the middle classes who, whilst wishing to resolve the political and economic problems to their own advantage, still championed their country's interests and independence, and the large landowners and middle-class reactionaries, intent only on safeguarding their own privileges, to the detriment of economic development, advocating an open-door policy towards foreign capital and laying the nation's economy open to being controlled by the latter. The main representative of the first group was Bishop Fan Noli, whose brief spell in government in 1924 (see Chapter 3) is given a generally positive appraisal by the historians; at the forefront of the second group, of course, was Ahmet Zogu.[30] One opinion of Zogu's reign which is generally more favourable is that of Skendi, who claims that, given the country's overall political immaturity and the traditional autonomy of the tribes of the north and the feudal beys of the centre and south, Zogu's authoritarian government was probably the only one which could follow through a solid unification of the country. In any case, decisive steps towards modernizing the country were certainly taken under this government.[31] The latter point could be debated, but the view that Zogu intended to secure his country a certain degree of independence, in spite of the burdensome ties he formed with Italy, seems accurate. The manner in which his reign ended in itself seems to confirm this.[32] A similar assessment of his reign appears in a recent biography. Noting that, after the Hoxha regime, Albania was still by far the poorest nation in Europe and had become the most brutally repressive, the Zogist dictatorship is seen in a more favourable light.[33]

In April 1923, the League of Nations appointed a Financial Adviser, in the person of the Dutchman Jan Hunger. Meanwhile, not only British and Italian companies were vying for access to the Albanian oil fields, but French and American ones also, and disputes were developing between them.[34]

It was against this backdrop that Mussolini, who had been head of the Italian government and Foreign Minister for just a few months, began to engage with the Albanian question.

It was a scenario in which the economic interests of other countries in the oil industry, especially Britain, played a role, but in which Italy was in prime position politically speaking, its vital security interests in the Adriatic having been acknowledged in an international forum. On the other hand, the Albanian government was still maintaining an attitude which was open and non-prejudicial towards any foreign power. Its main interlocutor in both political and economic matters remained the League of Nations, which recognized its role in assisting and protecting the young state.

However, the talk coming out of the various bodies of the League was not followed through by concrete actions, and in the final analysis we see the League of Nations to a great extent colluding in an economic and financial penetration which was almost exclusively Italian.

CHAPTER 2

The Albanian economy and the Balkan context: the Calmès Report

Economic and monetary developments in the Balkans in the early twentieth century

At the end of the First World War, Albania's economic and financial situation was in many respects similar to that of other Balkan states.[1] The main factor emerging in these economies was the low level of capital, resulting from the lack of any consistent process of capital accumulation. The consequences of this were twofold. The first was a heavy reliance on foreign nations, with a corresponding slowdown in development, since this became tied to the ability and willingness of foreign governments and capital markets to grant these countries loans. The second was a low standard of living amongst the population and a constant flow of emigrants out of the country, especially to the United States.

The countries also shared a similar pattern of production. With next to no manufacturing industry, it was essentially based on raw materials and agricultural produce. The agricultural system itself was organized on extremely outdated principles and, although in some countries (Greece, Serbia and Romania) some attempts had been made at agrarian reform,[2] elsewhere, such as in Central and Southern Albania, feudalism remained deeply entrenched. Where reforms had taken place they fragmented agricultural property, which led to a widespread decrease in its size, with the exception of that of the large semi-feudal landowners.

Another feature common to the Balkan states was the low profile of their foreign trade, both in absolute terms and relative to their income and population, and the fact that this was basically characterized by exports of raw materials and agricultural produce, and imports of manufactured or semi-manufactured products. The geographical distribution of international trade within the Balkan region in the post-war period shows an absence of any significant commerce between the countries of the region themselves, which points to the fact that the respective economies were not complementary to each other and therefore lacked any effective stimulus for a reciprocal process of integration.

One other feature which the Balkan countries had in common in the post-war period was that their external political dependence and the foreign loans themselves did not in fact influence the flow of imports and exports in any decisive way. In this respect, the Balkan nations proved that they were effectively independent in their choices of economic policy, in spite of these dependent relationships. Albania was no exception, as we shall see more clearly when we study the country's balance of trade and payments in greater detail.

Notwithstanding the similarities in the foreign trade of the Balkan countries outlined above, two important distinctions must be made. The first relates to the structure of their exports. Albania and Yugoslavia were exporting goods which were quite varied, whereas exports out of Greece, Bulgaria and Romania centred on a single product, which in the case of Greece and Bulgaria was tobacco and, in that of Romania, oil. The second distinction to make is between the countries which had a structural trade surplus except during periods of heavy foreign debt (these were Bulgaria, Yugoslavia and Romania) and Greece and Albania, which had a structural deficit. While in Greece's case a sizeable flow of emigrant remittances almost completely compensated for the deficit, for Albania the other entries in the current part of the balance of payments were never sufficient to fill the gap, which, as we shall see in more detail later, was filled instead by huge inflows of Italian capital.

As for the currency situation, before the war the Balkan states had adhered, either *de jure* or *de facto*, to the Latin Monetary Union. The gold content of the respective currencies was therefore 0.290322 grams of gold per unit of currency and they were tied to a 1:1 ratio with the French franc, the lira and the Swiss franc (the main parties to the Union) and a ratio of 25.2215 per sterling. The events of the war made it impossible, as in all the countries of Western Europe, to maintain this standard. After the war the rise in public spending in the Balkan countries produced serious rises in the rate of inflation and a depreciation of the respective currencies amidst confused situations such as that which arose in the newly created Yugoslavia, when different currencies were circulating simultaneously and their relative exchange rates[3] were uncertain. The problem of inflation reached a peak in 1924 but from then on a considerable inflow of foreign capital for stabilization purposes, and greater control of public spending were together able to hold back the domestic and external depreciation of the Balkan currencies.[4]

The policy of borrowing from abroad had in fact already been broadly pursued before the First World War and can be traced back to the Balkan nations' acquisition of independence. At that time, the majority of loans were granted to finance projects for the railways and to enable those countries to increase their military capacity. On their part, the major powers saw the loans as a means of increasing their political influence.

After the war, the foreign debt of the Balkan nations increased constantly. The years 1920–1931 were characterized by massive inflows of foreign capital. Four international loans were granted to Greece and Bulgaria under the auspices of the League of Nations. Other smaller international loans were made to Romania and Yugoslavia. Apart from these transactions, which mainly involved the markets of London and New York and to a smaller extent those of Amsterdam, Zurich, Brussels, Prague and Milan, Yugoslavia borrowed almost exclusively from France and the United States and Albania from Italy. The same alliance and political support strategies devised in the respective Foreign Offices were seen repeated in the financial arena.

The chief aim of the post-war loans was, as has been said, to provide stability. They were in fact used to increase the currency reserves of the central banks in order to sustain their respective currencies, but also to reduce public debt towards the respective central banks. In the case of Greece, for example, a loan was made for the purpose of 're-founding' the central bank itself. Another important purpose of the loans which connected them with those made before the war was to finance public works such as roads, railways and land reclamation.

This period of stabilization was accompanied throughout the region by a radical reorganization of the central banks, for which foreign experts were also brought in to help. This is what we see happening in Greece and Bulgaria in 1928, in Romania in 1927 and in Yugoslavia in 1931. This is also what happened in Albania.

The policy of borrowing from abroad and the growing independence of the central banks should be seen in the context of developments which took place on the international monetary scene during the 1920s, in which the Genoa International Monetary Conference of 1922 stands out as an important landmark.

During that period there was lingering international unease, stemming from the insufficiency of gold stocks in relation to the role which gold played in the international monetary system. In spite of the deflation which had occurred in some countries, prices were considerably higher than they had been before the war, while the price of gold had remained unchanged. Countries saw an opportunity to 'avoid the wide fluctuations in gold-purchasing power which could result from several nations all competing to replenish their metal reserves at the same time'.[5] The conference therefore recommended that, while gold should remain as the currency standard, an international convention should centralize and manage the use of gold by means of reserves held in some key currencies. For a currency to maintain its gold parity, guarantees were to be given in the form of reserves which did not have to be made up of gold. Countries which chose this option would hold all or part of their own reserves as foreign currency, rather than gold. Although this system, commonly known as the 'gold exchange standard', had to some extent been proved effective prior to this, it had never risen to the status of standard procedure.[6] In order to achieve currency stability, the issuing banks needed to be free from political interference, and foreign loans had to be granted which were intended precisely for the purposes of stabilization and putting the 'gold exchange standard' into practice.[7]

Fascism saw the outcome of the Genoa Conference as an attempt to establish an international monetary order governed in effect by the Bank of England.

> So that all countries would return to a gold standard, those responsible for monetary policy in Britain tried to introduce a system of currency stabilization by which the circulation of bank notes would be guaranteed not by actual reserves of gold but by credits held in foreign banks, English and American banks in particular. The banks of these countries, which were veritable reservoirs of gold, issued bonds throughout the world, cashed the proceedings of the issue and credited the amount, as stabilization loans, to the different countries, after having – of course – deducted their commission. . . . These credits at English and American banks then acted as guarantees for the circulation in the countries which had taken out the loans. But they were also used for circulation in England and America. It was in practice a single backing for two debts. This system, which under private law would be an offence carrying serious penalties, in international affairs went by the grandiose title of the 'gold exchange standard'.[8]

At the time these lines were printed Italy was on the verge of creating, in relation to Albania, a 'lira area', similar to the 'sterling area', according to the rules of the 'gold exchange standard', the difference being that unlike the pound the lira was not convertible into gold.[9]

In Albania the foundation of the issuing bank itself, the establishment of a new currency system and the loan granted by Italy in the mid-1920s all took place along much the same lines as the developments outlined above.

The Calmès proposals

In effect financial developments in Albania in the early 1920s to a great extent mirrored the wider scene and therefore followed a pattern which was sufficiently clear at an international level. They also, however, bore the unmistakable hallmark of the political position which the Fascists were adopting towards the country with increasing determination. The main aspects of this position will be outlined in Chapter 3. The report produced by Professor Calmès on behalf of the League of Nations, which we have already referred to, provides a useful starting point for examining these developments.[10]

In his discussion of the possibilities for Albania's economic development, Calmès distinguished between its finances and its economy, judging the finances to be in a healthy state and the economy to be in a poor one. He identified the positive aspects of the financial situation as being Albania's policy of maintaining the circulation of a gold-based currency in spite of the chaos of the wartime period, unlike its Balkan neighbours, and a public debt which was almost non-existent. He identified the causes of the economic backwardness as being: a state of extreme underdevelopment in the country (the result of five centuries of neglect by the ruling authorities); an uneducated population; the absence of infrastructures; and an inadequate level of production, all of which were reflected, as Calmès pointed out, in a trade balance heavily in deficit (see Table 2.1).[11]

According to Calmès, an explanation of how the country was able to withstand such an imbalance in its foreign accounts could be found in the fact that the Albanian people had stockpiled large quantities of gold and silver during the war, which had led to Albania being one of the few countries still relying on a metallic circulation and, in fact, on a gold-based one. We have already seen that the acquisition of independence had not brought with it, in spite of several attempts, the creation of a central bank for Albania and a currency system of its own. At the beginning of the 1920s, therefore, the country had no national currency, let alone a paper currency.

Table 2.1 Albanian foreign trade in 1920–1921, by country (thousands of gold francs)

	Imports		Exports		Balance	
	1920	1921	1920	1921	1920	1921
Italy	11,086	12,731	1,426	1,614	9,660	11,117
Greece	3,978	2,124	43	488	3,935	1,637
Turkey	782	665			782	665
United Kingdom	734	1,135			733	1,135
Austria	724	669			724	669
United States	123				123	
Yugoslavia	106	335	53	88	54	246
	17,533	17,659	1,522	2,190	16,011	15,469

Source: Calmès Report, pp. 15–16.

Its stock of precious metals, estimated by Calmès to be worth 50–100 million gold francs (excluding gold stockpiled in the form of jewellery), was mainly held in the form of gold 'napoleons' and silver 'crowns'. This particular format does not however mean that a bimetallic currency system existed, with a fixed price ratio between the two metals. In Albania, the coexistence of the two metals in circulation meant that pieces of silver were accepted in payment for their own intrinsic value, as bullion, and therefore had a variable exchange rate in respect to gold pieces.

Similarly, the little paper money which was in circulation also had a variable exchange value in relation to gold, especially Italian notes, which were exchanged primarily in the coastal region. Exchange rates were fixed weekly by the local prefectures and sub-prefectures. The fact that the Exchequer accepted payment in gold, silver or notes, but that payment in silver or notes was subject to a 5 per cent and 10 per cent premium respectively (to cover the risk of loss in exchange value), meant that in practice these payments were almost always made in gold.[12]

Apart from its 'healthy currency', Calmès identified another positive aspect of Albania's financial situation as being the absence of foreign debt and the controlled level of public borrowing,[13] another feature which set the country apart from others in the Balkan region. Here also, however, a degree of caution is required in assessing the situation, as it is an extremely rudimentary financial administration we are speaking of. The official public debt at the time Calmès was writing consisted in effect of two short-term loans, the first being for 1,500,000 francs at 5 per cent, on a three-year term, issued in 1920 and underwritten in part by the Albanians in America; the second was for 710,000 francs, at 6 per cent, issued in 1922 for repayment in the same financial year. Both were represented by bonds which were accepted as payment for taxes and customs duties and thus constituted an advance on these payments. Calmès also noted that, if we compare revenues and expenses in the state budgets for 1921 and 1922, a further deficit appears (see Table 2.2).

In his commentary on these figures and those of the following years, Di Nardi wrote in 1940:

> It is not clear from the financial documents open to the public how the country coped with its successive deficits, since there is no record of any loans having been made. It is well known, however, that the Italian Government has always contributed to rebalancing Albania's budget . . . and in any case the Albanian Treasury is notorious for its habit of abusing credit from the State's private suppliers, delaying payments for months and even years, and ignoring deadlines. It seems that manipulating the budget played an important role in the struggling equilibrium of Albania's finances.[14]

Table 2.2 Budget of the Albanian state, 1921–1922 (in thousands of gold francs)

	1921	1922
Revenues	18,809	19,747
Expenditures	21,471	22,195
Deficit	2,622	2,448

Source: Calmès Report, pp. 22–28.

Against this background, Calmès was of the opinion that development in Albania should be set in motion by mobilizing the country's stockpiled wealth, increasing its production capacity, reclaiming land and building a road network. But what kind of instruments did he envisage for putting all this into practice? Calmès was an astute observer and realized that Albania's political situation was very fragile. He was acting on an international mandate, that of the League of Nations, but was aware that, behind the League, Italy's interests had already received special recognition only a few months earlier. On the other hand, this was not yet the Italy of Mussolini. The recommendations in his report are therefore quite enlightening and give us an insight into why, after barely three years, the ideas being put into practice were far removed from his.

His proposals were as follows:

(a) To create an issuing bank. This would 'inspire the trust of the Albanian people', would encourage them to bring out their stores of treasure which were hidden away, stagnating and producing no return, and invest them in the bank in the form of shares and deposits. The bank would become the 'prime mover' in the as yet non-existent credit system in the country.[15] In keeping with the conventional wisdom of the time, the bank would be a private institution in which the state would have no chance of interfering. In order to emphasize its independence, a portion of its capital, perhaps half (the total of which Calmès recommended should be around 10–15 million gold francs), would be underwritten by foreign shareholders, either from countries which could not be suspected of having any political influence on Albania or from several different countries whose respective designs on the country would cancel each other out.

The backing for notes issued by the bank would follow the lines of the 'gold exchange standard' and would be partly in gold (30–40 per cent) and partly in assets held abroad, which he considered sufficient guarantee for a population who were traditionally wary of using paper currency and were attached to the method of carrying out transactions using actual metal. As for the latter, Calmès pointed out the inconvenience of circulating pieces of silver according to their intrinsic value and recommended that silver coins be reduced to the rank of a fractional or token currency with limited power of redemption and a face value higher than its intrinsic value.[16]

(b) To create a road network and develop agricultural potential by reclaiming the marshlands. (In Calmès's opinion, industrial development should be part of a later development phase.) The sum needed to implement these projects he estimated at 110 million gold francs. He warned that it was not prudent to count on a foreign loan, even if this would have been 'of great help' and 'would contribute towards political stability in the Balkans'. The existence of the Albanian state should not depend on help from abroad. For the marsh reclamation works, Calmès advocated, in place of a foreign loan, a plan to grant concessionary rights to private companies for exploiting the reclaimed land. For the construction of the roads, which would not provide a return on the investment in the same way, Calmès thought that the same solution would not be possible and that the Albanian government should 'rely on its own means' instead.[17]

To a large extent, Calmès still believed in finding an international solution to the Albanian problem, which should therefore not be hijacked by the vested interests of any single foreign country. From a technical point of view, he had faith in the ability of the Albanian state to rebalance its own foreign accounts without the need for stabilizing loans, not recognizing perhaps that the healthy state of the Albanian currency was inextricably linked with the country's backwardness.

CHAPTER 3

The League of Nations: a missed opportunity

The League plan and the British disentanglement

The creation of the Albanian bank of issue, the huge loan granted by Italy and, more generally, the beginning of a new currency regime and establishment of a preferential economic and financial relationship between Italy and Albania are all inseparable from the wide-ranging and complicated diplomatic approaches which Italy was making towards Zogu. It makes sense, therefore, to consider the complex diplomatic and financial relations maintained by the Fascist government (a term which is not always entirely representative of Italian positions at the time) on two fronts: that of Albania; and that of the other European governments, the British government in particular.[1] However, prior to this, another of Albania's important interlocutors, the League of Nations, was playing a substantial role.[2]

The Financial Adviser appointed by the League of Nations, Jan Hunger, arrived in Tiranë at the end of May 1923. He found that the Zogu government was being flooded by requests for concessions by foreign firms, while the Albanian constitution (the so-called Constitution of Lushnjë of 1920), which granted too much power to the parliament and the council of ministers, was preventing the Prime Minister from taking the necessary timely action. British, Italian and French interests were heavily involved in oil exploitation. There was also a German company which was interested in a railway concession, but as the railway business was not profitable it sought concessions in the exploitation of forests, coal mines and hydro-electric power instead and also some territory along the projected railway. Italians wanted to lease a large strip of coastal land between the Shkumbin and the Vjosë rivers, in order to drain the marshes. In addition, several concessions had already been granted, to Italians (for asphalt production and for copper mines), Germans (for foresting), Swiss and Americans (for the leasing of state land).[3]

However, Hunger noted that these requests were 'not supported by adequate capital', and what the Albanian government needed was money. Thus, the financial problem became a priority.

The League's Finance Committee, under the chairmanship of the Director of the National Bank of Belgium, Albert-Edouard Janssen, set about drawing up a legal framework for the constitution of a bank of issue, to be put before the Albanian parliament for approval.

The plan drawn up by the League of Nations,[4] dated 4 September 1923 but never carried out, makes interesting reading, especially when compared with the text of the legislation which was later issued and put into action under the influence of the Italians. The plan, although based on the guiding principle that the National Bank should be autonomous of the Albanian government (a principle which was also reaffirmed in the subsequent legislation), nonetheless gives the Bank a more clearly defined place in the country's socio-economic and political framework and, above all, makes no mention whatsoever of the Italians having any special interest in its management. This confirms that by the second half of 1923 Italian policy had not yet made a decisive shift towards Albania.

According to the League of Nations' plan, the task of supervising the new institution would be assigned to a commissioner to be appointed by the Albanian government, which would participate in the Bank's administration through a consultative vote. The headquarters of the Bank's board of directors would be in Albania and the Secretary-General would be resident there also. As to the provisions which were to govern the Bank's activities, they would be in accordance with Albanian legislation. Any changes to the Bank's Charter should be approved by the Albanian Finance Minister. All these provisions were to disappear, as we shall see, in the later texts, which were substantially drawn up by the Italian financial group.

Article 22 of the League's plan gives another interesting insight, stating that the Bank was to begin its first fiscal year 'as of the date of its constitution until 31st December 1924', which shows that, as far as the League of Nations was concerned, the foundation of the Bank would be taking place within a short period of time. The political troubles of 1924, however, meant that its foundation was postponed until September 1925.

According to the League's initial plans, British and French finance was to form the nucleus of the enterprise along with Italian finance, via a participation of 25 per cent each in the capital of the future Bank. Hunger had, in fact, approached Marcus Wallenberg, of the Stockholm Enskilda Bank, about the creation of an international bank which would be both a bank of issue and a commercial bank, and had stressed that the introduction of a paper currency in Albania would present serious difficulties without a strong gold backing. 'A first issue of paper money', he said, 'at a time when the manner in which it will be received by the population is uncertain, cannot be profitable to the government, for caution would demand the constitution at the same time of a gold bullion reserve, as to be able to buy back the paper, as soon as it depreciates in value.'

Wallenberg, on behalf of the League, worked on the idea of a bank of issue with a capital of 5 million gold francs, 75 per cent of which would be owned in equal portions by France, Britain and Italy, and the remaining 25 per cent allotted to Belgian, Swedish and Dutch banks and to Albanian individuals. The obvious place to start raising finance was the London market. Wallenberg consulted in London with Hambros, Lazard and the British Overseas Bank. Apparently, the negotiations broke down, and obtaining money from private quarters in Britain proved impossible.[5] So, at the end of 1923, Franco-British interest began to weaken, despite the favourable stance of the Finance Committee delegates from these two countries, Sir Otto Niemeyer of the British Treasury and Jean Parmentier of the French Ministère des Finances. Even the attempts made by the Imperial Ottoman Bank to open a branch in Durrës (with the intention of taking over issuing rights in the future) were only short-lived.[6]

The events that occurred at the end of 1923 and in early 1924 are crucial for an understanding of the bold approach of the Italian government and the retrenchment of the League of Nations. Britain, on its part, backed the League of Nations only insofar as there was no risk of opposing Italian interests: at the decisive moment, it chose not to consider Albania as a foreign policy priority, as long as its own important oil interests were protected.

In February 1924, the financial situation of Albania was – in the words of Harry Eyres, the British Minister at Durrës – 'desperate' and the outlook very bleak.[7] It was in this context that the controversial issue of Hunger's dismissal by the Albanian government occurred. Pandeli Evangjeli, the acting Prime Minister, revoked his contract on 29 February. Hunger reacted angrily: 'There is the vital question of the creation of a State bank and subsequently of a Crédit Foncier', he wrote to the League, and remarked that the Albanian government was unwilling to fall into line. Eyres, however, believed that Hunger lacked energy and drive and openly asked the Foreign Office to appoint a new British financial adviser, rather than an adviser from any country. The League, through its Secretary-General Sir Eric Drummond – also British – thought at first that the situation could be remedied, that a neutral adviser would do the best job and that Hunger could finally be reinstated. The Albanian government silenced the question of Hunger's dismissal once and for all, noting that Hunger had benefited from a very large salary (around 100,000 gold francs) for doing nothing.[8]

In reality, what was clearly emerging was a British disentanglement, a growing Italian involvement and a closer link between Italy and Albania.

According to the British, the worsening of the Albanian financial position was not seen unfavourably by the Italians: it was a kind of prerequisite for making their 'bail-out' more effective. 'I failed', wrote Eyres to MacDonald, the Prime Minister, 'to discover any sign of regret on his [the Italian envoy's] part. It was as who should say: "This is what we have been waiting for."'[9]

In response to his complaint of a lack of more decisive action to support the League, the Foreign Office wrote to Drummond, making its position plain: 'We seem to have done all that can reasonably be expected of us in a matter which is of its nature more of a League affair than our own.'[10] The following day, Otto Niemeyer told the League's Committee that his government was 'not however prepared to take the initiative in seeking to impose reforms upon an unwilling country, and is unable to support any further action'.[11] In the same vein, when in December 1924 two Italian destroyers were sent to Durrës and Vlorë, raising the concerns of Eyres ('British prestige in these waters seems to me to require some such pressure'), the British government gave no sign of involvement ('Our desire at present is to localise and not to internationalise the situation. Despatch of destroyer would only complicate situation').[12] A few months later, the Foreign Secretary, Austen Chamberlain, was still more explicit with Eyres: 'His Majesty's Government are anxious, from the point of view of general policy, to avoid either becoming involved to a greater extent than is absolutely necessary in Albanian affairs, or giving the appearance in any way of opposing the legitimate interests of Italy in that country.'[13]

The Italian involvement

According to the unanimous opinion put forward in the press during the Fascist era, however, the National Bank of Albania was founded on the basis of a mandate given to Italy by the League of Nations.[14]

Let us go over the sequence of events which led to the foundation of the Bank and the granting of the loan by Italy.[15] Italian enterprise in Albania during the years immediately following the First World War had remained mostly private, as it had been at the beginning of the century, and involved only a few groups of speculators. It was two private entrepreneurs, the Ligurian brothers Carlo and Gildo Pugni, holders of stakes in the Albanian oil business, who acted as intermediaries in Zogu's first approach of an economic nature towards an Italian public body, the Ferrovie dello Stato (the Italian State Railways). Zogu needed money to pay his troops and the militia of Mat (his home region) and offered to sell the Ferrovie dello Stato some woods which he owned in Mat. The contract was drawn up in November 1923 and Zogu received an advance of 700,000 lire on an agreed price of 1,700,000 lire.[16]

Eyres followed these developments with increasing concern. He saw the payment[17] as the result of 'Italian intrigues', ostensibly for the purchase of a property, consisting of 'forests insignificant and unsaleable, impracticable for exploitation'. According to Eyres, the Italians had understood that Zogu was 'the right horse to back'.[18]

Hunger's dismissal was perfectly in line with this trend in the financial field and, a few days later, Italian interests were given an important 'green light' by the League.

Hunger, now out of play, seems as usual to have understood the developments a little late in the day. 'As regards the creation of a bank of issue', he wrote to the League, back home in Amsterdam, on 15 May, 'it should be mentioned that Messrs Janssen and Alberti, the members of the Finance Committee of the League of Nations who were asked to obtain the balance of the share capital of the bank have, as I learnt in March last, almost succeeded in doing so.'[19]

Zogu made an important approach towards Italy at the beginning of 1924, with the signing of a trade agreement on 20 January and a settlement convention between the two countries on 29 February. The trade agreement was the first of its kind made by the Albanian government and named Italy in the most-favoured-nation clause, establishing full freedom of trade between the two states, the exemption of goods from transit duties and the obligation not to grant commercial monopolies to third parties. Zogu, however, did not present the agreement to parliament for ratification, for fear that it would be interpreted as being too biased in Italy's favour and would therefore not be approved.[20]

The Italian financial group, on the other hand, was becoming more and more influential, led by the Director of the Credito Italiano and delegate to the League of Nations' Finance Committee, Mario Alberti, who, as we shall see later, was acting hand in glove with Rome.

Finally, on 27 March 1924, the Chairman of the Finance Committee, Janssen, wrote a letter to Mario Alberti, in his dual role as leader of the 'Italian group' and Italian representative on the Finance Committee, announcing effectively that the League of Nations was withdrawing from the field. In this letter, we read, among other things:

> The Finance Committee has expressed its opinion as to the principles upon which it believes the foundation of an issuing bank in Albania should be based. It hopes that this advice may be of help to the government in its decision on the measures to be adopted and the parties to be involved in subscribing to the capital. However, the Committee's responsibilities and powers do not go beyond this. . . . In these circumstances, it is not the place of the Committee to stand in the way of any other solutions which may have been reached in a different manner, such as those put forward in your letter, providing these are practicable and in keeping with the wishes of the Albanian government.[21]

The attempts to create a capital base for the forthcoming bank of issue with the inclusion of a British participation were unsuccessful. A few days after the League of Nations had given a free hand to the Italian group, Giorgio Manzi-Fè of the Banca Italo-Britannica, an affiliate of the British Italian Banking Corporation, was urged by the Director-General[22] of the Bank of Italy, Bonaldo Stringher, to participate in the formation of a new National Albanian Bank. Manzi was not anxious to join, but at the same time felt that it might not be advisable for Britain to remain outside.

This idea, not unsurprisingly, was rather coolly received by the British authorities. Harold Nicolson, then a 1st Secretary at the Foreign Office, in charge of the Balkan region, consulted the Treasury, fully aware that it was not in British interests that Albania should fall completely into Italian hands, but recommending a 'no opinion' on the matter. Niemeyer, at the Treasury, sceptical about any real willingness of the British banking community to be involved, and unwilling to involve his government in what was considered by now an area of Italian influence, confirmed that they should stay neutral.[23]

However, an important development occurred in June 1924 that in some way contributed to reviving British interest in the area. A revolt led by the leader of the democratic party, the orthodox Bishop of Durrës, Fan Noli, overturned the government (in which Zogu had just been replaced by Vërlaci) and forced Zogu himself to flee to Yugoslavia.[24]

From exile, Zogu turned to the Fascist government, via an intermediary, for finance to help him regain power, but Mussolini, on the advice of his Foreign Ministry, chose not to become involved. This was during the months of the Matteotti crisis and Italian foreign policy was strongly influenced by the Secretary-General of the Ministry, Contarini, who believed in non-intervention, in keeping with Italy's pre-war policy towards Albania. It was no coincidence therefore that Mussolini refused at the same time to become involved with Fan Noli, who had also requested his help.[25]

Zogu therefore sought and obtained help elsewhere: military support from Yugoslavia and financial support from the British Anglo-Persian Oil Company, which, as we recall, had shown previous interest in Albania's mineral resources in 1920–1921. According to the pact he made with the latter, Zogu agreed, on his return to power, to convert a preferential option granted to the company into an exclusive concession to prospect and drill for oil, in return for payment by the company of 50 million dinars, half to be paid immediately and half to be paid on ratification of the concession by the parliament.[26]

It is against this background that Zogu regained power from Fan Noli in December 1924. Albania, which was born a principality, was proclaimed a republic in January 1925, with Zogu elected as President. His need for financial support was total. It had been denied him by the Italian government while he had been in exile, but he was aware that he would not get any money from Yugoslavia, which had even fewer financial means at its disposal and whose own immediate interests were in conflict with those of Albania. Zogu therefore began a round of impassioned negotiations with Italy and Britain.[27] The first indications from Italy, however, were not encouraging, and Italy now had British economic interests to reckon with as well;[28] but what exactly was the Italian position?

A distinction needs to be made here between two prevailing mind-sets in Italy's foreign policy towards Albania at the time. The first was the one embodied by the Secretary-General Contarini: given that Zogu had made assurances that he intended to respect Italy's economic interests, and considering that if he was under obligation to those who had helped him his strongest ties on gaining victory would be with his financiers, 'the strategy of economic penetration appeared to be the most advantageous'.[29] Di Nolfo notes that 'Contarini was thinking along the lines of a general pledge agreement between the Balkan countries, a "Balkan Locarno", which would form a truly solid and profitable foundation for Italian influence in our neighbouring peninsula'.[30]

The second mind-set was embodied by the Fascist member of parliament Alessandro Lessona, a native of Liguria like the previously mentioned Pugni brothers. He was more inclined to throw caution to the wind and intervene directly in Albanian politics. His sentiments were echoed amongst some of Italy's diplomats, especially by Vincenzo Lojacono, head of the Albanian Office. There is some debate as to exactly what role Lessona played, on Mussolini's personal mandate, and in the face of some scepticism from the Contarini camp. That Lessona was something of a wild card, acting totally independently from the Italian Foreign Ministry, was well known to the British: Robert Parr, Chargé d'affaires at Durrës, noted that Lessona dealt directly with Zogu, without even informing the Italian envoy, Marchese Durazzo.[31] The account given in Lessona's *Memorie* is not entirely in accord with the findings of historical research into the events in question.[32] Suffice it to recall the 'ambivalent nature'[33] of Italian diplomacy in Albania which appears repeatedly (and not without reason) in the Fascists' approach to Albanian affairs.

We do know that, on 25 January 1925, Italy's position towards Albania was summed up in a memo prepared by Contarini and approved by Mussolini, entitled 'Issues to be clarified between the Italian and Albanian governments'.[34] Italy was asking Zogu, among other things: to have the previously mentioned trade agreement and settlement convention ratified by Albania; to grant Italy concessions in the oil fields and public works contracts; to specify the terms of forestry concessions granted to Italian companies; and, last but not least, to agree to the establishment of an Albanian state bank.

Zogu, however, was mindful of his undertakings towards the Anglo-Persian Oil Company. What is more, a proposal for establishing a bank had been put forward by a private British group. In February 1925, Eyres received two people from a London firm, Gottlieb and Godwin of C. E. Tidswell, who wanted to negotiate with the Albanian government for the creation of the new bank. Specifically, the idea was to form an Albanian Development Corporation, with a capital of £150,000, 10–15 per cent of which would be allotted to the Albanian government as fully paid shares. This would be accompanied by a loan of £2 million sterling for public works, with contracts to be given only to British firms. A bank of issue would be established, under purely British control.

This attempt failed completely, on two accounts: the unreliability of the promoters and, above all, the strong wish of the British government to appease the Italians.

These two people, wrote the Foreign Office to Eyres, were 'of insufficient standing. . . . Their principals are second rate and several are Germans. . . . If they do get the concern, this will infuriate the Italians even more as the firm is partly German.' Also, at a certain point it emerged that Gottlieb did not actually represent Tidswell, but he was not forthcoming about who had sent him, and to complicate things further it turned out that there were two companies with similar names. The Foreign Office was adamant about the whole proposal, instructing Eyres to 'adopt an attitude of reserve'. The same attitude was taken later, in May, when a certain Ethelburg Syndicate of London approached the Foreign Office, taking up the negotiations started by Gottlieb. The opposition of the Italian government, which was taken for granted, was the overwhelming obstacle to the initiative.[35]

At the same time, first Sola, the Italian Chargé d'affaires, and then Durazzo, the Italian Minister in Albania, were taking part in negotiations with the Albanian Finance and provisional Foreign Minister, Libohova. The outcome of these was Italy's specification of an offer in the following terms: 500,000 gold francs to be paid immediately; another 500,000 before 15 March; a loan of 1 million gold francs on signing the agreements; and a subsequent loan of 2 million sterling, equal to the British offer.[36]

At the end of this diplomatic marathon played out with these powerful negotiators, and before agreeing to the Italian proposals, Zogu partially fulfilled his agreement with the British by granting the rights to sizeable oil deposits to D'Arcy Exploration Co., a branch of Anglo-Persian.[37]

As for the Italians, on 24 February Alberti arrived in Albania to finalize the technical details of the agreement with his Albanian counterpart. Not the least important of his tasks was to clarify for public opinion the fact that the operation of founding the issuing bank involved the Italian financial group and that the Italian government was not as yet involved in any precise way. He was to make clear to the Albanians, however, that the Italian government was behind him in any commitment he entered into.[38]

Having paid the final instalment to Zogu of the 1,700,000 lire for the previous purchase of the woods in Mat, the Italians obtained an oil concession (on 12 March), granted to the Ferrovie dello Stato in the provinces of Vlorë and Berat.[39] On 15 March, the agreement for the foundation of the issuing bank and for a large loan from Italy to Albania was signed at last.[40]

Alberti himself refers to an attempt on the part of the British, for which I can find no other evidence, to hinder the foundation of the Bank by the Italians. The opportunity to create an issuing bank through the channels of the League of Nations having been dismissed, he claims that the British tried to stop the Italian operation through Harry Eyres, the British Minister in Albania, by repeatedly pressing upon Zogu the services of an Anglo-Greek finance group, supposedly led by one Basil Zaharoff, described by Alberti with some polemical ardour as 'the Anglo-Oriental arms merchant and keeper of the gambling house in Monte Carlo'.[41] It is unclear if this initiative had some connection with the one planned by the previously mentioned Gottlieb and Ethelburg Syndicate.

We can infer from these events that the League of Nations, far from giving Italy an explicit mandate, chose to stand back and leave the way clear for direct negotiations between the powers concerned.[42] The problem was in fact resolved via a series of direct approaches to Zogu by the great powers, Italy and Britain in particular. This type of solution was not in fact new. It had been tried out less than a year before, in resolving the Corfu crisis, when Italian diplomacy, at that time with French support, had succeeded in transferring the management of the crisis out of the hands of the League of Nations and into the more benign and accommodating jurisdiction of the Ambassadors' Conference. The international approach to the Albanian problem which Calmès had advocated, in order to guarantee Albania's national autonomy, gave way therefore to a different approach, in which the deep-seated and direct interests of the great powers would no longer be filtered and mediated by the bodies of the League. Calmès had advocated the financial intervention of a nation with no direct interest in Albanian affairs, or at least of several nations whose interests would effectively cancel each other out. In his desperate search for money to keep himself in power, Zogu made advances to Italy and Britain but the competing interests of these two nations certainly did nothing to neutralize their respective political and economic influence in the new state. Britain eventually acquiesced, and Italy's predominance in Albania was finally confirmed.

At this point, a brief digression could be interesting, to consider whether the Italian financial community fully endorsed the regime's political moves in the Balkan chessboard, and what the standpoint was of the Italian banking sector in relation to the particular question of Albania.

According to Carocci:

> The foreign policy advocated by the dominant players in Italy's economy was one of collaboration with the major powers, with whom most of the foreign trade was carried out, but partly because exports into these markets were decreasing[43] they planned to move into markets in the Danube, Balkan and Mediterranean regions and approved of policies showing prestige and strength in these regions, which would indirectly facilitate economic penetration. . . . The tendency to create closed markets was a feature not only of trade relations between the major powers and their colonies (as it had been before the war) but also, especially during the 1930s, of their relations with other countries whose economy was weak, no matter where they were. The Fascist approach fits this pattern, and could almost be seen as its precursor, as it substituted for the Italian economy's meagre capacity to initiate neo-mercantilist trade relations its own emphatically imperialistic political aggression.[44]

Nonetheless, whilst there was support for the regime in the most qualified sectors of the economy, especially for its internal, economic and trade union policies, its foreign policy was felt to be of less immediate interest and was more accepted than positively encouraged. There was also a degree of reticence, especially in the banking sector, with respect to embarking upon foreign investments, deemed to be risky and less profitable.[45]

Another study tends to confirm this view.[46] The study looks at the mediocre results which Italy achieved in its economic expansion into the Balkans between the wars and suggests the root causes. The failure is identified as being due (as well as to errors in political judgement on the part of Mussolini, especially in his relations with France and Britain, and to the overall weakness of Italy's economic structure) to a 'lack of available capital and a consequent stickiness and obstructionism in Italy's banking structure'.[47] The theory has an interesting bearing on the present study. It is supported in the first place by a reference to Italy's contribution to the series of international loans which, as we have already seen, were granted with some generosity to the Balkan countries during the 1920s, for the purpose of currency stabilization. The limited amount of Italy's contributions highlights 'the slowness and even reluctance of the Italian banking community (including the Bank of Italy) to become excessively involved in Eastern Europe, in spite of continuous pressure from the government'.[48] In order to participate in the issuing of these loans, banks were invoking guarantees against the exchange risk and the right to turn to the discount window of the central bank, so we can imagine how relieved Italy's central bank must have been at the hesitancy of the Italian institutions to take part in the loans.

Amongst the financial markets involved in issuing the loans to the Balkan states between 1920 and 1931, the Milan market played a decidedly secondary role. Tranches were issued on the Milan market with nominal values totalling a modest $9.5 million plus £0.95 million sterling,[49] compared to an overall total of $216.08 million, £33.25 million and FF3,041.64 million.[50]

The negligible impact of Italy's financial contribution is also confirmed, still in the same study, by the extent of the Italian banks' presence in the Balkans and the type of transactions being carried out there. If we look behind the 'glowing exterior', the paltry amounts being invested, the cautious nature of the transactions (mainly involving the public and agricultural sectors) and the 'guarantee culture' cast the Italian presence (comprising the Banca Commerciale Italiana, Credito Italiano, and Banco di Roma) in a different light. Such cautiousness suggests that the banks were aware of how precarious their presence in the region was.[51] Entrepreneurial activity outside the banking sector also lacked substance, being aimed mostly at 'stimulating commercial transactions, or at the very most carrying out building and infrastructure works, only to up sticks and leave once they had made the gains they had been looking for'.[52]

Moving from the general Balkan framework to the specific Albanian case, we can look at how Albania fitted into this picture. There is no doubt that it was an exception and that Italy's presence in Albania was huge and influential. Nonetheless, certain developments would seem to indicate that, in some respects, Italy's economic penetration into Albania was similar to the way in which Italian economic forces were acting in the wider Balkan context.

As we have already noted, Italian enterprise in Albania after the war was mainly private, as it had been at the start of the century, and involved only a few groups of speculators, who acted in a similar way to that described in the study quoted above. When Mussolini decided to initiate economic penetration into Albania, however, he thought it wise to bypass these ordinary businessmen and turn instead to the more skilled players in the economy, making use of Mario Alberti of the Credito Italiano. It is significant to note that the latter was against economic penetration in that country and 'only agreed to it under the coercion of Mussolini'.[53] He was sure that the costs involved in the expansion would outweigh its advantages, from which he deduced the necessity for financial intervention by the state, which could be far greater than any which the Credito Italiano would have been able to sustain on its own.[54] It was no coincidence, then, that Alberti, in his inaugural speech for the National Bank of Albania, interspersed his oration for the occasion with emphatic references to the Italian government, expressing his conviction of its 'sure protection', which would give the enterprise 'certain assurance of a prompt and effective defence of its legitimate interests'. Subsequent developments proved Alberti right, and saw an ever greater and more influential presence of the Italian state in Albania.

The anxious murmurs in economic and financial quarters were in contrast with the perhaps forced optimism of those closer to the government. The Chargé d'affaires, Ugo Sola, who conducted the technical negotiations for the foundation of the Bank together with Alberti, expressed the hope that the purchase of profitable oil and mineral resources would amply compensate for the costs of the enterprise.[55]

CHAPTER 4

The creation of the National Bank of Albania and the SVEA

The new monetary system

On 15 March 1925, the Agreement for the creation of the Albanian National Bank and for a large loan to the Albanian government for public works was signed by Mario Alberti, as representative of the government-approved Italian financial group, and by Mufid Bey Libohova, Albanian Finance and Foreign Minister, representing the Albanian state. The Agreement was approved by the lower and upper houses of the Albanian parliament on 23 June and 5 July 1925 respectively. At the same time, the Organic Law for the National Bank and the Law on Monetary Organization were also approved. In accordance with the provisions of the Agreement, the Bank was incorporated in Rome on 2 September, in the form of a joint-stock company, and its Charter, based closely on the contents of the Organic Law, was approved.[1]

Both the formation of the National Bank of Albania (Banka Kombëtare e Shqipnis), at the centre of a new monetary regime, and the loan made for carrying out public works created an institutional and economic structure which, on paper, fulfilled the two main recommendations put forward by Calmès. In practice, however, they could not have been further removed from them. A summary inspection of the body of regulations upon which the Bank was founded is enough to identify the main features of its structure and operations, and to see the unusual and onerous ties which were being formed with Italy.

The first and highly determinative condition was the way in which the distribution of the company capital, equivalent to 12.5 million gold francs, affected the principle of the Bank's independence. Not only was the Albanian government barred from having shares in the capital, but the participation of Albanian citizens was also set at a maximum of 49 per cent (point 2 of the Agreement). This is only a discrepancy of 1 per cent compared with the figure proposed by Calmès, but in substance the difference was much greater.

The provisions of the Agreement appeared to favour the Italian authorities, in that the remaining 51 per cent of shares in the capital seemed implicitly to be reserved for the Italian financial group, as the second party to the Agreement, but the situation was actually more problematic. There were banks in other countries (Belgium, Switzerland and Yugoslavia) which also had an interest in the enterprise and had no intention of withdrawing. Any British involvement, which had always been unlikely, was finally ruled out. 'This is all to the good', Nicolson commented.[2] For political reasons these countries could not be ignored, but, if a certain quota of shares were to be allocated to them, the Albanians would end up as majority shareholders, with everything which that implied for the management of the Bank.

The Yugoslavs in particular had been pressing their case quite strongly. A few days after the signing of the Agreement, Alberti had met with Antonievič, the Yugoslav Minister in Rome, who in a memorandum to the Italian Foreign Ministry had expressed his government's keen interest in being a major shareholder. Pressure had also been brought to bear by Lalé Zuber, Chairman of the Serbo-Albanian Bank in Cetinje, one of the Yugoslav banks interested in the enterprise. Alberti had rebuffed these attempts, on the grounds that, with the League of Nations' blessing, Italy's interests now had priority, but still it seemed that the total holding of the Yugoslavs, Swiss and Belgians could not be brought to less than 20 per cent.[3]

This meant in practice that the 49 per cent of shares reserved in the Agreement for Albanians would have to be reduced. Clear instructions to this effect were sent by Mussolini on 30 March to Durazzo, the Italian Minister in Albania.[4] According to these, 30 per cent of the share capital was to be allocated to Albanians living in Italy, who were actually dummies for the Italian financial group.[5] As for the remaining 19 per cent, since no Albanians had come forward by the last official date for subscriptions, this quota was also filled by the Italian group. Minimal allocations were subsequently made to Albanian civil servants, which did nothing to change the existing balance. The outcome was that, after 25 per cent of the capital had been allocated to the Yugoslav, Swiss and Belgian banks, 75 per cent of it went directly or indirectly to Italy, by means of the transactions outlined above.

The country did not fail to recognize the serious implications of this capital ownership structure, which in the event had excluded Albanians from any real involvement in the running of the Bank. The British immediately suspected that something was amiss in the allocation of the Bank's shares. 'I have little doubt', wrote the British Chargé d'affaires to the Foreign Office, 'that the shares thus subscribed [by Albanians] will very shortly come on to the market and that Italian interests will be able in course of time to buy up.' Eqerem Libohova, Albanian Minister in Rome and brother of Mufid, who had signed the Agreement, was appointed as a director of the Bank.[6] Mufid Bey Libohova was accused of corruption and forced to resign.[7] Specific allegations – that Mufid had been corrupted by the Italian negotiators – led to the commissioning of a parliamentary enquiry committee. The report submitted by the committee to the Albanian parliament on 7 December caused uproar. Challenges were raised against the committee on procedural grounds, the investigation was postponed and, as far as we know, everything ended without further consequences.[8] In August, Marchese Durazzo left the country, annoyed by Lessona's interference and personal dealings with Zogu.[9]

It is in this light that we read Table 4.1, which shows the formal distribution of the capital between the Bank of Albania's shareholders.

Note that, even though the founding shares, reserved for the Credito Italiano, were only valued at 1.25 Albanian francs each, they carried the right to one vote as did the ordinary shares, valued at 25.00 francs. This meant that, in terms of voting rights, the percentages representing each participating group, as shown in Table 4.1, were altered as follows:

A. Italian financial group: 37.8 per cent (as opposed to 26 per cent);
B. Yugoslav holding: 8.4 per cent (as opposed to 10 per cent);
C. Swiss and Belgian holdings: 12.6 per cent (as opposed to 15 per cent);
D. 'Private individuals', in the sense described above: 41.2 per cent (as opposed to 49 per cent).

Another important question is that of the effective ownership of the capital. We have already seen that Italian financiers, including Alberti himself, were reluctant to take on financial burdens in Albania. It was immediately clear that in practice it was the state which would bear the burden. Mussolini, as Foreign Minister, gave instructions to this effect to the Bank of Italy's Director-General, Bonaldo Stringher, in his capacity as Chairman of INCE, the Istituto Nazionale per i Cambi con l'Estero (the Italian national foreign exchange institute), in a confidential letter dated 11 May 1925. INCE was to deposit in a Swiss bank, on behalf of the subscribing Italian banks, the sum due for their quota of the capital. The payment was also to be extended to cover the subscription quota of the dummy shareholders, with deposits made at certain branches of the Credito Italiano.[10] In the end, the total cost of the transaction for the Italian state was 3,159,620 gold francs (13,915,154 Italian lire).[11]

The Bank's 'independence' was also supposed to have been safeguarded through the various company bodies. According to the Organic Law (article 2), the board of directors and the executive committee, a restricted body made up of the Chairman, Vice-chairman, Secretary and Managing

Table 4.1 Distribution of capital shareholdings in the National Bank of Albania

		No. of shares
A. Italian financial group (26% of capital):		
Credito Italiano, Genoa	Founding shares	100,000
	Ordinary shares	15,000
Banca Commerciale Italiana, Milan	Ordinary shares	30,000
Banco di Roma, Rome	Ordinary shares	30,000
Banca Nazionale di Credito, Milan	Ordinary shares	30,000
Other minor banks	Ordinary shares	20,000
		225,000
B. Yugoslav holding (10% of capital):		
Banque Zadrouga, Belgrade; Banque Serbe, Zagreb; Banque Adriatique-Danubienne, Belgrade; Banque Serbo-Albanaise, Cetinje	Ordinary shares	50,000
C. Other foreign holdings (15% of capital):		
Banque Commerciale de Bâle, Basel	Ordinary shares	50,000
Banque Belge pour l'Etranger (a branch of the Société Générale de Belgique, Brussels)	Ordinary shares	25,000
		75,000
D. Private holdings (49% of capital):		
30% of capital	Ordinary shares (Ajet Bey Libohova)	40,000
	Ordinary shares (Eqerem Bey Vlora)	58,000
	Ordinary shares (N. Vlora)	52,000
19% of capital	Ordinary shares (Ugo Viali)	40,000
	Ordinary shares (Vincenzo Azzolini)	25,000
	Ordinary shares (Massimo Aureli)	30,000
		245,000
	Giving the total number of shares as:	595,000

equivalent to 12,500,000 gold francs, to be paid in full on the founding shares and at one-fifth on the ordinary shares (point 1 of the Agreement, art. 4 of the Law and the Charter).

NB:

Value of ordinary shares: 25.00 francs.

Value of founding shares: 1.25 francs.

Director, to whom the board's powers were delegated, would have been allowed to hold meetings either in Albania or in Italy. The Charter (article 2), however, stated that they should meet in Italy. Central management would be made up of two Albanians and two Italians, with the chairmanship always reserved for an Italian (point 9 of the Agreement and article 42 of both the Law and the Charter). Meetings were to take place in accordance with Italian company law. The Bank's administration would comply with 'Italian banking procedure and practice' (point 15 of the Agreement). All the provisions, whilst they can be justified in part by the complete absence of any credit structure or standard banking practice in Albania, are unmistakable evidence of Italy's deliberate intervention in the running of the Bank. The only involvement conceded to the Albanian government was the right to appoint one board member and one internal auditor (point 10 of the Agreement, articles 37 and 48 of the Law and the Charter).[12]

A syndicate of the National Bank's majority shareholders was formed on 1 September 1925,[13] the day before the incorporation of the Bank. Under its terms the shareholding banks (Italian, Yugoslav, Swiss and Belgian) undertook to tie up the shares they owned until 1938, that is, not to sell them without the other syndicate members' consent and, even then, to transfer them only to other syndicate members or to individuals or bodies approved by them. This reinforced (if reinforcement were needed) the unassailable position of absolute dominance which Italy had acquired, and the only subsequent alteration it underwent was when ownership of shares in the Bank was officially centralized in the Italian state, when, as a consequence of the Royal Decree Law of 28 August 1935, the shares of the National Bank of Albania, with few exceptions, were taken over by INCE, on behalf of the Italian Treasury. Therefore, from 1935 onwards, almost the entire capital of the Bank was owned by the Italian state.

The Bank had the sole right to issue notes and coins, in keeping with the principles of the prevailing gold exchange standard which had been sanctioned by the Genoa Conference a few years earlier. According to the Agreement of 15 March (point 11), the Bank was in fact to have built up a metal reserve equal to one-third the value of the banknotes to be issued, whilst the Bank's own Charter was to have set the rules governing the remainder of the backing, based on the League of Nations' guidelines for newly formed issuing banks. The Organic Law and the Charter, however, moved away from the concept of full backing for the paper circulation. The Bank would issue notes against a reserve, which would be equal to at least one-third the value of the notes issued. It would be made up of gold, foreign notes from countries in which convertibility was in force, and readily available financial assets held with foreign banks belonging to countries whose currency had a stable and liquid market. The non-gold quota was not to exceed two-thirds of the total (articles 22 and 23 of the

Organic Law and the Charter).[14] If the overall reserve were to drop below one-third of the circulation, the Bank would have to increase interest rates on its own transactions by 1–1½ points, depending on the size of the drop (article 23 of the Charter). Although there was a Charter provision for meeting requests for conversion with foreign currency rather than gold, gold was actually used as the convertibility guarantee for a long time, with the size of requests being relatively modest. Although in terms of the breakdown of its reserves Albania was operating on the gold exchange standard, in practice, in its internal affairs, it applied an actual gold specie standard, a fact which was certainly boasted of by the Albanian government, but even more so by the Italian government. The greater part of the metal reserve was nonetheless held in Rome, not in Albania, further proof of the ties which bound the Bank to Italy.

The Bank and the state were to receive 50 per cent each of the proceeds from the rights to issue notes and mint coins (point 6 of the Agreement, article 15 of the Law and the Charter). Alberti, who, as we have seen, regarded the economic aspect of the whole operation with much misgiving, considered this margin insufficient for the Bank, 'in view of the fact that the current situation of the Albanian economy would preclude the Bank from almost all the ordinary profit-making transactions which credit institutions usually carry out'. He added that, with a 50 per cent share of the profits, the Bank would be worse off than it would have been under the terms envisaged in the League of Nations' plan for the foundation of an issuing bank.[15]

The monetary system had as its basis the Albanian gold franc (article 1 of the Monetary Organization Law). Its chosen parity was the same as that which had been in force before the war in the countries of the Latin Union (including Italy), though by then these countries had been progressively moving away from that rate and suspending gold convertibility, which had been equal to 0.290322 grams of fine gold to the franc.[16]

The Monetary Organization Law provided for the minting of gold coins in 100, 20 and 10 franc denominations, silver coins of 5, 2, 1 and 0.5 francs, nickel coins of 1 and 0.5 'leks'[17] (5 leks being equal to 1 franc) and, finally, bronze coins of 0.25 and 0.05 leks (article 2 of the Monetary Organization Law). Silver coins were accepted in private transactions as fractional (token) coins, but the National Bank and the Exchequer were to accept them without fixed limits (article 7).[18] The paper currency, to be issued in multiples of leks, was in all respects on a par with the coin currency (article 16).

Later on, when we move on from this examination of the Bank's institutional aspects to consider the operational side, we shall attempt to test a thesis which had already been put forward by opponents of the Fascist regime and which was later taken up at a historiographical level. According to this thesis, the Bank attempted to round up the gold which had previously been stockpiled by Albanian citizens, via the issuing of bank notes; in this way, the Bank was used, ultimately, as a vehicle to siphon Albania's gold off into Italy.

Following these notes on the National Bank of Albania's structure and the monetary system which it was intended to set in motion, it will be helpful to take a brief look at the Bank's principal activities.

Whilst the Agreement provided that in its relations with the Treasury it should be allowed to take on the services of state treasurer and to negotiate government and municipal loans (point 6), and whilst the Bank's Law and Charter confirmed these provisions, article 15 of both these sources reiterated the intention that the Bank should be autonomous, and confined its financing of the state to two very limited types of transactions: advances of up to 2.5 million francs for temporary Treasury imbalances, to be repaid within the same financial year; and discount on 60-day Treasury bills in 20,000 franc denominations, with the Bank having the right to keep the proceeds from customs and excise duties and to decide on the overall total of the bills to be discounted, in keeping with the total sum in circulation at the time.

As for relations with the public, these were established with the almost total absence of other banks in mind, and hence the need to have direct contact with the country's commercial activities, by accepting deposits and extending credit in the form of discounts on bills of exchange and advances, while refraining from any type of transaction which carried a locking-up risk.

In the same vein, the Bank was to avoid granting medium- or long-term loans, which therefore left the task of financing the country's infrastructure and industry to other bodies (article 15 of the Law and the Charter).

Hence, the currency in circulation would find its backing in a portfolio of commercial loans, as well as in reserves of gold and foreign currencies.

The sequence of events in the National Bank's foundation raises certain questions, for which we will try to find answers in the course of the following chapters. These can be summed up as follows:

- To what extent did the exceptional link with Italy influence the way the Bank was managed? What was its relationship with the Italian and Albanian governments? What were the respective conditions they imposed, and what role did the Bank of Italy play?
- How was the monetary policy managed, especially in consideration of the trends of Albania's balance of trade?
- To what extent was the exchange rate of the Albanian franc and the reserves affected by this management?

The SVEA loan

However, before investigating these points, we shall take a look at the institution which complemented the central bank, the SVEA.

As mentioned above, the Banking Agreement drawn up between the Italian group and the Albanian government provided for the issuing of a considerable loan to the latter.

This was intended to take place within a short period of time, via the formation of a company by the National Bank, namely the 'Società per lo Sviluppo Economico dell'Albania' (the company for economic development in Albania), or SVEA (point 18 of the Agreement). The capital for this company was to be 15 million lire, of which approximately 7 per cent would be allocated free of charge to the Albanian government. The company's fundamental task was to issue to the latter a loan of 50 million Albanian gold francs, to be paid in stages and at an interest rate not exceeding 7.5 per cent, or higher if market conditions dictated, with a maturity up to 40 years. The loan was destined essentially for the construction of road and rail networks and ports, and for the reclamation and draining of the marshes (points 19–22 of the Agreement). The Albanian state was to guarantee the capital and interest repayments with the proceeds from customs and excise duties and state monopolies and, in the event of these falling short of the total, with the proceeds from other taxes (point 25 of the Agreement).

SVEA was formed on 23 April 1925, which was before the actual foundation of the National Bank. As in the Bank's case, the capital was subscribed to by the major Italian banks, plus the Istituto Nazionale per la Colonizzazione e le Imprese di Lavori Italiani all'Estero (the Italian national institute for colonization and for enterprises and works abroad), minor banks and private individuals. It was to INCE, however, that the whole burden actually fell. The capital of 15 million lire stipulated in the Agreement was soon raised, and three-tenths of it were paid.[19]

As for the loan, Alberti attempted to place the relative bonds abroad, on the guarantee of the Italian government, but his attempt was not successful. In the first place, the Finance Minister de' Stefani was less than enthusiastic about the idea,[20] but, more importantly, Alberti came back empty-handed from a mission to the J. P. Morgan house in New York. As Morgan's pointed out, having only just arranged a sizeable loan to Italy of $50 million for stabilization purposes,[21] a further, smaller transaction (50 million francs would be equivalent to $9.6 million), which was 'indirect and complicated', would have made an unfavourable impression on American investors and damaged the Italian 'brand', with no advantage in return. According to Morgan's, the Italian government would be jeopardizing its own creditworthiness 'for a mess of potage'.[22] They did not succeed in placing the bonds in Italy either, which meant that these had to be taken on by INCE.[23]

Once again, the market's lack of enthusiasm meant that the financial burden for penetration into Albania fell to the public purse.

The bonds' nominal value was 70.5 million francs.[24] The loan was to be repaid within 40 years, at interest of 7.5 per cent, a rate which Alberti considered 'excessively low'.[25] An opposite view has been taken by some Marxist historians: this rate was too high and contributed to strangling the Albanian economy. The statistical information on this point is rather scattered. If we look at the long-term interest rates prevailing in Europe at that time, the rate of 7.5 per cent can be compared with 6.37 per cent on French, 5.38 per cent on Italian and 4.43 per cent on British paper (yearly average, 1925).[26] We also notice that, for foreign debtors, borrowing long-term money (other than Dominion and colonial debtors) on the London market in 1925 meant paying an 8 per cent interest rate.[27] We may argue that a risk premium on a loan to Albania should hardly be surprising and even the 7.5 per cent charged on the SVEA loan was below the London rate for similar issues. On the other hand, it is true that, because of the sheer size of this loan, even a very small interest rate would have made servicing the loan very problematic.

As the Albanian government's solvency was questionable, its guarantee was supplemented by a guarantee from the Italian government. The net amount of the loan, 50 million francs, was earmarked for paying for those public works for which the loan was intended, which meant that it would be issued in stages. On 25 November 1925, the total amount was deposited with the National Bank of Albania, in its lire equivalent of 242,794,000 (168 million euros, in today's money), so that the interest made on it could alleviate the burden of repayment for the Albanian government.[28] The value of the SVEA loan should not be underestimated. The Albanian GNP at that time is extremely uncertain but, according to some calculations,[29] it could have been between 120 and 170 million francs. The SVEA loans, therefore, might have formed between 30 and 40 per cent of Albania's total income. From the Italian viewpoint, the transaction was not negligible, either, being 0.15 per cent of the GDP for 1925.[30]

The Bank of Albania in turn deposited the sum with INCE. As Gambino pointed out, however, no immediate disbursements were made from the loan fund, by SVEA, the Treasury, or INCE on the Treasury's behalf.[31] Owing to the appreciation of the lira, the loan fund reached the equivalent of 62.1 million Albanian francs, which subsequently grew to 62.7 million through other measures. Out of this sum, an initial disbursement was made in payment for partially completed works which had already been carried out on the Albanian government's initiative, and a further sum to cover the first two six-monthly instalments and interest payments. This left 57.8 million francs available for public works, to be carried out in collaboration with the SVEA.

In 1925, then, a solid economic foundation and an articulated institutional structure formed the basis on which the economic and financial relations between Italy and Albania would rest. With the concession of 12 March, Italy had gained access to Albania's oil resources; with the Agreement of 15 March, the foundations of the Albanian Bank had been laid, mainly at the behest of the Italians and certainly with their funds. At the same time, it was decided to invest sizeable Italian financial resources in the country, through SVEA. Whilst the trade and settlement agreements of 1924 were made with strictly commercial interests in mind, the oil and banking agreements were made in a completely different spirit, which represented a quantum leap in attitude. With the Banking Agreement in particular, Italy demonstrated its interest in Albania not only from a commercial point of view but also from the point of view of the country's production mechanisms and its monetary and financial system.[32]

Closer political ties between Italy and Albania

This series of financial agreements was followed by certain political developments. It is in the light of these that we can gain a better understanding of the relatively autonomous economic policy which Zogu was able to follow during the 1930s. After the agreements on the National Bank's foundation and Italy's loan to Albania had been finalized, a secret military treaty was made between the two countries in August of that year. This was in spite of opposition from Contarini, who tried to convince il Duce of Zogu's bad faith, in the light of rumours that he had secretly renewed contacts with Yugoslavia.[33]

Shortly after Contarini's resignation as Secretary-General to the Foreign Ministry, Mussolini intensified relations with Zogu. The negotiations for a new treaty benefited from the favourable stance adopted by the British government. Whilst Austen Chamberlain, the Foreign Secretary, refused to acknowledge that Italy should have any exclusive rights and privileges, and gave the Italian government endless formal reminders to respect Albania's independence, he nonetheless wished to be the faithful executor of the decision made in 1921 by the Ambassadors' Conference, which had recognized that Italy had vital security interests to defend at the entrance to the Adriatic.

Chamberlain finally came round to considering Albania as an 'Italian Belgium',[34] in other words a small country to be protected against aggressive neighbours. Wrongly interpreted as connivance, this appeared to give Italy the green light in Albania. On 27 November 1926, a 'friendship and security pact' was signed by Aloisi, the Italian Minister in Tiranë, and the Albanian Foreign Minister, Vrioni. Under the terms of the pact, the two countries: recognized that any act liable to disturb the status quo in Albania would be contrary to their reciprocal interests; undertook to give each other mutual support and cooperation; and agreed not to enter into any pact with third powers which could be prejudicial to the other party. There was no reference in the text of the pact to League of Nations jurisdiction – the link being established between the two countries was direct and without the mediation of any international assembly.[35]

It should be noted that, regardless of the pact, Zogu was in no way prepared to allow any Italian interference to compromise Albania's sovereignty. It has been said that 'he was sure he would be able to manoeuvre his way between the most openly imperialistic Fascists, his own internal opponents, and the intrigues of the Yugoslavs, while at the same time minimizing his dependency on Mussolini'.[36] The wording of the pact was actually quite generic and flexible. Mussolini adopted an approach which was mid-way between that of the Contarini school, who were opposed to a reciprocally exclusive treaty with Albania, and that of the more openly imperialistic school, which aimed to turn Albania into a true colony. However, whilst the flexible nature of the wording allowed Zogu to call on Italy's support for his irredentist claims in the Kosovo region of Yugoslavia, and to suppress internal insurrections against his regime, it also left Italy ample room for interfering in Albania's internal affairs, in spite of the assurances it had given.[37] The Yugoslavs were not slow in noticing the sinister implications of the pact. Britain maintained a position of benign neglect towards the whole question and accepted the explanations furnished by Italy, which aimed to pass the pact off officially as nothing more than a confirmation of Italy's special position, as recognized by the Ambassadors' Conference of 1921. Meanwhile, Yugoslavia was determined to strengthen its diplomatic standing against Italy and to find a power which could act as a counterweight to Italy's growing influence in the Balkan area, and to this end it began to gravitate more towards the French.

On 11 November 1927, an accord was finally signed between France and Yugoslavia, approximately one year after the Italo-Albanian pact. The counter-response was not late in coming. On 22 November, a new treaty was signed in Tiranë between Italy and Albania, aimed at further consolidating the relationship between the two countries, the signatories this time being the new Minister in Albania, Ugo Sola, and Vrioni for Albania.[38] The treaty was defined as a 'defensive alliance treaty', and in official terms it placed the two countries on a par with each other and contained reciprocal obligations to give the other military assistance in the event of attack by a third power. However, it was viewed not only by the French but also by the British, who were reluctantly coming round to the French point of view, as a factor which seriously jeopardized the status quo in the Balkans and placed Albania dangerously within Italy's sphere of influence. This was in spite of the Italian diplomats' continuing protestations as to the reciprocity of the Agreement and its resemblance to the treaty of alliance between Britain and Portugal.[39] The 1927 Treaty of Tiranë is still a controversial issue among historians today, who disagree over its interpretation as did the political observers of the time. In the more positive interpretations, the treaty did nothing to change Albania's status, firmly placed as it had been since 1921 within Italy's sphere of influence. Albania's independence was not in question, since it was guaranteed by the League of Nations. According to this viewpoint, the treaty was a natural complement to the pact of the previous year and was mainly aimed at protecting Albania from the long-standing aggressive intentions of its dangerous neighbour, Yugoslavia. It is not surprising that the analogy which Sola had drawn with Britain's relationship with Portugal, at the time that the treaty was drawn up, appears also in De Felice's work.[40] According to the most negative interpretation, the treaty was a prelude to the clear establishment of Albania as an Italian protectorate and was the final stage of an evolving process by which Mussolini had been slowly but surely moving away from the policies of the 'old guard' in Italian diplomacy. According to this interpretation, the Treaty of Tiranë of late 1927, far from being the definitive expression of a moderate stage in Mussolini's foreign policy, was rather the outcome of a typically imperialistic approach: a foretaste of his foreign policy of the 1930s and, as such, the first step towards Italy's occupation of Albania in 1939.[41]

Roughly one year later, on 1 September 1928, Ahmet Zogu had himself proclaimed 'King Zog of the Albanians' by an ad hoc assembly, in an act inspired by Italy which constituted 'a bare-faced encouragement of Albania's irredentist claims in the Kosovo region of Yugoslavia'.[42] Italy was the first country to recognize the constitutional change in Albania.[43]

CHAPTER 5

The balance of trade, the balance of payments and the exchange rate of the Albanian franc

A gold parity for the new currency

The Albanian franc has long been remembered as one of the strongest currencies of the inter-war period. According to the authoritative *International Currency Review* of July 1977:

> Before the Second World War, the Albanian franc was the strongest currency in Europe. The strength of the Albanian franc – established on 25 June 1925 with a gold content of 0.290323 grams, was associated with its gold cover of 100%. The notes of the Albanian National Bank, issued from March 1926 onwards, were, in effect, bullion certificates. The currency was never devalued, in spite of the 1931 devaluation of sterling, the dollar's devaluation in 1933 and the Swiss franc's depreciation in 1936. Even when Albania was occupied by Italy in 1939, the rate of exchange, although pegged to the Italian lira, was maintained within a tiny fraction of the earlier rate.[1]

It is worth emphasizing, therefore, not only the pegging of the Albanian franc to the former gold parity of the dissolved Latin Monetary Union, during the period of widespread and enduring currency instability that was the post-war period, but also the fact that it maintained its value during the 1930s while the major currencies were forced one by one to abandon the gold standard (see Figure 5.1).

In this chapter, we shall try to identify the reasons behind this strength and to understand the effect it had on financial relations with Italy, by examining Albania's foreign accounts during the period from the early 1920s to the Italian occupation of the country in 1939.

As we have already mentioned, the gold content of the Albanian currency was set at 0.290322 grams to the franc, which was the gold content used by the former Latin Union. The Union had by then effectively dissolved. Already before the First World War and even more as a result of it, the

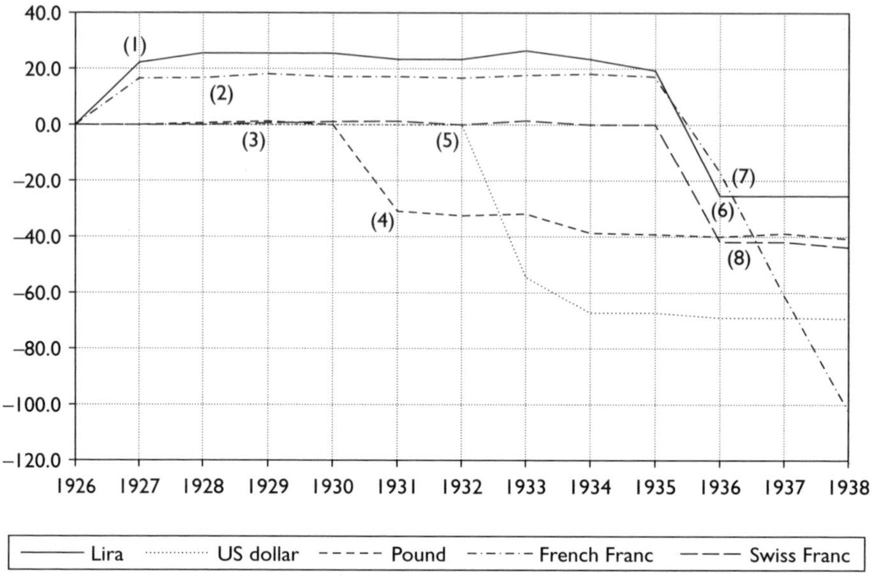

Figure 5.1 Devaluation (–) or revaluation (+) of certain currencies in relation to the Albanian franc (starting from 1926)

Key:
(1) 21 Dec. 1927: stabilization of the lira;
(2) 25 June 1928: stabilization of the French franc;
(3) 20 Dec. 1929: return to pre-war parity of the Swiss franc;
(4) 24 Sept. 1931: sterling abandons the gold standard;
(5) 31 Dec. 1932: devaluation of the dollar;
(6) 5 Oct. 1936: realignment of the lira;
(7) 1 Oct. 1936: adoption of inconvertibility by the French franc;
(8) 27 Sept. 1936: adoption of inconvertibility by the Swiss franc.

Note:
1926–1928: annual average exchange rate;
1929–1937: December average exchange rate;
1938: mean of average June, September and December exchange rates.

Source: Société des Nations, *Annuaire Statistique 1933–1934*, Geneva, 1934, and *Annuaire Statistique 1938–1939*, Geneva, 1939.

countries belonging to the Union had been progressively abandoning the gold standard, with the introduction of their currencies' inconvertibility. It was not only the currencies within the Latin Union which had been involved in moving away from the gold standard, but all the major Western currencies, including those of Britain, the United States and Germany.

It is true that, with the end of the war, the problem which dominated the currencies was that of stabilization and that, in the prevailing opinion of the time, stabilization equalled a return to gold. The Genoa Conference of 1922, of which we have already spoken, enshrined this principle, advocating a return to gold as the cornerstone on which to rebuild the international monetary system. It is also true, however, that, while acknowledging the need to stabilize currencies and to restore gold convertibility, there was a recognition that the events during and after the war had led to a huge expansion in national budgets, especially on the expenditure side, and a violent acceleration in inflation, which would make a straightforward return to the pre-war gold content an arduous task.

A distinction began to be made therefore (this tendency emerges clearly from the records of the Genoa Conference[2]) between a group of countries which had been less severely hit by inflation and which could therefore envisage a restoration of pre-war parity, and another group which had suffered more violent inflation and could only stabilize their currencies at gold contents representing a fraction of the previous ones. We know that, while a few countries managed, albeit amid violent polemics, to stabilize their currencies in the first sense (the United States in 1919, Britain in 1925 and Switzerland in 1929), most of the other major countries arrived at stabilization in the late 1920s, at the cost of heavy deflation, reaching a level well below the pre-war level (Italy in 1927 and France one year later). Meanwhile, the Latin Union, already effectively disbanded, was abandoned by Belgium in 1925 and formally dissolved in 1927.[3]

Returning to Albania, it is puzzling that in 1925 one of the poorest and most backward countries in Europe adopted a currency with the same gold content as the Latin Union, which had by then been effectively abandoned with little prospect of renewal. The available documentation does not offer any clear explanation of the rationale behind the adoption of this parity, but certain factors can be taken into account.

In the first place, there was no former parity to be restored. The country quite simply did not possess a currency regime of its own before the First World War. Its independence only dated back to 1913. The troubled months of Prince Von Wied's government, followed by the events of the war years, which had witnessed the Albanian territory first as the theatre of some bitter battles and then occupied by several warring countries, certainly had not created an ideal climate for the consolidation of any system. The fact remains, however, as previously mentioned, that the little circulation which did exist in the country was for the most part made up of coins from countries belonging to the Latin Union. The gold franc was the unit of account adopted by the Exchequer.[4] These facts alone constituted reasons enough for basing the new regime on the framework of the former Union.

Another factor was that, wartime vicissitudes aside, Albania had not experienced (probably because of its very lack of an effective central power), the process of expansion in public spending which had been a primary cause of monetary collapse elsewhere. The rudimentary nature of the economy also played a part. Self-sufficiency, and hence the fragmentation of the system into countless self-contained units, was more or less the norm, and there had therefore been no means for a price system to develop.[5] Consequently, there had been no severe inflationary trend which could pose any serious dilemma regarding the level at which the currency should be set. The only reliable and consistent point of reference, as Calmès was quick to emphasize in his report,[6] appeared to be a sizeable store of precious metals which had not yet been gathered into a central bank, as there was none, but had been stockpiled by Albanian families.

However, while we may presume that at an internal level there was no dilemma in choosing the gold content of the new currency, at an external level the factors for valuation were more conflicting.

In the early 1920s, the years immediately preceding the creation of the National Bank of Albania and the law which founded the new monetary regime, a marked imbalance existed in Albania's balance of trade. Referring to 1921, Calmès observed that the emigrant remittances had not been sufficient to outweigh the deficit, which had instead been covered by an outflow of precious metals worth 7.5 million gold francs.[7]

However, this imbalance began rapidly to be absorbed thanks to a considerable increase in exports, so that in 1925 it represented only 4.7 million francs (as opposed to the 15–16 million of a few years earlier), while the ratio of exports to imports rose and in 1925 exceeded 3/4 (see Table 5.1).

Table 5.1 Albanian balance of trade, 1920–1925 (in millions of Albanian francs)

	Imports	Exports	Total	Balance	Percentage exports/imports
1920	17.5	1.5	19.0	–16.0	8.6
1921	18.2	2.2	20.4	–16.0	12.1
1922	12.1	3.0	15.1	–9.1	24.8
1923	23.4	8.1	31.5	–15.3	34.6
1924	20.5	12.4	32.9	–8.1	60.5
1925	21.8	17.1	38.9	–4.7	78.4

Source: L. Lenti, Gli scambi internazionali dell'Albania, in *Principii di economia albanese* (Padua, Cedam, 1940), pp. 165–185.

There are no data available during the years in question for the other main entry on the current account side, the emigrant remittances, but we can presume (and the pattern of the remittances in the years following 1925 supports this) that they tended to outweigh the gap in the trade figures, which in any event was rapidly closing, and this encouraged the adoption of a relatively strong exchange rate.

While we are lacking in reliable sources of information, it is safe to assume that assigning that particular gold content to the Albanian franc was also influenced by factors of a more political nature: the creation of the National Bank of Albania and the Albanian currency regime was the product of an operation which had been led by Italy. Those responsible for establishing Albania's currency certainly intended to show that the regime being created was a 'healthy' one, and, within the accepted norms of the mid-1920s, this meant choosing (or returning to) a system which was soundly anchored to gold, and adhering as closely as possible to a body of norms and procedures which had been in place before the First World War. Setting a parity equal to the pre-war parity of many countries was a clear and ostentatious way of expressing such an approach.[8]

Albania's foreign accounts: the first phase (1926–1929) – trade deficits and capital surpluses

The next question is whether this parity can be seen as justified in the light of the subsequent development of the Albanian economy. Let us briefly analyse the situation in the light of the pattern of the balance of trade and the balance of payments. Later on in the chapter we will also examine the strength of the Albanian franc by taking into account the movement of the real exchange rate, with reference to the evolution of prices in Albania and Italy, Albania's main trade partner. It must be borne in mind, however, that this assessment is problematic, especially as far as the balance of payments (for which we possess statistics which are partial and for certain years only) and the real exchange rate are concerned. A high degree of caution is therefore needed in interpreting the unfinished series of statistics and those with gaps.

One difficulty in assessing the period under discussion in this chapter – that is from 1926, when Italy began its lending activities to Albania, until 1938, the year preceding Italy's occupation of Albania – is, in fact, the lack of statistical evidence regarding the balance of payments from 1934 onwards. It is, however, reasonable to assume that, in the presence of a structural deficit in Albania's balance of trade, capital inflows from abroad, mostly from Italy, were the defining element that conditioned the Albanian foreign accounts and, ultimately, the relative strength of the Albanian currency.

Relying mainly on balance of trade figures, we can divide the above period into three phases, preceding, coinciding with and following the Great Depression respectively. This is done purely for the sake of convenience, because the flow of financial resources from Italy – which is what the capital account of Albania's balance of payments essentially was – was not synchronized with the cyclical pattern of Albania's foreign trade now outlined (see Tables 5.2 and 5.3).

The first phase covers the years 1926–1929, preceding the Great Depression. Albanian foreign trade expanded vigorously,[9] especially on the import side. Even though the 'invisibles', mostly emigrant remittances, produced a sizeable surplus, the current account deficit expanded over time.

On the capital account side, the periodic SVEA loan disbursements emerged quite clearly, as does, in general, the net inflow of capital from abroad, evidence of the financial contributions which Italy was making to Albania.

The capital account surplus not only compensated for the negative balance in the current account but also allowed the accumulation of foreign assets, which is what caused the Albanian franc to hold its value so well on the foreign exchange market. In 1929 the capital account registered a surplus of 15.6 million francs, and the overall balance also showed a surplus, of 4.8 million francs.

Table 5.2 Albanian balance of trade, 1926–1938 (in millions of Albanian francs)

	Imports	Exports	Total	Balance	Percentage exports/imports
1926	24.9	12.1	37.0	–12.8	48.6
1927	24.7	11.1	35.8	–13.6	44.9
1928	32.1	14.9	47.0	–17.2	46.4
1929	38.6	14.7	53.3	–23.9	38.1
1930	33.3	12.4	45.7	–20.9	37.2
1931	29.5	7.5	37.0	–22.0	25.4
1932	22.8	4.5	27.3	–18.3	19.7
1933	15.9	5.7	21.6	–10.2	35.8
1934	12.3	4.3	16.6	–8.0	35.0
1935	13.7	6.0	19.7	–7.7	43.8
1936	16.8	7.4	24.2	–9.4	44.0
1937	18.9	10.2	29.1	–8.7	54.0
1938	23.0	9.7	32.7	–13.3	42.2

Source: Lenti, Gli scambi internazionali dell'Albania, pp. 165–185.

Table 5.3 Albania's balance of payments, 1926–1933 (in millions of Albanian francs)

	Current account				Capital account					
	A	B	C	D	E	F	G	H	I	L
1926	−13.6		+11.9	−1.7	0.6		1.6		2.2	0.5
1927	−14.5	−0.2	+11.9	−2.8	1.4		2.2		3.6	0.8
1928	−17.6	−0.2	+12.7	−5.1	2.4		3.5		5.9	0.8
1929	−24.8	−0.2	+14.2	−10.8	9.6		6.0		15.6	4.8
1930	−20.8	−0.2	+10.3	−10.7	11.8		4.5		16.3	5.6
1931	−22.4	−0.2	+10.1	−12.5	15.8	1.0	2.2		19.0	6.5
1932	−18.7	−0.2	+9.0	−9.9	7.0	7.0	2.0		16.0	6.1
1933	−12.3	−0.5	+2.7	−10.1	4.0	3.4	0.6	2.1	10.1	0

Key:
A: trade balance;[a]
B: interest and dividends on foreign capital invested in Albania;
C: services balance;[b]
D: total balance of current account;
E: SVEA loan;
F: 1931 loan;
G: other long-term capital inflows;
H: short-term transactions;
I: total balance of capital account;
L: overall balance.

[a] These totals do not coincide exactly with those in Table 5.2 as they include adjustments for errors and for non-registered goods.
[b] Emigrant remittances, tourism, land returns, diplomatic services.

Source: Société des Nations, *Balance des paiements*, Geneva, 1932, 1933, 1935.

In spite of the noticeable correlation between the deficit in the balance of trade and the surplus in the capital movement, as seen in Figure 5.2, which meant that the latter took on *ex post facto* a compensating role in Albania's balance of payments, this did not mean that the Italian financial authorities regarded the movement of capital into Albania as a means of closing the deficit in Albania's foreign accounts. The inverse was actually the case – the movements of capital were prompted by the regime's policy of penetration into Albania which was more than purely economic and they acted therefore as an 'exogenous variable' within the Albanian economy.

In fact, Italy was not deterred from pouring capital into Albania by the country's limited capacity to repay it. Difficulties emerged almost immediately in servicing the SVEA loan. The first annuity had been deducted from the proceeds of the loan, but the annuity for 1926, which

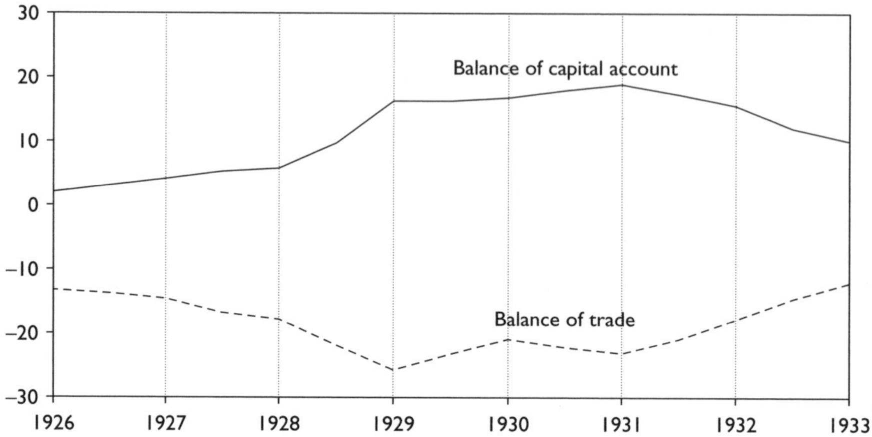

Figure 5.2 Albania: movement of capital and balance of trade, 1926–1933 (in millions of Albanian francs)

Source: Lenti, Gli scambi internazionali dell'Albania, pp. 165–185.

was the first to be paid out of ordinary state revenues, was not forthcoming. An adjustment was made to the loan repayments in an agreement of 26 February 1926, under which a moratorium was granted for the years 1926 to 1929. However, in 1930, out of repayments owing worth 10 million Albanian francs, only 0.9 million had been actually paid, after which the repayments went into complete default.[10]

Another worrying development (for the Italians) was that not only were the Albanians not servicing the loans but the money they received was being spent on buying goods from other countries, not from Italy. Had Albania spontaneously decided to spend the money received from the loan on imports from Italy or had it been obliged to do so by some clause in the loan agreement (in other words if it had been a tied loan), the inflow of capital would have generated an equivalent widening of its trade deficit with Italy. This however did not happen. As Italian lending activity intensified, the overall trade deficit increased, but the deficit with Italy remained static or decreased. This was because the proceeds from the loan were being spent on purchases from third countries (see Tables 5.4 and 5.5).

We can see from Tables 5.4 and 5.5 that Italy was the main market for both Albania's imports and its exports. However, while Albanian exports going into Italy made up a considerable portion of the total, thus allowing an Italian commentator to say that 'only Italy increased its purchases on the Albanian market, which was being progressively deserted by all the other

Table 5.4 Geographical distribution of Albania's foreign trade, 1921–1929 (in percentages)

	1921	1922	1923	1924	1925	1926	1927	1928	1929
Albanian exports:									
Italy	73.7	68.7	60.3	51.5	58.7	45.8	50.5	61.2	60.4
Other countries	26.3	31.3	39.7	48.5	41.3	54.2	49.5	38.8	39.6
Albanian imports:									
Italy	72.2	79.3	68.1	75.5	75.2	67.1	61.7	49.0	45.7
Other countries	27.8	30.7	31.9	24.5	24.8	32.9	38.3	51.0	54.3

Sources: for 1921–1926, *Situazione economica dell'Albania*, Report presented to the International Chamber of Commerce, Stockholm, 1927; for 1927–1929, Frasca Polara, Il commercio estero e la politica degli scambi in Albania.

Table 5.5 Albania's trade with Italy, 1921–1929 (in millions of Albanian francs)

	1921	1922	1923	1924	1925	1926	1927	1928	1929
Exports	1.6	2.0	4.9	6.4	10.0	5.5	6.3	9.1	8.9
Imports	13.2	8.4	15.9	15.5	16.4	16.7	15.3	15.7	17.6
Balance	−11.6	−6.4	−11.0	−9.1	−6.4	−11.2	−9.0	−6.6	−8.7

Source: for 1921–1926, *Situazione economica dell'Albania*; for 1927–1929, A. Gambino, Le relazioni economiche fra l'Italia e l'Albania, in *Rivista internazionale di scienze sociali*, 1940.

countries',[11] the proportion of Albania's imports coming from Italy was being constantly and drastically reduced, and this dates from the time when Italy's political interest became more pressing. While in 1924 and 1925 it was still around the 75 per cent mark, by 1928 it was below 50 per cent. In the bilateral trade relationship between Italy and Albania, the Albanian deficit began in the latter part of the decade to show a reduction.

The second phase (1930–1934) – the Great Depression and the increasing trade disagreements between Italy and Albania

Moving on to the second phase (1930–1934), it is marked by separate but crucial events: the Great Depression, Zog's most serious attempts to pursue a policy of independence, and a growing Italian perception of Albania as a political, economic and financial liability. The 1930s saw a worsening in Italy's relative position. However, it is worth making a few general observations on the changes taking place on the economic and financial scene in the Balkans during those years, since it is this wider scene which provides a reference for developments in Albania.

At the beginning of the 1930s, the Balkan states were severely hit by the world crisis.[12] Albania was no exception, but once again developments in Albania took a particular turn, owing to its close links with Italy.

The starting point of the crisis in the Balkans can be identified in the widespread drop in the price of agricultural produce. Although the wholesale price index had already begun to fall in 1929, in Albania, as elsewhere, the worldwide crisis of 1931 accelerated the fall. Since the Balkan countries depended on agricultural exports in a major way, they were consequently obliged to drastically reduce their imports. All this was happening while the collapses in the banking sector in the major Western countries and the fall of the pound (which abandoned the gold standard in September 1931) were leading to an abrupt interruption to the flow of foreign capital into the Balkans and the withdrawal of short-term capital investments, especially in Yugoslavia, Romania and Greece. All this in turn led to a continuous decrease in the currency reserves of the central banks, the imposition of currency restrictions aimed at maintaining exchange rates at the levels at which they had previously been 'stabilized' (thanks to those very foreign loans), and finally a widespread abandoning of the gold standard. Greece moved away from it in 1932. Elsewhere, while the currencies kept a theoretical parity, their external depreciation was tacitly accepted. Finally, it became clear that servicing the foreign debts was going to be impossible: the Balkan states were in default.

The fall in prices had brought serious consequences for the agricultural classes, who had freely taken on debts while the price of their produce had been higher. Their purchasing power was now greatly reduced. Given the relevance of the agricultural sector to these countries' economies, tax receipts were consequently greatly reduced, which led to a crisis in public finances. In several countries, drastic measures were introduced to deal with the debt problem of the agricultural sector, by allowing moratoriums or cancelling debts outright (as in Bulgaria, Yugoslavia, Romania and Greece), and by supporting the price of wheat by state purchases at higher than market prices (in Bulgaria, Yugoslavia and Romania).[13] The other major problem described above, that of the deterioration of the external position caused by the export crisis and the interruption to the flow of foreign capital, was tackled almost everywhere by attempts to start a painstaking process of industrialization, in other words diversifying the economy which until then had been primarily agriculture based.

Moving on to look at Albania, its foreign trade did not escape the dramatic deterioration encountered by the other Balkan states; in fact, it suffered even more noticeably in this area (see Table 5.6).

Table 5.6 Trade balance of certain Balkan countries (in millions of the national currency)

	Albania (Albanian franc)			Romania (leu)			Yugoslavia (dinar)			Greece (drachma)			Bulgaria (lev)		
Yearly average	a		b	a		b	a		b	a		b	a		b
1926–1929	100.0	43.3	44.3	100.0	66,166	99.7	100.0	14,729	94.3	100.0	18,194	51.0	100.0	13,031	92.8
1930	106.2	46.0	37.2	77.8	51,468	124.3	93.3	13,735	97.5	89.5	16,291	54.8	82.7	10,774	134.9
1931	85.5	37.0	25.4	56.8	37,615	143.8	65.1	9,594	100.2	71.1	12,928	47.5	81.3	10,591	127.4
1932	62.4	27.0	19.7	42.6	28,161	145.9	39.9	5,879	108.2	68.3	12,427	58.3	52.6	6,852	97.4
1933	50.8	22.0	35.8	39.2	25,905	120.7	42.2	6,211	119.2	74.6	13,569	61.0	38.7	5,047	129.2
1934	39.3	17.0	35.0	40.6	26,865	103.4	49.8	7,330	110.5	78.4	14,265	62.3	36.7	4,782	112.8

Key:
a: total trade and index number of total trade;
b: percentage coverage of imports by exports.

Source: Société des Nations, *Annuaire statistique 1927*, Geneva, 1928, and *Annuaire Statistique 1936–1937*, Geneva, 1937.

Where Albania finds itself in a markedly worse situation compared with the other countries is in the persistence of a very low export/import ratio. This feature can probably be put down to the fact that, while in the other countries the contraction of exports due to the Great Depression entailed a corresponding reduction in imports, in Albania imports were maintained for as long as the inflow of Italian capital continued; hence the gap between exports and imports widened. Here we see how Italian capital inflow conditioned the Albanian trade balance. When, for reasons that will shortly be made clear, that inflow ceased, Albanian imports also went down, and the trade gap was correspondingly reduced.

The data for the balance of payments stop, as we have said, at 1933. Up to that year, in spite of the positive balance on the services side, the current part ended in deficit. The positive overall balance, which remained until 1932, was cancelled out in 1933 owing to the reduced inflow of capital. In the following two years, the statistics on money supply, which we will look at in Chapter 6, demonstrated a destruction of liquidity under the 'foreign' component, which supports the hypothesis that the overall balance of payments was likewise negative.

The period 1930–1934 is actually a crucial phase in the relationship between Italy and Albania, not only in financial terms, and it will be useful to give it more detailed attention. The beginning of the 1930s saw the Fascist regime still heavily committed to the payments to Albania, in spite of the difficulties which Albania had clearly been having in coping with the repayments. These difficulties were foreseeable, and in fact had been foreseen. It was known that Albania would have great difficulty in repaying the loan, but the intention was to use this fact in order to gain some control over the Albanian administration, in particular over its customs and excise.[14] Albania was therefore granted successive moratoriums on the SVEA loan, of which a large portion was never repaid. Through successive agreements between SVEA and the Albanian government, reductions were granted in Albania's capital and interest repayments. By the end of 1938, the Albanian government had repaid only 1.1 million francs to SVEA.[15] However, the underlying political intentions meant that the debtor's breach of the repayment terms did nothing to discourage the lender from making further loans.

On the contrary, the Albanian government, encouraged by Italy's generous assistance, paid little attention to the rapid fall in ordinary revenues at the beginning of the 1930s and maintained expenditure at 30 million Albanian francs per year, 45 to 50 per cent of which was for military purposes.[16] Thus, in 1931, a new ten-year loan of up to 10 million Albanian francs per year was granted by the Italian government, interest free and with no fixed term for repayment, aimed primarily at financing Albania's balance of payments deficit. An Italian Foreign Ministry memorandum of 8 July 1931 illustrates the political nature of this loan also, stating that the deficit had:

> caused a concern that the administrative and military organization of the young state might not live up to the Fascist government's expectations. Moreover, in view of the SVEA loan having been used up, there was a clear need to generate new activities to boost Albania's anaemic economy [a sort of deficit spending] and to extend our penetration into the country.[17]

The Italian Minister in Tiranë, di Soragna, observed for his part that 'ours is a loan by name only. In reality, it is a free annual contribution.'[18]

Only two annual disbursements of the loan were made, before it was suspended on 1 April 1933. The suspension must be explained partly on technical and partly on political grounds. What had actually happened was that many obstacles had been met within the joint Italo-Albanian Commission which had been appointed to pay out and distribute the loan and especially to supervise the way in which the payments were put to use. This entailed having some control over Albania's public administration, which Albania rightly saw as interference in the country's internal affairs. The official reason given for suspending the loan was 'the difficult times towards which the world economy is heading', but in reality political motives were never far away.[19]

This massive transfer of resources into Albania was, in fact, a cause for serious concern within Albania's administration – on a political level because of the implicit link it was creating between the two countries and the potential interference in Albania's internal administration; and on a financial level because of the objective difficulty in servicing the loans given a balance of trade heavily in deficit and exports which had been severely hit by the Great Depression.

There were clearly two conflicting interests: Italy needed a boost to its exports to Albania, in order to obtain a trade surplus which could repay capital expenses in Albania. In turn, Albania's primary objective was to fill its trade gap. This happened in the midst of the worst economic crisis of the century.

Albania saw the need for a decisive drive on exports, in the first instance to Italy which had long been the destination of choice for Albanian goods. 'Open the doors for our produce to come into Italy', Prime Minister Pandeli Evangjeli had said, 'and our economy, thus revived, will be more able to deal with the SVEA loan.'[20] An Albanian Royal Commission set up to study the economy's problems therefore advocated, in a report presented to the government in 1932,[21] the adoption of a policy 'based on the principle of balanced imports and exports and quota restrictions', to deal with the huge gap in the balance of trade.

The Italians were thinking along very different lines, however. Ignoring the overall deficit in Albania's balance of trade and concentrating on bilateral Italo-Albanian trade, they aimed for a drive on Italian exports into Albania, in order to offset their own increased financial commitment in the country. Tables 5.7 and 5.8 illustrate how, in the 1930s, this goal was far from being reached. Italy's interests are clearly explained in an essay by Frasca Polara of 1932.

After the trade agreement signed with Italy in 1924,[22] Albania had signed other treaties for special bilateral tariffs with Greece, Yugoslavia and France and had extended the relative benefits to other countries, by means of various types of trade conventions, all of which demanded the most-favoured-nation clause.[23] The consequence of all these treaties had been, as Frasca Polara pointed out, the persisting serious imbalance in Albania's foreign accounts, but, even more, a position of advantage for 'many countries which on their part have done nothing to ease Albania's burden in these very arduous years of economic revival, during which Albania's goods have found a sole outlet in Italy'.[24]

Table 5.7 Geographical distribution of Albania's foreign trade, 1930–1938 (in percentages)

	1930	1931	1932	1933	1934	1935	1936	1937	1938
Albanian exports:									
Italy	59.8	66.2	62.7	79.6	63.4	61.1	66.6	78.6	68.4
Other countries	40.2	33.8	37.3	20.4	36.6	38.9	33.4	21.4	31.6
Albanian imports:									
Italy	50.2	46.9	39.5	41.9	34.1	28.4	24.9	24.0	36.3
Other countries	49.8	53.1	60.5	58.1	65.9	71.6	75.1	76.0	63.7

Source: Gambino, Le relazioni economiche fra l'Italia e l'Albania.

Table 5.8 Albania's trade with Italy, 1930–1938 (in millions of Albanian francs)

	1930	1931	1932	1933	1934	1935	1936	1937	1938
Exports	7.4	5.0	2.8	4.6	2.7	3.7	4.9	8.0	6.7
Imports	16.6	13.9	8.9	6.7	4.2	3.9	4.2	4.9	8.3
Balance	–9.2	–8.9	–6.1	–2.1	–1.5	–0.2	+0.7	+3.1	–1.6

Source: Gambino, Le relazioni economiche fra l'Italia e l'Albania.

Frasca Polara observed, in reference to the proposals by the Albanian Royal Commission, that if the policy of balancing imports and exports was meant in a *relative* sense, in other words if the percentage of purchases and sales was related to the total imports and exports of each state, this would have meant that Italy, which absorbed two-thirds of Albania's exports, would have to provide two-thirds of Albania's imports, which would substantially improve Italy's own position. If, however, the expression 'balanced imports and exports' was intended in an *absolute* sense, in other words that of a balanced trade between one state and the other, then Albania's export into Italy should increase dramatically, or its imports from Italy should be drastically reduced. However, given the 'necessity' of the current level of Albanian imports for economic development and the impossibility for Albania greatly to increase its exports, Frasca Polara concluded, in his critique of the Commission's report, that Albania's trade deficit was insurmountable, and therefore the composition of Albania's imports should be modified in favour of those countries which were of most benefit to Albania (in other words Italy).

More particularly:

> Where country *X* cannot and most probably will not be able to buy from Albania, why should Albania favour *X*? Country *X* would thus become a competitor to those few countries [Italy] which buy generous quantities of Albanian goods and . . . can be of most benefit to Albania. What is needed therefore is a complete revision of Albania's foreign trade relationships.

As we can see, Frasca Polara took it for granted that Albania would find it impossible to increase its exports.

At a diplomatic level, Albania's intention to close the trade gap by means of a substantial increase in exports to Italy was exploited politically by Italy with a decision to create a customs union between the two countries, which would make Albania's bond to Italy stronger and more permanent. The Italian government thought that the political benefits of a customs union would, in this approach, outweigh the disadvantage of increased imports from Albania.

In March 1932 meetings began, which were to remain private, between the Italian Minister in Tiranë, di Soragna, and King Zog and his government, to negotiate this customs union between the two countries. They did not go well, one obstacle being the king's insistence on being independent from his 'great ally'. Di Soragna was trying to prove: a) that for geographical and political reasons only Italy could be an effective destination market for Albanian goods; b) that the current system of Italian trade agreements, based as it was on the most-favoured-nation clause, did not allow Albanian exports to Italy to be given preferential treatment over exports from third countries; c) that inevitable international repercussions made any kind of reimbursement (as Albania had proposed) out of the question; and d) that a customs union therefore seemed to be the only solution.[25]

The solution proposed was not without its pitfalls, which on Albania's side were of a political nature and on Italy's side of an economic nature. Zog was actually afraid that, with the formation of such a union, Albania would be bound 'hand and foot' to Italy, so although he did want the substantial advantages which would come with the union he would not admit it. Italy, however, could see few advantages from an economic point of view. The Director-General for production and trade, Anzilotti, put forward a series of observations on the matter. In the context of Italy's overall trade figures, the volume and value of trade with Albania was minimal; extending customs tariffs to the Albanian border would necessitate extending inspection procedures accordingly; it would be necessary to keep in check any Albanian interference in Italy's commercial dealings with other countries; and Italy's tariff system would have to be adapted to the primitive nature of Albania's economy. However, Italian politicians were attached to the political aspects of the union, seeing it as a symbol of closer ties between the two countries. In short, 'while Albania supported the substance of the union . . . Italy supported its form'.[26]

An international press campaign at the beginning of 1933 disclosed the negotiations taking place and this, added to the above factors which in truth were not very encouraging, delayed the project by obliging Zog to deny that negotiations were under way.[27]

Thus 1933 was a somewhat awkward year in the political relationship between the two countries, with the failure of the negotiations for a customs union coming in the wake of the interruption to the 1931 loan.[28]

It was during this period that Zog made complicated attempts to obtain loans elsewhere, all of which failed. Although he acted discreetly, news of his attempts reached Rome and it is worth reporting word for word Mussolini's response and his instructions to the Italian Minister in Tiranë:

> With respect to the information gathered and the hints we have been given on Zogu's proposal to enlist the help of the League of Nations in obtaining a loan for Albania [writes Mussolini on 12 August 1933] it will be useful for you to choose a suitable occasion, when your remarks will seem completely natural and spontaneous, to point out how, for obvious reasons, Albania would not be able to obtain any loan without the participation, or rather the positive support of Italy. Among other reasons, the Geneva process is long and requires the consensus of all the major powers before a decision of this kind can be made; but I must emphasize that all this should be said in such a way that the

> Albanians will not guess that Italy might have concerns as to the success of such a project.[29]

King Zog's precarious position, however, made him hold out for guarantees which other countries were unable to grant, and he was thrown back on his own resources, curtailing public expenditure and leaving projects unfinished.

The final year of this phase, 1934, saw a considerable contraction in Albania's foreign trade, owing partly to the drop in imports which until then had been sustained, in spite of the world depression, by the Italian loans (see Table 5.2).

The final phase (1935–1938) – increasing Italian financial commitments and no returns

The final period before the occupation is from 1935 to 1938. Reconciliation with Italy began in the early part of 1935 and by March 1936 Albania was able to secure renewed assistance at the price of fresh concessions and increased political intervention.[30] Italy promised to make substantial loans and grants, and in return Albania agreed to accept greater Italian influence. The first clear sign of the political rapprochement between Mussolini and Zog was Albania's distancing itself from the League of Nations' sanctions on Italy following the war in Ethiopia (November 1935).[31] On 19 March of the following year, the governments of Rome and Tiranë came to a new series of financial agreements (a 'package' of around 14 million Albanian francs, 45 million euros in today's money), whose substance can be summed up as follows:[32]

1	Payments in 'liquidation of the 10 year loan of 1931', over a two-year period	890,946
2	Funding of the Albanian state budget deficit 1934–1935	1,700,000
3	Capital refinancing of the National Agricultural Bank, over a three-year period	2,800,000
4	'Agricultural loan', over a three-year period	6,000,000
5	'Loan for the tobacco monopoly', over a two-year period	3,000,000
	Albanian francs	14,390,946

with an additional two loans for the port at Durrës. These loans were granted by the Banco di Napoli. 'Even in this case, however, it must be supposed that the Italian government are backing the transactions, as the interest provided for is at the wholly uncommercial rate of 1%.'[33]

In 1936 the Albanian government agreed to provide 250,000 Albanian francs for the service of the SVEA loan, but it was understood that payment would not be claimed by the Italians while financial difficulties persisted (further agreements provided for moratoriums, postponements, and cancellations of annuities).[34]

In this connection, an agreement was also signed between the Albanian government and the EIAA (Ente Industri Agrarie Albanesi): 'its general effect was to give EIAA a preponderant, and to some extent monopolistic, position in regard to the trade between the two countries'.[35]

Albania's balance of trade began to fare better: imports grew, owing to the resumption of Italian loans, but exports did also, owing to a revival in external demand (see Table 5.2).

At a bilateral level, however, in spite of the resumption of capital mobilization in favour of Albania, Italy's position within Albania's trade continued to worsen, to the point that in 1936 Albania's balance actually developed a surplus (see Table 5.8).

The deterioration of Italian exports into Albania was affected by competition from other countries, in particular Germany (iron, chemical products, clocks), Britain (wool products, rubber), Yugoslavia (cement, wood products) and the United States (transport), but especially from Japan.

> Not only has the treaty with Japan robbed our cotton textiles trade of several hundreds of thousands of gold francs, but it has also done damage to the Albanian traders themselves, who have been obliged to purchase and sell on goods which previously came from Italy and other countries.[36]

At the end of the 1930s it was clear, therefore, that Albania was an economic liability for Italy. Back in 1932, an American review, *Foreign Policy Reports*, had observed: 'Italy is not exploiting poor Albania economically. At present, it would be more true to economic reality to say that Albania is exploiting Italy.' This was just as true at the end of the decade.

A few statistics might give us a clearer view of the situation. In the period 1926–1929, the overall deficit in Albania's balance of trade with Italy was 35.5 million Albanian francs, higher than the movement of capital into Albania for the same period, recorded in the balance of payments as 27.3 million.

In the period 1930–1933, however, this relationship was drastically reversed: compared with an aggregate trade deficit (still with relation to Italy) which had gone down to 26.3 million francs, the inflow of capital rose to 60.2 million. If we presume that the vast majority of this inflow was

Italian, we can understand the deep dissatisfaction which the financial relationship with Albania was arousing in Italian economic and political circles. We can also understand how this feeling grew in the following years, especially after 1936 when, in the face of heightened Italian spending in Albania, the bilateral trade balance further improved in Albania's favour. A few years later, in 1940, Gambino put it very plainly:[37]

> The pattern of Italian capital investments in Albania was not matched by the pattern of trade between Italy and Albania. . . . Italy was still the main destination market for Albania and also – in spite of the reductions of recent years – its main supply market. However, the Albanian trade deficit with Italy, which at first grew with the expansion of Italian investments in Albania, subsequently receded, until it was replaced in 1936 and 1937 by a surplus. Thus the contributions of Italian capital, instead of increasing the volume of Italian goods destined for Albania, ended up as foreign currency at Albania's disposal. This currency was used for importing produce from third countries which, moreover, did not accept any exports from Albania.

From a political standpoint, these words indicate that, towards the end of the 1930s, King Zog was still far from seeing his country as being so tied to Italy as to allow the latter to dictate his choices of economic policy and demand a preferential trade relationship involving the absorption of Italian goods. They also explain, in economic terms, the reasons behind the regime's subsequent political actions, which culminated in the occupation of Albania and the establishment of a 'union' between the two monarchies. In fact, the article continues as follows:

> It would not have been possible to sustain, in the long term, the process of divergence between the pattern of Italy's investment in Albania and the evolution of the trade between the two countries. . . . It was necessary to put the relationship between the two countries on a different footing, in order for Albania to continue benefiting from Italian contributions of capital and Italian enterprise and to make firm steps towards economic progress.[38]

In terms of the overall size of Italy's financial commitment in Albania prior to the occupation, the only official figure recorded is the one supplied by the Foreign Minister, Galeazzo Ciano, in his speech to the Italian Chamber of Fasces and Corporations[39] on 15 April 1939 (immediately after the expulsion of Zog); Ciano boasted of the Italian 'legacy of hard work and trust' in Albania. More factually, he estimated the 'monetary' legacy at 1,837 million lire (approximately 1.8 billion euros in today's money).[40]

He did not provide a breakdown of the figure. However, we can work out how that figure was arrived at, and examine, in overview at least, the nature of the expenses and the use to which they were put.[41] On 28 May 1938, Ciano had written to his colleague di Revel, the Finance Minister, to inform him that a highly confidential report was being prepared on the main activities under way in Albania and their respective costs, 'borne by the Royal Exchequer'.[42] Approximately one month later, the inventory was ready. It is extremely interesting, as it enables us to form a picture of the extent and nature of Italy's financial involvement and, to some extent, the ways in which it evolved with time.

Gathering the countless expense entries into homogeneous groupings where possible, we can, with due caution and approximation, calculate the following percentages:[43]

Current expenses:

- (a) military expenses – approximately 35 per cent;
- (b) contributions to archaeological missions, churches, Catholic schools, earthquake victims, etc. – approximately 4 per cent;
- (c) political expenses – approximately 6 per cent.

Capital expenses:

- (d) mainly 'financial' (loans and shareholdings in banks) – approximately 28 per cent;
- (e) direct investments – approximately 21 per cent;
- (f) miscellaneous – approximately 6 per cent.

Entry (c) – political expenses – probably gives an indication of the Fascist regime's more direct political involvement with Albania's authorities and with those it intended to favour. For the sake of simplifying matters, we could perhaps say that the 6 per cent was the 'kickback' paid by the regime.

It is important to note that only a small part of the above-quoted figure of 1.8 billion lire was recorded in Albania's balance of payments, which leads us to the conclusion that the majority of the expenditure (for example under the 'military' heading) either did not give rise to any movement of currency or escaped official registration.

It is not impossible, however, that a fraction of such huge expenditure might have been concealed behind other entries in the balance of payments: for example, we might query the noticeable surplus for the 'services' entry on the current account, which the official statistics basically attribute to emigrant remittances.

The strength of the Albanian franc and the Italian interests

We can attempt to verify the 'strength' of the Albanian franc by measuring its overvaluation, in terms of how far its quotation differed from its purchasing power parity, in other words by examining the evolution of the real exchange rate and therefore taking into account the movement of relative prices. The exchange rate referred to here is that with the Italian lira, which is justified because of the dominant role Italy played in Albania's foreign trade. Once again, the lack of available statistics obliges us to adopt certain working hypotheses, which should prompt a degree of caution in evaluating the results.

In the first instance, it should be noted that, for the period in question (i.e. the period from 1925, when the National Bank of Albania was founded, to 1939, the year of Italian occupation, which caused fundamental changes in Albania's monetary system and in its relations with Italy), the first two years of data on the exchange rates of the Albanian franc are unavailable, which means they start from 1927. Furthermore, since we do not have any historical statistics on the exchange rate of the Albanian franc to the lira, it has been necessary to determine the 'cross-rate', calculated on the quotations of the Albanian franc and the lira in relation to the US dollar, as recorded in the League of Nations' statistics.[44] As regards the wholesale price index, the available series takes 1927 as equal to 100, since it was the year in which records began.[45]

We are taking 1926 as a useful base (so that we can take into account the influence of lira stabilization in 1927) and assuming, for 1926, an Albanian franc–US dollar quotation in line with the declared parity of 29.3 cents to the Albanian franc. For the price index, we are assuming that, between 1926 and 1927, the index of Albanian prices remained unchanged.

On this basis, Table 5.9 shows the evolution of the Albanian franc–lira exchange rate and the wholesale price index in Albania and Italy.

Table 5.10 and Figure 5.3 illustrate, on the basis of the data in Table 5.9, the evolution of the bilateral Albanian franc–lira real exchange rate in the period in question.

Tables 5.9 and 5.10 demonstrate, in the first place, that the fall in prices due to the world crisis was more gradual in Italy than in Albania. In the latter, it was most acute in the years 1931–1934, when the index fell from 90.25 to 51.07. In both countries, however, the turning point came in 1934: from then onwards, the level of wholesale prices started to pick up again, more so in Italy than in Albania, so that, while by 1939 the level in Italy had reached that of the late 1920s, in Albania it was still considerably lower.

The exchange rate showed a devaluation of the Albanian franc against the lira which stayed at around the 25 per cent level until 1934: a

Table 5.9 Albanian franc–Italian lira exchange rate and wholesale price index in Albania and Italy, 1926–1939

	A Lira–Albanian franc rate (lire per 1 franc)[a]	B Wholesale price index in Albania	C Wholesale price index in Italy
1926	4.96	100.00	100.00
1927	3.84	100.00	84.49
1928	3.67	104.08	81.39
1929	3.66	99.99	77.52
1930	3.68	88.11	69.77
1931	3.79	90.25	60.46
1932	3.78	73.57	56.58
1933	3.65	57.26	51.94
1934	3.78	51.07	50.39
1935	4.00	56.19	55.81
1936	6.22	62.67	62.01
1937	6.22	64.94	72.87
1938	6.22	63.55	77.52
1939	6.22	69.15	80.62

[a] 1927 and 1928: yearly average;
1929–1937: December average;
1938: June/September/December average;
1939: March/June/December average.

Sources: Column A is taken from Société des Nations, *Annuaire Statistique 1931–1932*, Geneva, 1932, and *Annuaire Statistique 1938–1939*, Geneva, 1939; Column B from Borgatta, Moneta e credito in Albania; Column C from C. M. Cipolla, *Le avventure della lira* (Milan, Comunità, 1958) (based on ISTAT figures).

repercussion of Italy's action of late 1927 to set the new parity of the lira by means of a 'return to gold', and abolish the lira's inconvertibility, thereby giving the lira a substantial overvaluation, which was to last until the mid-1930s.[46]

The exchange rate then got worse for the lira in 1935 (and the devaluation of the Albanian franc, still in relation to the 1926 rate, fell to less than 20 per cent). In fact, in 1935, the difficulties of the lira led to the first step towards devaluation: in July of that year, its gold convertibility was 'temporarily' suspended.[47] Then in 1936 the rate of the lira suffered a formal devaluation of 40.94 per cent – equal to the devaluation of the dollar two years before – with the prospect that it could be devalued a further 10 per cent should conditions make this necessary.[48] This action caused the exchange rate of the lira against the Albanian franc to plummet from 4 lire to 6.22 lire to the franc, and overturned the situation which had existed since the 'stabilization' of the lira in 1927, resulting in a substantial

Table 5.10 Real exchange rate of the Albanian franc in relation to the Italian lira

	Price differential (%)	Albanian franc in relation to Italian lira (%)*	Real exchange rate of Albanian franc (indices, 1926 = 100)**
1927	+18.4	–22.6	91.6
1928	+27.9	–26.0	94.6
1929	+29.0	–26.2	95.2
1930	+26.3	–25.8	93.7
1931	+49.3	–23.6	114.1
1932	+30.0	–23.8	99.1
1933	+10.2	–26.4	81.1
1934	+1.3	–23.8	77.2
1935	+0.7	–19.4	81.2
1936	+1.1	+25.4	126.7
1937	–10.9	+25.4	111.8
1938	–18.0	+25.4	102.8
1939	–14.2	+25.4	107.6

* With respect to 1926 value. The sign – indicates a devaluation; the sign + indicates revaluation.
** An increase indicates a loss of competitiveness.

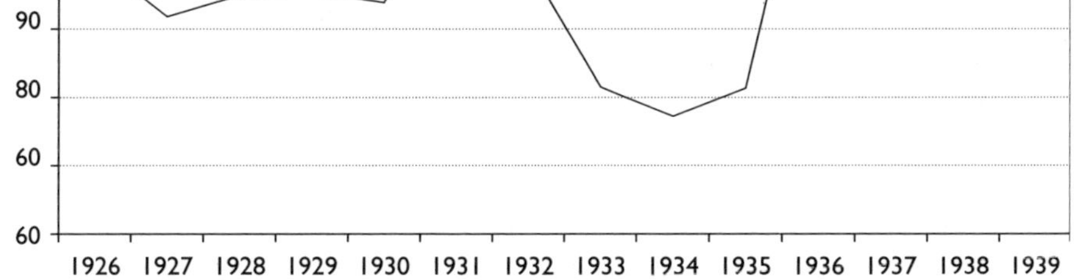

Figure 5.3 Real exchange rate of the Albanian franc in relation to the Italian lira (indices, 1926 = 100)

Note: An increase indicates a loss of competitiveness.

revaluation of the Albanian franc, which would remain intact at around 25 per cent until the Italian occupation.

From this evolution of the exchange rate, and the evolution of the relative prices, we can deduce that, in real terms, the overvaluation of the Albanian franc in relation to the lira was fairly contained for most of the years in question. For three of those years, it was even undervalued, until the 'realignment' of the lira in 1936; and it was only substantially overvalued during three other years – in 1931 and then in 1936–1937, following the realignment of the lira.

At the end of the 1930s (1938–1939), the rapid growth in the wholesale price index in Italy brought the real overvaluation of the franc to the lira within more narrow limits once again.

An analysis of the evolution of the Albanian franc leads, therefore, to certain conclusions:

(a) From the point of view of the balance of trade, the Albanian franc's strength was undoubtedly unjustified.
(b) Capital movements, mainly from Italy, do however give an adequate explanation for that strength, having compensated, and often more than compensated, for the deficit in the current account of the balance of payments.
(c) The exchange rate of the Albanian franc does not, however, appear excessively overvalued if, setting aside the foreign accounts and looking at the movement of internal prices, it is compared with the Italian lira. A large part of the period in question is influenced by the overvaluation of the lira itself, in the wake of the 'stabilization' of 1927. It was basically a case of two currencies which were both stubbornly attached to relatively high exchange rates. The evolution of the exchange rate mirrors that of the relative prices quite closely. Only in 1936, the year in which Italy was forced into a considerable devaluation, does a substantial overvaluation of the Albanian franc emerge, which in any event tends to diminish with the subsequent price increases in Italy.

In 1938, a marked reduction in the value of the Albanian franc would in the circumstances have made Italian exports into Albania even more difficult, and 'undervalued' the real exchange rate of the franc against the lira.

So in 1938, a logic is revealed behind the apparently perverse mechanisms of the financial relations between Italy and Albania. The transfer of such a massive volume of resources was a way of financing Albania's balance of trade deficit. This deficit, however, mainly showed up in relation to third countries, while it was quite small in relation to Italy, actually turning into a surplus in 1936 and 1937. In this context, since it was difficult to reduce the amount of capital investments in Albania, for reasons closely linked with the regime's policy of economic penetration, the central problem for the Italian authorities was not that of closing Albania's trade deficit, but rather of alleviating the burden of the capital transfers into Albania.

This pointed to altering the geographical distribution of Albania's trade, in the sense of increasing the percentage of Albania's imports from Italy, as Italian investments in Albania continued to grow. In other words, the challenge for the Italian authorities was to ensure that their spending on Albania was directed towards the purchase of Italian goods and services, rather than being addressed towards purchases of goods from other countries.

This need appeared particularly pressing in 1938, both because, as mentioned above, Italian exports in Albania were losing out to competition from other countries and because, by 1938, the regime was preparing for action which would be much more relevant on a political level but more costly on an economic level. In the summer of that year, a note from the National Bank of Albania spoke of 'a hoped-for intensification in political relations' and of 'a foreseeable increase of grants and direct investments in Albania on Italy's part'.[49]

From this perspective, we can see that a devaluation of the Albanian franc, which would have been justified by the trends in the current account of the balance of payments, would have been of no use to Italy, and in fact would have been counter-productive. The note from the National Bank of Albania quoted above highlights Italy's interest in maintaining the old parity of the Albanian franc:

(a) In the first place, quite simply, a devaluation, while bringing advantages for Albania, would have entailed corresponding disadvantages for Italy. The hindrance to Albania's imports which a devaluation would have caused would have affected imports from Italy also, the exact opposite of what was desired.
(b) A devaluation of the franc would have also led the Albanian government to ask for the capital gains deriving from the revaluation of its reserves. The National Bank estimated that this would have involved a transfer from Italy into Albania of something between 13 and 32 million lire.[50]
(c) The 'most probable mistrust' which the Albanian people would have shown towards the currency if had been devalued could have led to a run on withdrawals and a flood of returned banknotes to the National Bank, the latter estimating that this could have resulted in a exodus from Italy of 'several tens of millions of lire'. This would in turn have obliged the Bank to reduce its investments in Italian Treasury securities, and

its deposits kept at the Italian state's disposal at the Istituto Nazionale dei Cambi con l'Estero, investments and deposits which in June 1938 amounted to the equivalent of 13,582,000 Albanian francs.

(d) Finally, there was an overwhelming political motive for not devaluing the franc: devaluation would have hit anyone who held banknotes and bank deposits – 'all those people who have put their faith in this specially created currency, backed by Italy's moral guarantee'. In Albania, before the creation of the franc, a genuine, albeit limited, gold circulation had been in force. The National Bank had issued banknotes which were exchangeable for gold. A devaluation would have failed to 'reinforce in the minds of the very particular Albanian population a sense of the greatness of the Italy of today'.

This leads us, therefore, to the conclusion that the so-called strength of the Albanian franc, far from implying a healthy state of the economy and stability in the balance of trade, coexisted, especially during the 1930s, with a heavy imbalance in the foreign current accounts. Technically, this strength can be explained by the massive inflows of Italian capital and the need to prevent the trade relationship with Italy, which was already unfavourable for the latter, from deteriorating further. Politically, the currency's strength reflected the Italian authorities' intention to demonstrate to the international financial community that Albania's currency, under Italy's protective wing, was flying higher than others, and to show the Albanian people that their country's link with Italy was a source of security and safeguarding for their savings.

All these reasons converged to push into the background any plans for 'realigning' the franc, in the same way as the major currencies, to a level which was more in keeping with trends in the current account of Albania's balance of payments.

CHAPTER 6

Albanian monetary policy

Two dramatis personae: Alberti and Gambino

A respected body of opinion sees Mussolini's concept of power as involving a gradual centring of the political decision-making process in the person of the Duce himself, by means of the progressive removal of authority from parliament, the party and even the Grand Council of Fascism. A consequence of this tendency was a rise in the role of technocrats, who were responsible for dealing with the technical core of specific problems, leaving the political substance exclusively to the personal judgement of the Duce. The process was one of depoliticizing the machinery of state and turning it into a technocracy, in which the state bureaucracy and the major public bodies eventually became the most constant and reliable factors of the regime's stability.[1] In fact these technocratic aspirations had been part of the Fascist approach since the early years of its rise to power, and the appointment of de' Stefani – a typical technocrat – to the Finance Ministry was the first significant expression of this 'vocation' of the regime.[2]

It has also been observed, however, that, while this policy had certain favourable implications for the regime, in that it exploited the more positive elements of bureaucracy, it also had its negative side, in that it allowed a good deal of technical power to become centred in that bureaucracy, which in the end enabled the latter to form its own policies and brought it into direct contact with economic forces and interests which were not always in sympathy with the Fascists' policies.[3]

This body of opinion is useful to recall, as it has a bearing on our subject. The regime appointed individuals of unquestionable competence to the National Bank of Albania, who intended to maintain a clear divide between economic or financial evaluations and political judgements, which were to stay outside their remit. Thus, during the negotiations for the SVEA loan, it had been made very clear by the Italian negotiators that 'the undertakings in Albania represented no financial advantage whatsoever, but only huge burdens, which could only be compensated for by political gains, to be left up to the judgement of the Foreign Ministry'.[4] This technical competence went together with independence in decision making, which came to the fore on more than one occasion, even in the face of political pressure.

It was of course unthinkable that the Bank's management would ever question the regime's strategic choices. For example, later on, towards the middle of 1938, we see the Bank of Albania working actively (probably under politicians' instructions) on projects for monetary reform which presupposed Albania's loss of independence. The fact remains, however, that the National Bank's policies were implemented under rigorous technical criteria which sometimes brought it into opposition with both the Albanian and the Italian authorities. If anything, the technical emphasis of the criteria contributed towards the adoption of monetary policies which were conditioned not by the public interest, as one would expect from a modern central bank, but by narrower concerns for the interests of the Bank's shareholders or for the institution's profitability.

It is helpful to bear these factors in mind, even though another body of opinion links the managements of the Bank and SVEA to the most extreme and militaristic wing of Fascist policy in Albania. For example, Pastorelli, in emphasizing the divergence of opinion between those who believed that 'Albania should be seen as an area for Italian economic and political expansion' and those who upheld the more extreme view that it should be 'a base for military operations at the doorstep of the Balkans, directed in particular against Yugoslavia', adds that 'those responsible for the Bank of Albania and SVEA (Alberti, Gambino and Minister Lojacono, who was in charge of Albanian affairs at the Foreign Ministry) clearly based their actions on the latter viewpoint'. Pastorelli supports this view with the problem of the moratorium on the SVEA loan mentioned in Chapter 5, seeing Alberti's resistance to granting the moratorium as an expression of this approach. Pastorelli points out that, as King Zog well knew, Albania's defaulting on its debt would have led, via the guarantee mechanisms inserted in the loan agreement, to 'Italy having close and direct control over all Albania's finances'.[5]

However, it is possible to explain Alberti's attitude in terms of the 'technical' bias described above. His resistance to the moratorium (which was in the end granted) can be attributed more to a wish to run the Bank within the bounds of good and prudent management, attempting, as any sensible manager would, to avoid a loss for the business, than to a political wish to remove Albania's financial independence.[6]

The life of the Bank essentially revolved around two people: Mario Alberti, who was its first President and filled the post until 1931, and Amedeo Gambino, Secretary to the Board and then, from 1927, Managing Director. The first was a highly experienced banker, a brilliant personality judging by his numerous writings,[7] who among other things was a member of the Italian delegation which obtained satisfactory war debt terms for Italy from the negotiations with the United States, and was, as we have mentioned, the Italian representative on the Finance Committee of the League of Nations. As we have seen, when Mussolini decided to make the penetration into Albania more thorough and organic, the person he turned to was Alberti, who was Central Manager of the Credito Italiano at the time. We have also seen that Alberti, banking expert that he was, realized that the Albanian affair was not going to succeed financially. He was dragged into it reluctantly and realized that the support of the state would be indispensable if the enterprise was to go ahead.[8]

Gambino, a professor of corporative political economy, was really the brains behind the Bank of Albania for the entire life of the institution. He vigorously defended its interests, even during the troubled events which followed the Second World War.[9]

A scheme of monetary policy analysis

In the current chapter, a brief attempt is made at analysing the monetary policy pursued by the institution.[10] We will look first at the changes in money supply in Albania and at the relative importance of its components (internal and external). We will try to assess the restrictive or expansive stance of its policy, having in mind the specific nature of the Bank as a central bank, not a commercial enterprise, and taking into account the movements of its discount rate. The analysis of the money supply is also useful in assessing a charge levelled against the Italians: the use of the National Bank of Albania as an instrument to take gold out of Albania. We will then consider the correlation between trends in the money supply and in prices. We will also take a brief look at the reserve management policy.

We will end the chapter with a description of the controversy over bimetallism which upset the Bank towards the end of the 1920s, which is probably more relevant from a political than from a purely financial standpoint, but which gives a sufficiently clear idea of the relative autonomy which the National Bank was trying to maintain, with the backing of the Bank of Italy, in relation to both the Albanian and the Italian governments.

The analysis of the trends in money supply and its components is in a way made easy by the almost total absence of a developed banking system during the period in question,[11] which covers the years from 1927 (the year from which we have a homogeneous series of statistics) until 1938 (the final year of Albanian independence before the Italian occupation and the 'union' between the two monarchies, which radically altered the monetary system in Albania). In fact, an investigation which only takes into account the central bank's assets and liabilities would not be too misleading, and we will not need to pay much attention to the monetary base multiplier.

Our analysis will also need to take another factor into account, that is the absence of the 'treasury' component of the money supply. We have already seen that the National Bank's Charter precluded any significant transactions to finance the government, other than very short-term ones. The absence of a capital market also ruled out the possibility of any debt management activity which could influence the money supply.

However, it is important to see this lack in the right perspective, in the sense that the loans made by Italy not only played a determining role in the balance of payments, but also acted, in several instances, as a vehicle to cover the persisting wide deficit in the state budget.

Finally, another fact to bear in mind is that, in Albania's case, the central bank's purchasing of foreign assets was made possible not only by a surplus in the foreign accounts, but also by a gradual gathering (the extent of which is not known) of the pre-existing coined gold into the Bank's reserves, via its substitution by the new paper circulation.[12]

Our analysis is carried out within a simplified monetary base scheme (Table 6.1): on the 'money sources' side (the assets side of the central bank's balance sheet), we will only consider two classes of assets: the 'foreign' and the 'economy' components. The first registers the central bank's foreign assets, deriving from a surplus in the country's foreign accounts. The second registers the central bank's credit transactions: basically, credit granted via the 'discount window' and other advances (as we have just seen, the usual third component, the 'treasury', as credit granted to the Treasury by the central bank, was virtually non-existent in Albania).

On the 'money uses' side (the liabilities side of the central bank's balance sheet), we will first place currency in circulation and then deposits at the central bank and other minor liabilities.

Bearing these factors in mind, the present study takes as its basis Table 6.1, which shows the influential role which the 'foreign' component played in creating money. Its size in comparison with the total creation (or destruction) of money supply is such that, in all the years being observed (with a minor exception in 1931), the figures for the 'foreign' component and the total are both either plus or minus.[13]

Until 1932 the balance of payments created liquidity (with the minor exception of 1931). During this period, the creation of money via the 'internal' component, or the 'economy channel', also played an active role, through the discount window and advances made by the central bank; in fact, in 1931, in the face of a slight destruction of money supply via the 'foreign' channel, it was the 'economy' component which enabled a net creation of money.

This was a period, therefore, in which the gold standard seemed to work according to the 'rules of the game'. Every time the central bank was a net purchaser of gold and foreign currency, it expanded the money supply by discounts and advances to the economy (the 'economy' component) in order to achieve the external adjustment[14] (it is however difficult to deduce *ex post facto* from this trend whether, in Albania's case, such a policy was deliberately pursued by the Bank's management).

The year 1932 acted as a kind of watershed. As against a significant inflow of currency from the 'foreign' component, which created another corresponding increase in money supply, we see the beginning of the drop in the 'economy' component (a contraction in credit from the central bank), due at least in part, apparently, to a discount rate which in real terms reached 26.5 per cent.[15]

The period from 1933 until 1938 was characterized by a continuous contraction in the money supply (apart from an exception in 1936, when, as seen in Chapter 5, massive new loans came in from Italy). During this period, the 'foreign' component was constantly negative (except of course in 1936). The behaviour of the 'economy' component highlights two distinct phases during this period. The years 1933 and 1934 were those in which the effects of the Great Depression were most keenly felt. All the entries on the 'assets' side of the balance of payments diminished, the use of the Italian loans fell and emigrant remittances dropped, as did internal demand. Internal prices dropped also, partly as a result of the relative revaluation of Albania's currency. For its part, the National Bank pursued a policy of high 'real' interest rates. As Borgatta observes,[16] the aim of deflation was to avoid a 'relative inflation' which could have compromised the stability of the exchange rate. What emerges very obviously is the highly restrictive policy pursued by the monetary authorities, which was influenced by a wish to maintain the overvalued exchange rate. In 1933 and 1934, it seems the 'rules of the game' of the gold standard were once again confirmed, by a positive correlation between the variations in the two components ('external' and 'internal') of the money supply.

The second phase was from 1935 to 1938. In 1935, the 'economy' component resumed a creative role, with an increase in discounts and advances (when the 'real' discount rate became negative due to prices picking up), though it mostly did not succeed in offsetting the 'foreign' component, which was acting in the opposite direction. At this point, the 'rules of the game' of the gold standard stopped working, and in 1935 a reflationary phase began. In fact, 1935 was the year in which reflation also started in Italy.[17]

Tables 6.2 and 6.3 demonstrate in detail the relative importance of the 'external' and 'internal' components of money supply creation, and the official discount rate, both nominal and real (i.e. deflated by the wholesale price index), for the period 1928–1938.

Table 6.1 Sources and uses of money in Albania, 1928–1938

	1928	1929	1930	1931	1932	1933	1934	1935	1936	1937	1938[a]
Flows, in millions of Albanian francs											
Sources:											
1. Foreign											
1.1. Currency	3.38	1.99	4.08	–3.30	5.54	–3.63	–2.68	–1.77	7.56	–1.59	–2.90
1.2. Gold	0.10	0.59	0.28	3.26	0.52	1.83	–0.10	0.44		0.10	0.21
1.3. Silver	0.31	–0.22	–0.10								
1.4. Total	3.79	2.36	4.26	–0.04	6.06	–1.80	–2.78	–1.33	7.56	–1.49	–2.69
2. Economy	1.77	2.95	1.34	0.70	–1.31	–2.41	–0.29	0.75	0.60	0.44	1.79
Grand total (1.4+2)	5.56	5.31	5.60	0.66	4.75	–4.21	–3.07	–0.58	8.16	–1.05	–0.90
Percentage variation of total on previous year	39.3	26.9	22.4	2.2	15.2	–11.6	–9.7	–2.1	29.0	–2.9	–2.6
Uses:											
3.1. Circulation (notes and coins)	4.03	1.55	1.71	–0.80	1.50	–0.92	–1.04	1.80	–1.54	0.86	0.46
3.2. Liabilities (current accounts, savings deposits, cheques in circulation)	1.30	2.88	3.69	1.13	2.09	–4.23	–2.01	–0.67	8.70	–2.05	–1.17
3.3. Other sectors	0.23	0.88	0.20	0.33	1.16	0.94	–0.02	–1.71	1.00	0.14	–0.19
Total (3.1+3.2+3.3)	5.56	5.31	5.60	0.66	4.75	–4.21	–3.07	–0.58	8.16	–1.05	–0.90

	Dec. 1927	Sept. 1938		Dec. 1927	Sept. 1938
Stocks, in millions of Albanian francs					
1. Foreign					
1.1. Currency	11.92	18.60	3.1. Circulation	7.28	14.88
1.2. Gold	1.93	9.16			
1.3. Silver	0.01				
1.4. Total	13.86	27.76	3.2. Liabilities	3.10	12.75
2. Economy	0.28	6.60	3.3. Other sectors	3.76	6.73
Grand total (1.4+2)	14.14	34.36	Total 3.1+3.2+3.3	14.14	34.36

[a] For 1938: January–September.

Source: Based on National Bank of Albania documentation in ASBI, Baffi papers.

Table 6.2 Relative importance of the 'foreign' and 'economy' components as sources of money supply (in percentages of the total)

Year	1928	1929	1930	1931	1932	1933	1934	1935	1936	1937	1938[c]
Foreign	68.2	44.4	76.1	[a]	[b]	–42.7	–90.5	[a]	92.6	[a]	[a]
Economy	31.8	55.6	23.9	[a]	[b]	–47.3	–9.5	[a]	7.4	[a]	[a]

[a] In 1931, 1935, 1937 and 1938, the creation of money was due solely to the 'economy' component.
[b] In 1932, the opposite was true, the 'foreign' component being the only one to create money.
[c] January–September.

Table 6.3 Official discount rate in Albania (yearly averages)

Year	1928	1929	1930	1931	1932	1933	1934	1935	1936	1937	1938[a]
Nominal rate	9.0	9.0	9.0	8.5	8.0	7.9	7.5	7.5	7.2	6.1	6.0
Variations in wholesale price index	4.0	–4.0	–11.9	2.4	–18.5	–22.2	–10.8	10.0	11.5	3.6	–2.2
Real rate	5.0	13.0	20.9	6.1	26.5	30.1	18.3	–2.5	–4.3	2.5	8.2

[a] For 1938, the figure for the discount rate is the average for January–June.

Sources: Discount rates: League of Nations, *Annuaire Statistique 1931–1932*, Geneva, 1932, and *Annuaire Statistique 1937–1938*, Geneva, 1939. Price index: Borgatta, Moneta e credito in Albania.

We can get an idea of how modest the reflation which began in 1935 was, if we consider:

(a) that it barely managed to offset the destruction of money supply through the foreign component (apart from the sizeable exception of 1936); and
(b) above all, the total lack in Albania of the use of fiscal policy for countercyclical purposes. The state budget, as we have seen, was confined to a role of complete neutrality by the National Bank's unwieldy Charter and by the absence of an adequate domestic capital market capable of absorbing state bonds.

It is clear, therefore, that without the aid of the Italian loans the Albanian government would have had serious difficulty in covering the budget deficit. We should add that even the Albanian government's attempts to make the issuing bank's policies more accommodating met a rather lukewarm reception from the central bank itself. The unbending position of the Bank of Albania in this respect is clearly illustrated by an episode of 1934, when political tensions with Italy prevented any loans from being made. The Albanian government turned to the institution: (i) to obtain an advance of 1.5–2 million francs; and (ii) to request the Bank to take on as trustee a forthcoming issue of Treasury bills.

In spite of the insistence by Zurani, the Albanian government's representative on the board, that the institution had a 'moral duty to help the state', the Bank's board of directors voted to substantially reduce the amount of the advance to be granted, to 300,000 francs, and insisted that, under the terms of the Charter, the advance should be repaid before the end of the financial year and should be guaranteed 'in the appropriate manner, by assets of sufficient substance which are not otherwise tied up'. On the matter of the Treasury bills, the board insisted that they should be devised with features making them true credit certificates (such as a fixed term, a large denomination, the discretion as opposed to the obligation to accept them as payment) and not simply a substitute for money, 'of which the right to issue is by law reserved solely and exclusively for the Bank'.[18] One must bear in mind in this respect that 1934 was the year of greatest deflation in Albania's monetary policy. On the whole, this confirms that the state budget did not act in a countercyclical way. Its deficits were covered, at least in part, by inflows of capital from Italy which were entered accordingly, in the records on the creation of money supply, under the 'external' heading.[19]

Criticism of monetary management

Overall, it seems hasty nonetheless to draw from this whole period an impression that monetary policy in Albania was fundamentally restrictive, or more restrictive than elsewhere, a recurring accusation which commentators at the time, especially the Fascist regime's opponents, were already levelling at the National Bank's management. According to its critics, it did not give credit freely enough to meet the needs of Albania's developing economy (bearing in mind once again that the Bank was practically the only significant credit institution in Albania). There are several observations to make on this point:

(a) In the first place one factor to take into account, which is structural rather than linked to the economic cycle, is that the Bank itself justified its prudence in giving credit not only in terms of the underdeveloped situation in which it was operating, but also by the need to distinguish between short-term credit, which came within the Bank's institutional remit, and long-term credit, from which it was barred owing to its function as an issuing bank.

President Alberti observed in 1928, in a sort of statement of the Bank's programme:

> The protests against the policy of a healthy monetary system were many and lively. On the other hand, whenever we head towards inflationism, when credit is given liberally and easily, and concessions of every kind are granted instantly without a second thought, then the complaints against the Issuing Bank's policy die down. . . . There is a kind of credit which the Bank can give with confidence and there is another kind which the Bank should not give at any cost. . . . The Bank cannot provide capital for constructing buildings, putting up factories and buying machinery, because it cannot wait for years before its money is repaid. . . . The Bank has a very large number of creditors, that is every holder of its banknotes. It has to exchange for gold and foreign currency any bills which are handed over to it. If its cash is invested in houses or factories, the Bank certainly cannot say to holders of its notes that it will not give them gold or currency, but a piece of x's house, or y's factory, or z's machinery instead. . . . Instead, the Bank will put every effort into making commercial credit as easy as possible . . . within the limits of that credit supply which is comfortably within its means, and without jeopardizing the backing of its circulation.[20]

We have however seen that the Bank went through an expansionary phase until 1931. We should also remember that, in the years preceding those we have surveyed here, the discount rate had been quite rapidly reduced from the 12 per cent with which the Bank had begun its activity, to 10 per cent in February 1927, and then to 9 per cent in April of the same year.[21]

(b) One clearly restrictive phase is certainly the period 1932–1934, during which the central bank's credit activity contracted and the 'real' discount rate rose, owing to the sharp decrease in prices, to reach a maximum of 30.1 per cent in 1933. This brought interest rates close to the level they were at before the Italian 'presence' (a level which, of course, the Fascist regime had harshly criticized as being associated with backwardness and tantamount to usury).

(c) During the whole period in question, the level of the 'real' discount rate was generally higher than in Italy (which was also pursuing a restrictive policy);[22] however, a comparison on an international scale points to different conclusions, if the comparison is made with countries which were more on a par with Albania, in other words the Balkan countries.

We see (Table 6.4) that in the Balkan countries, unlike Albania, nominal rates rose at the beginning of the 1930s (with peaks between 1930 and 1932), but constantly decreased in the following years. The rise in nominal rates, combined with a widespread fall in prices, brought the real rates in the other Balkan countries to prohibitive levels also, with peaks not far from the Albanian 30.1 per cent (29.2 per cent in Bulgaria in 1930; 31.4 per cent in Romania in 1931; 22.6 per cent in Yugoslavia in 1931; and 21.5 per cent in Greece in 1930). In the other Balkan countries, as in Albania, the real discount rate underwent a sharp drop in the second half of the 1930s.

Of the countries in the Balkan region, Greece probably had the greatest relative stability in real terms in its discount rate, which had the lowest peak (21.5 per cent in 1930) and the highest of the low-points (–1.7 per cent in 1937).

The trends in money supply, in particular its foreign component, can also go some way towards responding to another criticism of monetary management in Albania which we have already mentioned, that is that the system of complete convertibility (the gold standard) was used by the Italians as a means of getting their hands, via the issuing of banknotes, on the gold which had been stored up by Albanian citizens and then channelling the gold into Italy, thus stripping Albania of its supply. This criticism was later taken up, as a direct charge against Italy, by the Albanian government after the evacuation of German troops from Albania in November 1944, and still appears in historical writings.[23]

On this point, it is important to remember, above all, that the main purpose of the National Bank was, in fact, to introduce the new banknote and to gather in the old metal and paper currency. 'The Bank must act',

Table 6.4 Discount rates in certain Balkan countries

	Bulgaria			Greece			Romania			Yugoslavia		
	A	B	C	A	B	C	A	B	C	A	B	C
1928	10.0	7.3	2.7	9.9	4.3	5.6	6.0	2.8	3.2	6.0	2.9	3.1
1929	9.5	6.5	3.0	9.0	2.9	6.1	8.2	7.0	1.2	6.0	–4.7	1.3
1930	10.0	–19.2	29.2	9.0	–12.5	21.5	9.0	–21.6	30.6	5.7	–13.9	19.6
1931	9.0	–17.7	26.7	9.8	–0.8	10.7	8.2	–23.2	31.4	6.5	–16.1	22.6
1932	8.6	–12.5	21.1	10.6	6.1	4.5	7.2	–10.3	17.5	7.5	–10.6	18.1
1933	8.0	–5.8	13.8	8.0	–7.3	0.7	6.3	–3.2	9.5	7.5	–1.2	8.7
1934	7.0	–5.7	12.7	7.0	1.7	5.3	5.9	0.2	5.7	6.8	–1.9	8.7
1935	6.6	1.6	5.0	7.0	0.1	6.9	4.5	14.5	–10.0	5.1	4.3	0.8
1936	6.0	1.4	4.6	7.0	3.7	3.3	4.5	13.7	–9.2	5.0	3.8	1.2
1937	6.0	12.8	–6.8	6.0	7.7	–1.7	4.5	14.7	–10.2	5.0	9.3	–4.3
1938	6.0	3.6	2.4	6.0	–0.6	6.6	4.2	0.1	4.1	5.0	4.7	0.3

Key:
A: Average nominal discount rates.
B: Variation in the wholesale price index, except for Greece (for the whole period) and Romania (for 1928–1929), for which the cost of living index has been used, in the absence of the wholesale price index.
C: Average real discount rates, deflated ex-post using the data from column B. For 1938, the discount rate figure is the average for the period January–June.

Source: Société des Nations, *Annuaire Statistique 1931–1932*, Geneva, 1932, and *Annuaire Statistique 1942–1944*, Geneva, 1945.

Formentini stated in 1927,[24] 'on this stock of gold and silver coins present in Albania (which according to Calmès's estimates could have been between 50 and 100 million francs),[25] and try to draw it into its coffers in order to build up the reserves on which its own paper circulation will be based.'

The accusation of clearing Albania out of its gold was expressed very quickly.[26]

The Bank of Albania and, later, the Italian government consistently reacted to this charge by saying that:

> the [gold] backing [for Albania's circulation] was built exclusively from purchases of gold on foreign markets (not in Albania), particularly in London (the Bank can give evidence of this for each gram of its gold); those purchases were made possible through the proceeds of the SVEA loan. In other words this backing was built up without exporting a single gram of fine gold from Albania and with foreign currencies almost totally provided by Italy. This [gold] backing was always held, in a free deposit, at the Bank of Italy and the Mint in Rome.[27]

If we look at the money supply (Table 6.1), we can see that, during the period in question, the stock of gold increased constantly, with the sole exception of 1934, so that, by the end of the period, there was a stock worth 9.2 million Albanian francs, compared with the initial 1.9 million. It is not actually possible to say with any certainty that this sum represented the gold rounded up on the internal market, rather than a surplus in the foreign accounts. It is, however, certain that the status of the balance of payments was solid, and the way in which the Albanian franc held its market value, which we have looked at previously, is ample witness to this. It is also certain, as we have seen, that the only reason for this solid position was the large inflow of funds from Italy.

At least for the years for which we have statistics on the balance of payments, we can actually observe that the creation of money supply via the 'foreign' component was due, except in 1928, to surpluses in the balance of payments (see Table 6.5). This means that, while we can put forward the hypothesis that for 1928 the 'foreign' component was actually fed by influxes of gold coming from the Albanian market, such an assumption does not hold for the other years.

On an historical level, it is difficult (and futile) to imagine what might have happened had the inflow of Italian capital been absent. The answer which immediately springs to mind is that a serious deficit would have emerged, which would have shown up in the first instance in a trade deficit, followed by an exodus of gold out of Albania. However, as has been said, such an answer is pointless from an historical point of view, and we cannot rule out other hypotheses, such as the possibility that, in order to handle

Table 6.5 Trends in the 'foreign' component of money supply (in millions of Albanian francs)

Year	Variation in 'foreign' component	Balance of payments surplus
1928	+3.8	+0.8
1929	+2.4	+4.8
1930	+4.3	+5.6
1931	0	+6.5
1932	+6.1	+6.1
1933	−1.8	0

the trade deficit, the Albanians could have proceeded to adjust their foreign accounts by reducing imports and thus restoring equilibrium without the need for foreign loans.

Leaving aside these speculations on 'counterfactual history', what does seem certain is that the National Bank of Albania's management increased its gold stock, alongside a favourable evolution in the foreign accounts, brought about by Italy's policy of granting loans.

A separate question, of a political rather than a financial nature, is obviously that of the physical location of the gold itself. We know that, supposedly for security reasons,[28] it was mainly held in Rome. However, contrary to the assertions coming from various quarters, no legal transfer of Albania's gold from the Bank of Albania to the Italian monetary authorities ever took place, not even in the wake of the political developments of 1939.

Price trends

We will now take a closer look, still with reference to the period 1927–1938, at the money supply and wholesale prices, in order to see how closely correlated they are.

Taking the definition of money supply in its narrowest sense (as paper and metal circulation, plus current accounts with the central bank and cheques in circulation), Table 6.6 and Figures 6.1 and 6.2 show the changes in the money supply and in the wholesale price index.

There is clearly very little correlation in the first years under consideration. In 1928, the large increase in the money supply was due to the start-up phase of the new system.

The negligible impact it had on price levels can be explained, at least in part, by the fact that the new circulation was, as previously stated, a replacement for the pre-existing one.

Table 6.6 Prices and money supply in Albania, 1928–1938

	Annual percentage changes	
Year	Wholesale prices	Money supply
1928	+4.0	+50.2
1929	–4.0	+26.1
1930	–11.9	+26.9
1931	+2.4	+1.7
1932	–18.5	+13.2
1933	–22.2	–18.1
1934	–10.8	–12.8
1935	+10.0	+3.8
1936	+11.5	+34.3
1937	+3.6	–5.3
1938	–2.2	–3.2

Source: Based on documentation in ASBI, Baffi papers.

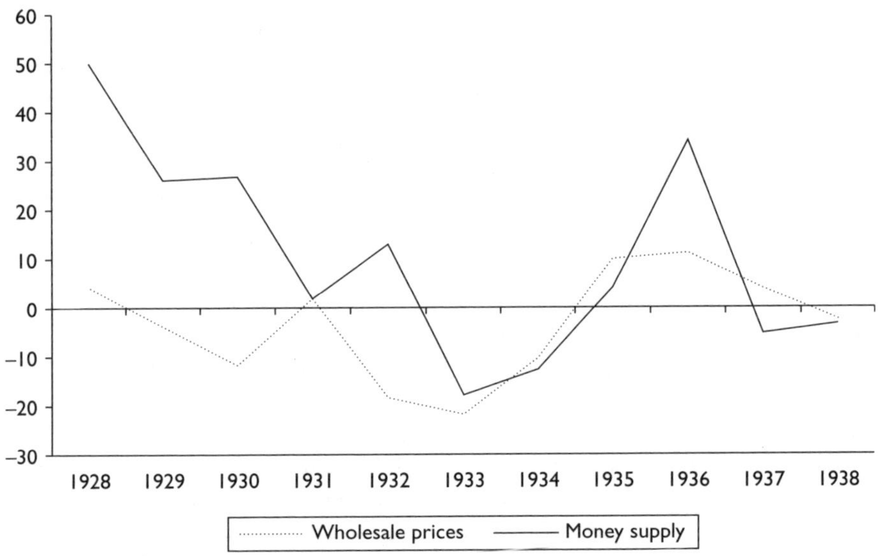

Figure 6.1 Prices and money supply in Albania, 1928–1938 (annual percentage changes)

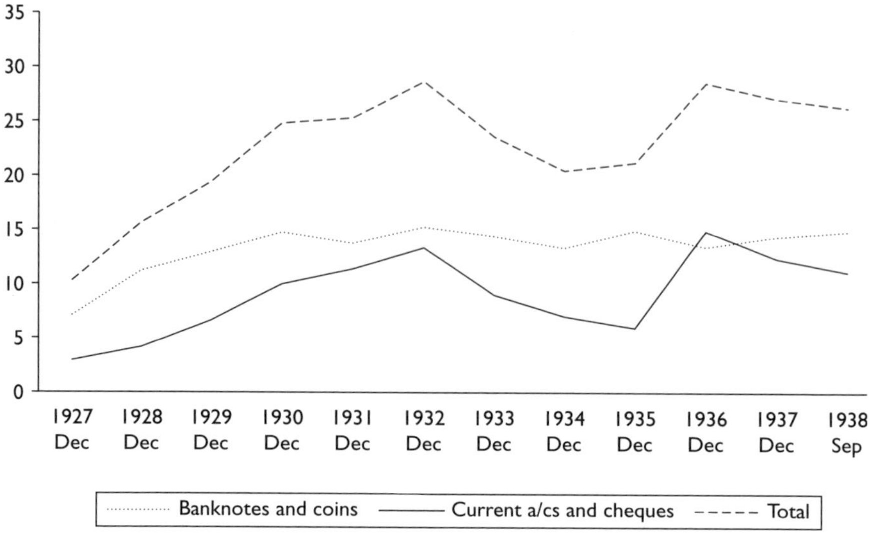

Figure 6.2 Money supply (paper and metal circulation, current accounts, cheques in circulation) (in millions of Albanian francs)

The scene is then dominated until 1934 by major decreases in the price index, reflecting the Great Depression and in particular the repercussions of the devaluation of other currencies, which lowered the cost of imported goods. It is more difficult to explain the correlation between the increase in the money supply and the decreases in prices in 1929, 1930 and 1932. Borgatta, a keen observer of Albania's monetary system, attributes this in part to stockpiling phenomena and to a reduction in the velocity of currency circulation.[29] Again according to Borgatta, the minor rise in prices in 1931 can be explained by a poor harvest and the renewed flow of Italian capital.[30] It is easier to understand the figures for the following years, in which the money supply and prices were affected more directly first by the economic depression and the restrictive monetary policy and then by the small reflation.

All of the above can be expressed by calculating the correlation coefficient between the two series, which is very high for the last six years (0.6335), but is considerably lower if taken over all 11 years (0.1419).[31]

Reserve management

We have referred several times to the prudential criteria, but also to the special consideration of the Italian interest, which were behind the monetary authorities' decisions. These are confirmed again by the reserve management policies.

As mentioned in Chapter 4, the Charter stated that the backing for the National Bank of Albania's paper circulation should be composed of reserves equal to at least one-third of the banknotes in circulation. These reserves, in turn, were to consist of gold and foreign financial assets, which could not exceed two-thirds of the total reserves. In practice, the gold reserve had to be at least 11.1 per cent of the circulation.[32]

If we look at the data for the paper circulation and other liabilities of the National Bank (Table 6.7), we can see that, during the whole period in question, tensions deriving from excessive expansion never occurred. The only year in which a considerable increase (+59.7 per cent) was recorded was the first year of the period in question (1928); but the figure is not very significant, as this was the start-up phase in the life of the new currency system and, as stated previously, the new circulation, at least in part, was not adding to the pre-existing one, but replacing it.

This meant that the backing for the circulation (composed, as we recall, of metal and foreign financial assets) proved always to be more than sufficient and certainly exceeded the statutory minimum of one-third. Also, the backing associated not only with the circulation but also with the Bank's other liabilities (deposits in current and savings accounts and cheques in circulation) was very ample (see Table 6.7 again).

However, the most interesting aspect of the backing for the circulation is that the percentage composition of the assets actually reflects, over time, precise monetary policy criteria as well as the degree to which Albania was tied to Italy.[33]

It seems appropriate to study this aspect in more detail, using a scheme for analysing the gold exchange standard proposed by Grubel.[34] The gold exchange standard, advocated, as we have seen earlier, by the Genoa Conference, was successfully put into practice, especially in the second half of the 1920s. In 1927 and 1928, according to an estimate quoted by Grubel, foreign currency reached a level of 42 per cent of the total reserves of the 25 major countries. During the course of the 1930s, however, the system began to decline for two main reasons. The first was that the system was highly charged politically. Countries were convinced that their national prestige would be strengthened if their own currency was used as an international reserve and hence if the country was admitted into the restricted group of 'world bankers'. To be able to fulfil this role, the country's currency had to be freely convertible to gold, which in turn involved keeping a large proportion of the reserves in gold as opposed to currency. This meant that countries which aspired to this more important role began to move away from the gold exchange standard, and converted part of their currency reserves to gold.

The second reason was that the real economic incentive which might have led countries to keep their reserves in currency rather than gold was

Table 6.7 Banknote circulation, liabilities and backing (in thousands of Albanian francs)

	Circulation and other liabilities			Backing						
	Circulation	Deposits in current and savings accounts, cheques in circulation	Total	Gold	Silver	Foreign currency	Foreign Treasury bills	Total	A (8:1)	B (8:3)
	(1)	(2)	(3)	(4)	(5)	(6)	(7)	(8)	(9)	(10)
Dec. 1927	6,320	3,111	9,431	1,302	115	11,893		13,310	210.6	141.1
Dec. 1928	10,095	4,423	14,518	1,249	315	15,306		16,870	167.1	116.2
Dec. 1929	11,536	7,275	18,811	1,760	99	17,157		19,016	164.8	101.1
Dec. 1930	12,925	10,966	23,891	1,933	3	20,465		22,401	173.3	93.8
Dec. 1931	11,869	12,096	23,965	5,038	3	15,409		20,450	172.2	85.3
Dec. 1932	13,052	14,189	27,241	5,407	2	18,753		24,162	185.1	88.6
Dec. 1933	12,165	9,959	22,124	7,225	3	13,825		21,053	173.0	95.1
Dec. 1934	11,019	7,948	18,967	7,122		11,296		18,418	167.1	97.1
Dec. 1935	12,243	7,278	19,521	7,556		11,515		19,071	155.7	97.6
Dec. 1936	10,653	15,978	26,631	7,556		16,255		23,811	223.5	89.4
Dec. 1937	11,131	13,923	25,054	7,583		12,576	2,412	22,571	202.7	90.1
Dec. 1938	10,529	n.a.	n.a.	7,574		8,912	2,408	18,894	179.4	n.a.

A: Ratio of total backing to circulation.
B: Ratio of total backing to circulation plus other liabilities.

Source: Documentation in ASBI, Baffi papers.

the fact that the former produced a return. However, during the Great Depression which marked the 1930s, the series of competitive devaluations of the currencies in relation to gold tended to make the latter more appealing, as it led to a capital gain which amply compensated for the absence of any return on the metal stock. Added to this, the frequent devaluations meant that the value of the currencies in the reserves was uncertain, which contributed to the reserve holders shifting their preference from currency to gold.

Moving on to the case of Albania, until 1930 its system complied fully with the gold exchange standard, with the greater part of its reserve being made up of foreign currency. Between 1928 and 1930, only a small fraction of the overall reserves (less than 10 per cent) was made up of gold. It was decided to hold interest-bearing assets in preference to locking them up in gold. However, 1931 was the year of sterling's devaluation and in Albania, as elsewhere, the gold exchange standard suffered from the confidence crisis in currency stability. We then see a sudden leap in the gold component, which jumped to 24.6 per cent in 1931 and continued rising gradually until it peaked at the end of 1938 at 40.1 per cent of the total reserves (see Table 6.8). The gold reserve, always above the threshold of 11.1 per cent of the circulation, climbed in 1938 to more than 73 per cent.

Although the first reason cited by Grubel certainly had no influence on the increase in the gold component of the reserves (it was out of the question for Tiranë to aspire to being a prime international finance centre), the second reason had considerable influence (that is, protecting the value of the reserves). It should be added, however, that, in spite of the Albanian

Table 6.8 Percentage composition of the reserves

Year	Gold	Foreign currency[a]	Italian Treasury bills
1927	9.8	90.2	
1928	7.4	92.6	
1929	9.2	90.8	
1930	8.6	91.4	
1931	24.6	75.4	
1932	22.4	77.6	
1933	34.3	65.7	
1934	38.7	61.3	
1935	36.6	63.4	
1936	31.7	68.3	
1937	33.6	55.7	10.7
1938	40.1	47.2	12.7

[a] Including silver, which is only present in negligible amounts.

Source: Documentation in ASBI, Baffi papers.

government's 'long-standing wish to see the Bank's reserves converted to gold bullion', as well as 'moved physically into Albania',[35] a sizeable portion remained invested in foreign currency, especially Italian lire. In December 1932, which was when the dollar was devalued, the percentage invested in dollars was barely 7.3 per cent of the gross foreign currency reserves.[36] In October 1935, the net lira stock totalled 41.2 million, around 10.3 million francs at the average exchange rate of that year, and almost 90 per cent of the total foreign currency reserves.[37] In the Bank's accounts, to further emphasize the importance of the investments in lire, three-month Italian Treasury bills appeared in the 1937 financial year, which in 1937 and 1938 were equivalent to 10.7 per cent and 12.7 per cent respectively of the whole reserves (see Table 6.8).

The problem of the time, therefore, especially towards the middle of the 1930s, was hedging the foreign currency component of the reserves against exchange rate risks, and the Albanian government, together with representatives of the foreign shareholders, put the matter to the Bank's management with some urgency.

The Bank's management, solicitous 'always to take Italian monetary policy into account',[38] but also mindful of its duty to protect the interests of the institution, doggedly pursued the policy of asking the Italian authorities for guarantees on its foreign currency holdings. By 'Italian authorities', we mean the Foreign and Finance Ministries and the Bank of Italy. The Foreign Ministry, in keeping with its aim to revive the 'cordial cooperation' with Zog which the events of the early 1930s had placed in jeopardy, was anxious for the guarantees to be granted; the Bank of Italy, which, it seems, had advised the Bank of Albania to limit the extent of its conversion of lire to gold,[39] maintained a neutral position, although it was anxious for the guarantees not to fall on its own reserves; the Finance Ministry gave in to pressure from the Foreign Ministry and granted the guarantees.

The issue first came up in a concrete way in May 1935, with the devaluation of the US dollar. The National Bank of Albania suffered an exchange loss because it had in its portfolio a relatively small amount in dollar bonds from the Morgan loan to Italy (around 2.5 million gold francs).[40] However, the issue arose again in a more serious way a few months later.

On 22 July 1935, as related in Chapter 5, the lira's performance on the foreign exchange market caused the authorities to abolish the rule which set the minimum backing for 'sight' liabilities at 40 per cent and to 'suspend' *de facto* the gold convertibility of lira notes, which effectively meant abandoning it.

The Bank of Albania's management, which, as we have seen, held the huge sum of 41.2 million Italian lire in its own reserves, a small part of which was invested in Treasury bills and the rest deposited with Italian banks, was faced with the dilemma of whether or not to go ahead with a massive conversion of this reserve to gold or to another currency with full gold convertibility. Judging by reports that in October 1935 Zog hurriedly exchanged 500,000 Albanian francs for dollars in Switzerland,[41] it seems that a fear was spreading in Albanian circles that the Albanian franc might drop in the same way as the lira. Faced with a choice between avoiding a conversion to gold, 'in the greater interest of the lira', and the opposing duty to protect the interests of the institution, loudly voiced by the Bank's non-Italian board members, especially the Albanians, the management chose a middle way. In a private memorandum to the Finance Minister, Thaon di Revel, the National Bank pointed out the considerable depreciation of its reserves (which in the period January 1934 to October 1935 had been equal to more than 1 million gold francs), caused by the drop in the lira exchange rate, and firmly requested a guarantee from the Italian government for the 41 million lire in its reserves, based on the level of 0.07919 grams of refined gold per lira (the level set in December 1927, with the stabilization of the lira, the so-called 'quota 90').[42]

The Finance Minister issued the guarantee, on condition that the Bank of Albania should maintain its lira holdings at their existing level.[43]

The problem came up again, even more drastically, less than a year later, in the wake of the Italian decision to formally devalue the lira by 40.94 per cent, on 5 October 1936.

On the same day, the Albanian government, without any prior consultation with the National Bank, issued a communiqué stressing that, in the light of the devaluation of the French franc, the Swiss franc and, most recently, the lira, the Albanian gold franc was 'insured by strong reserves which guaranteed it 100%'. It was only afterwards that the Albanian Finance Minister, Gera, wrote to the Bank of Albania to verify this assertion! The Bank's President, Mosconi, together with Gambino, reassured Gera, but at the same time felt it necessary to contact the Bank of Italy in order to call on the gold guarantee which had formerly been made on the lira reserves. Since the sum guaranteed was set, as we have seen, at 41.2 million lire, the lira's devaluation had led to an exchange difference equivalent to approximately 1,335 kilograms of gold. The Governor of the Bank of Italy, Azzolini, in turn referred the matter to Minister di Revel, pointing out that the guarantee had been given by the government and therefore should not rebound on the Bank of Italy. The government had no choice but to authorize the Bank of Italy to set aside in its own reserves the quantity of gold needed to cover the Bank of Albania's entire lira reserves (3,262.6 kilograms of gold). In the event, the Bank of Italy avoided any gold outflow, as the Bank of Albania decided against claiming it, requesting instead the equivalent stock in lire, around 69.7 million, which moreover was to be reinvested in Italy. The Finance Ministry gave its consent. Not one gram of gold left Italy, but the Bank of Albania's lira reserves saw a considerable increase, from 41.2 to 69.7 million.[44]

The debate over bimetallism

To close this chapter, it seems appropriate to mention the debate over bimetallism which took place between the Bank of Albania's management, the Albanian government and the Italian government, between 1928 and 1929.

We have already seen that before the monetary reform of 1925 gold coins ('napoleons') and silver coins ('crowns') were both in circulation in Albania. The silver coins were exchanged at their intrinsic value and hence at a rate which varied in relation to gold coins. The Exchequer did accept payment in silver coins but only at a 5 per cent premium, to cover the risk of a loss in their value following any variations in relative prices. The new monetary system of 1925 wanted to maintain the simultaneous circulation of both gold and silver. It was decided however to relegate the silver coin to the rank of fractional currency, together with nickel and bronze coins, with limited redemption power in private transactions ('token coins'): the face value of the silver coin was therefore fixed well above its intrinsic, or market, value. While on the market the ratio between the prices of the two metals was around 32, the legal ratio was fixed at 15.6.[45]

At the same time these silver coins had unlimited redemption power with respect to the Exchequer and the National Bank: an unlimited number of silver coins could be taken to them and exchanged for gold coins at the legal ratio ('mint ratio').

As the experience of the previous century had amply demonstrated, bimetallism can only survive when the mint ratio is close to the market ratio: otherwise, if – for instance – the market value of silver is much lower, as in our case, then it is convenient to buy silver on the market, have it coined at the mint, exchange the silver coins for gold coins at the inflated legal price and cash the difference. The monetary authority loses out, as it is forced by law to accept the overvalued silver against its gold. Bimetallism was a case-study in Gresham's Law, with silver as the 'bad money' driving out gold, the 'good money', and was consequently dismissed.[46]

It seems that the Albanian system was flawed: considering silver as a token coin, and at the same time permitting its conversion into gold coins at the 'mint ratio', had two main negative results: a scarcity of token money, and losses for the Central Bank.

It is therefore not surprising that in Albania the bimetallic standard could not survive. Not only was there a huge discrepancy at the very start between market and mint ratios, but, in a period such as the 1920s, marked by falling silver prices (between November 1919 and November 1929, the price of silver on the London market fell from 73 to 23 pence per ounce), the intrinsic content of coins in relation to their face value diminished rapidly. The ability to convert silver coins at their legal value encouraged the public to exchange them for gold coins at the issuing bank, to which the loss was passed on, amidst a growing shortage in fractional coins. This induced the Bank of Albania to withdraw the silver circulation.[47]

The Albanian government had a different viewpoint: it wanted first to restore the old local custom of using silver, as well as gold, as a monetary standard. But, above all, it could not easily give up the share of minting profits (1/2) that the law accorded to the government.

In order to reach this double objective, new legislation was enacted in 1928 (Law of 12 June): it set a new metal content for silver coins, almost doubling it in order to bring the intrinsic value of the coin closer to the legal value, thus bringing the market and mint ratios closer together. Secondly, it stated that silver coinage would be carried out not by the National Bank, but 'through the Bank', upon authorization of the Albanian government: this was the starting point for claiming a larger profit share than that assured by the Agreement of 1925 (1/2).

In practice, leaving aside the far-from-insignificant matter of the minting profits, it was actually a case of restoring the former bimetallism, that is, a system based on coins of two different metals, with a legal value not far from their market value. In May 1929, the board of the National Bank made a stand against the above-mentioned law, which had not as yet been put into practice, claiming that in effect it was an anachronistic return to bimetallism.[48] The directors of the Bank made their hostility to the project known to the Albanian government. The Governor of the Bank of Italy, Stringher, wrote to Mussolini[49] expressing his support for the National Bank of Albania's position and reiterating that the attempt to return to a bimetallic system was an anachronism which would damage Italy's credibility in the international banking community.

In Stringher's words, 'very dubious opinions'[50] would be formed 'as to our own competence in managing circulation'. On a more concrete level, the return to bimetallism would have involved serious losses for the Bank of Albania if the foreseeable further devaluations of silver made it desirable for people to hand their silver coins in at the Bank and withdraw gold. According to the Bank's directors, if the coins minted reached a value of 5 million francs and there then followed a 50 per cent depreciation in the price of silver (as had happened in the previous decade), the losses involved would have been such as to absorb the entire capital and reserves of the Bank. According to Stringher, there would be no advantage for the Bank of Albania even in the reverse case of a revaluation of silver, since private individuals in Albania would stockpile silver coins if their intrinsic value exceeded their nominal value and Albania would once again face a shortage in its token circulation.[51]

However, the Albanian government was insistent and, at the end of May 1929, it requested the Bank of Albania to begin minting the new silver coins immediately, to a total value of 2 million Albanian francs, on the basis of an alleged agreement reached between the Finance Minister, Tutulani, and the Bank's directors. According to the Albanian government's plans, the old 'crowns' would have to be completely withdrawn from circulation and exported to Italy, while the new coins would be minted in Rome, imported and put into circulation. Once the full 2 million francs' worth of new coins had been imported, the circulation of the old 'crowns' would be forbidden.[52]

At this point, a strange kind of role-play took place, which demonstrates how Mussolini, intent on pursuing excellent relations with the Albanian government (Italy had only recently given its support for Zog's coronation as King of the Albanians, and Italian foreign policy, in spite of a lingering mutual mistrust, sought his complete support), did not hesitate to block the solutions put forward by the Bank of Albania, with the Bank of Italy's backing. The Bank of Albania called on Italy's Foreign Ministry to intervene, denying that any agreement had been reached with the Albanian government, stressing that it was against the project and wanted nothing to do with it, and placing the responsibility for the agreement with the Italian Legation in Albania (and hence indirectly with the Italian government). The National Bank also pointed out that the project had come from 'narrow circles of low-level Albanian politicians', and that the largest sections of the population did not care about it. Lastly, the Bank underlined the need for the Italian government to distance itself from the project, which would otherwise seriously discredit Italy in international circles, not to mention amongst the foreign financial groups which, although in a minority, had a share in the institution's capital.[53]

Mussolini's reply to these remonstrations on the part of the 'technocrats', while seemingly long-winded and sibylline, is in fact clear enough:

> I am confident that while the steps which the Bank [of Albania] is about to take may not, by *force majeure*, be completely in keeping with the monetary principles which seem to hold sway nowadays in the more advanced nations, they will nonetheless enable monetary reform to take place without incurring those financial dangers to which Your Excellency [Governor Stringher] has referred and will help to overcome the long period of stagnation which, to the considerable detriment of our political interests, has long been apparent in the matter in question.[54]

In other words, I really want a good rapport with Zog, so don't go upsetting my plans with these technicalities!

On 4 December 1929, the bimetallism affair ended in a compromise, with an agreement made in Tiranë, under the auspices of the Italian government, between Minister Tutulani and the Managing Director of the Bank, Gambino. The victory for the 'technocrats', in which the new silver coins would, if necessary, be minted according to the system laid down in the 1925 Monetary Law rather than the one set out in the Law of 1928 (which was soon repealed), was heavily counterbalanced by the National Bank's giving up its rights to the minting profits in favour of the Albanian government. Minting was to be carried out 'on behalf of the state', thus accepting the principle of the 1928 Law. These profits, even if they were to be deposited with the Bank of Albania as backing for the new circulation, would bear interest for the Albanian government at 4 per cent.[55]

In fact, having learnt its lesson from the unsuccessful experiment in silver circulation, the Bank replaced the new issue of silver with a larger issue of nickel coins. The old silver coins, the 'crowns', continued to circulate in the interior regions of the country, which caused imbalances in the price levels. When, from 1929 onwards, prices in Albania began to decline in keeping with the trend in the world market, the persisting devaluation of silver caused an increase, in those regions, in the cost of living, that is, in the price of consumer goods purchased with silver coins on the basis of their intrinsic value.[56]

To bring this episode on bimetallism to a close, we can draw the following conclusions:

(a) In 1929 the Fascist government was not as yet using a firm hand over the small nation, since, in order to win Zog over, the Italians felt the need to hold back from insisting on 'healthier' financial options.
(b) Throughout the controversy, the Bank of Albania maintained a position of independence and responsibility towards its minority foreign shareholders.
(c) The Bank of Italy, mindful of the 'critical eye' of the international banking community, resolutely supported the position which seemed most technically correct.
(d) The Albanian government's position remains somewhat ambiguous. It claimed to be acting in the interests of the population and for the purpose of remedying the shortage in the token circulation. It is uncertain, however, whether, in proposing a new issue with an intrinsic value close to its face value, the government was really intending to meet circulation needs, or to use the revision of the existing law to appropriate a greater proportion of the minting profits for itself, leaving

the Bank of Albania to bear the brunt of any losses caused by further possible devaluations of silver.

A more successful attempt to introduce silver coins was made by the Albanian government in 1935. Again, the issues at stake were a shortage of token currency, made worse by the exportation of the old 'crowns' out of Albania in order to cash in on a rise in the price of silver, and the question of the share of minting profits to be allocated to the Albanian government. Once again the Italian government commented that it was necessary 'sometimes to subordinate financial interests to a more general and realistic vision of the situation'.

A Law of 28 March 1935 opened the way for the new coinage, and the circulation of silver coins, initially at 590,000 francs, increased to 1,216,000 francs by the end of 1938.[57]

CHAPTER 7

The occupation of Albania and the union between Italy and Albania

Invasion and union

Towards the end of the 1920s, this was the view of Albania in Fascist Italy:

> In addition to being a fervent patriot, King Zog has shown himself to be a devoted servant of his country and an enlightened ruler, worthy to wear the crown. . . . The Albanian ruling class will benefit from our valuable advice, and from the assistance provided by a flourishing institution such as the National Bank of Albania, and a well-functioning, lively organization such as SVEA. Thus this small nation is rising up and enjoying a rebirth; the painful traces of its cruel history are disappearing; all the old sectarian prejudices of caste, political factions and religious hatred are dissolving one after the other in the shadow of the past.[1]

Less than ten years later, the view had changed radically:

> The people, whose miserable living conditions call to mind those of Chinese villages scattered along the banks of the Yangtse river, are reluctant to tolerate the existence, growth and ostentation of a Court whose members are like the characters in an operetta in their ways, but which is weighing on public finances in an intolerable manner. . . . If Italy were to assert itself, possibly in a conclusive and totalitarian way, it would serve as a counterbalance in the Balkan region to the undeniable increase in influence which the Reich has acquired in that area, following the implementation of the *Anschluss*.[2]

Even though these extracts have been taken from two very different sources – a propaganda book on the 'help given by Italy to the small but strong and important state', and a confidential report from Ciano to Mussolini – they give an idea of the regime's clear change in policy towards Albania in the course of less than a decade.

Ciano's view was exactly echoed by Sir Andrew Ryan, the British Minister in Albania: 'The Italian government have shown a distinct tendency this year to be critical of the extravaganza of Albanian financial expenditure[; they] assert the principle that, as they so largely finance Albania, they are entitled to expect that the money should be well administered and that expenditure abroad should as far as possible be directed into Italian channels.'

Indeed, in 1938, political developments were already clearly indicating that Zog's days were numbered. Once again, we will refrain from dwelling on these developments, which have been described in detail elsewhere.[3]

The main aspect to emphasize here is that in 1938 the change of policy took place which then led, in spring 1939, to the Italian occupation of Albania. The seeds of this change were sown in Ciano's report to Mussolini, referred to above, and in the latter's acceptance of the report's conclusions which pointed to annexation as the preferred solution to the Albanian question, through the establishment of a union between the two monarchies, sharing the head of state in the person of Victor Emmanuel III. The change was motivated by considerations both of an economic nature (the need to take full advantage of the country's resources and thus make the affair, which had been disappointing until then, profitable for Italy) and of a political nature (first and foremost the need to contain German expansionism in the Balkans).

We have dealt with the first point earlier on, and it was a particularly sore point for the regime.[4] We may note here that King Zog's expenses added insult to injury, in this respect. According to a British memorandum, written a few days after the occupation of the country:

> Italy's own increasing financial difficulties . . . led to severe criticism of Albanian extravagance during the past twelve months, and it appears that the Italians actually went back on some of their promises much to the displeasure of the King, who is said to have courted the idea of seeking help elsewhere. Whether the Italians had come to distrust the King, or whether they regarded his administration as inefficient and an impediment to the rapid realization of their programme, it is impossible to say.[5]

The British government, always particularly sensitive to developments in that area, was aware that the huge amounts of money spent by Italy in Albania were not producing results, for various reasons: bad administration and extravagant expenses, and a disregard for directing expenses 'into Italian channels' on the part of the Albanians. This was all the more so, since 'Italy pays a secret subsidy of 3.5 million gold francs towards Albanian military expenditure'.[6]

As regards the political situation, it is worth remembering that historians stress Mussolini's lukewarm attitude towards Germany during the course of 1938, especially after the *Anschluss*. In relations with the Germans, there emerged in 1938, along with the Alto Adige (or Southern Tirol) question, that of a 'serious and precise delimitation of the respective spheres of influence in the Danube–Balkan area, in which Germany's over-activism did not augur well and showed no intention of respecting Italy's hunting ground and the rights Italy had acquired'.[7] Faced with the Nazis' annexation of Austria, Ciano believed that the occupation of Albania would serve as a form of counterbalance and a retaliation on Italy's part.

It was against this background, with Italy maintaining a divide between its own foreign policy and that of Germany, that the Munich agreements of September 1938 were reached. They represented 'the brief Indian summer of Mussolini's life', or 'the high point of Mussolini's new politics'.[8] Mussolini was aiming to become the pivotal force in Europe and, according to De Felice,[9] was planning to create an axis of a different sort alongside the Rome–Berlin Axis, this time a Rome–London axis, which would be the central support for the whole system and would serve to maintain its fundamental equilibrium. It would be used to restrain the excesses of the other two mutual partners (Germany and France), and would act as the nucleus of an 'executive board' made up of the four great powers, now that the League of Nations (from which Italy had pulled out at the end of 1937) had been set aside.

This idea was never carried out, for reasons which lie outside the present study. It is worth noting, however, that the annexation of Albania fitted well into this political scene (as far as London and Paris were concerned, an Albania in Italian hands could present an effective obstacle to German penetration along the Danube).[10] In the event, the occupation took place as a counter-move to another German initiative, that of the occupation of Bohemia which took place on 15 March 1939. Mussolini stepped up the pace accordingly: it was time to put a stop to German scheming in the Balkans and to show the French and British that, after the taking of Prague, Italy was not going to wait around.[11]

The occupation was carried out within two days, 7 and 8 April. Zog fled to Greece. On 12 April a Constituent Assembly unanimously decided to offer the Albanian crown to the King of Italy. On 16 April, Victor Emmanuel III assumed the title of King of Albania. An Under-Secretariat for Albanian Affairs was set up at the Foreign Ministry, with a close friend of Ciano's, Zenone Benini, appointed as Under-Secretary. Benini had been Vice-President of the Fascist Corporation for the Iron and Steel Industry until then and, as we read in the official notice of his appointment,[12] 'a Fascist and *Squadrista* [member of the Fascist Squads] since 1920'.[13] A few days later, on 23 April, Starace, the Party Secretary, travelled to Tiranë to set up the Albanian National Fascist Party and Albanian Fascist Youth.[14] Later, with the Law of 13 July 1939, a General Lieutenancy of Albania was established in Tiranë. Francesco Jacomoni di San Savino, another of Ciano's friends and Italian Minister in Tiranë, was nominated Official Representative of the King (Lieutenant General).[15]

The process of turning Albania into a Fascist state continued with the formation of the Central Council for the Corporative Economy, established with the Lieutenant General's Decree of 14 March 1940; the Council had a consultative role and, together with the Central Council of the Albanian Fascist Party, formed the Supreme Corporative Fascist Council, which replaced the parliament.[16]

The financial press was not above indulging in the rhetoric of the time, proclaiming that 'the destinies of the Italian and Albanian peoples are now joined for ever',[17] nor was the Bank of Italy shortly after, in the language of its Annual Report for 1939, usually much more measured and technical. Dedicating ample space to the 'historic event', it felt the need to link it to Italy's 'ancient' culture, to 'Imperial Rome', Amalfi, Naples and the Venetian Republic, and declared that Italy's contribution to Albanian culture was 'unparalleled in the history of relationships between nations'.[18]

In constitutional terms, the bond between Italy and Albania was defined as a 'union of realms', that is a union in which the communality of the head of state was not accidental, due solely to the fact that the laws of the two states, each acting of its own accord, had simultaneously brought the same person to the thrones (which would be a union of persons), but an event brought about by specific legal rulings. Relations between the two states remained international in law, but common diplomatic and consular services were established and the armed forces were unified.[19]

In practice, there was a certain confusion surrounding relations between Italy and Albania after the formation of the union. We read, for example, that, although Jacomoni was acting as Albanian head of state (for King Victor Emmanuel), as a diplomat he was still under the jurisdiction of the Italian Foreign Ministry, and Jacomoni found himself 'in the absurd position of signing agreements in the name of Victor Emmanuel III, with the Albanian government, that is, with his own government'.[20] The financial Agreement between the two governments, which we will be looking at shortly, is a typical example. It was signed by Jacomoni as Italy's representative, and put into force in Albania by the very same Jacomoni acting as Albanian head of state.

Within this political framework the time was soon ripe to set up a much closer economic and financial link between the two countries, with the creation of an 'economic, customs and currency union', on the basis of the Agreement of 20 April 1939. Before examining this Agreement, and the resulting effects on: (a) Albania's monetary system and the Central

Bank's Charter; and (b) the regulations governing exchange rates, foreign trade, travel abroad and the movement of banknotes into and out of the country, it is worth considering some of the projects which had already been planned in 1938 with a view to bringing relations with Albania more into line with Italy's interests.

These were ideas developed in June 1938 (which thus emerges as a 'pivotal year' from an economic as well as a political point of view), in close connection with the gloomy picture of relations between Italy and Albania which Ciano had painted for Mussolini barely a month earlier.[21] In fact, these projects, found in the archives of the Bank of Italy,[22] all have one obvious thing in common: their incompatibility with the status quo of the time. In other words, the different economic solutions being suggested with a view to safeguarding Italian interests were extremely unlikely to have been accepted by Albania, were it to remain an independent state.

The first proposal looked at the possibility of simply extending the circulation of the Italian lira to Albania. The second looked at creating a 'lira area' similar, as the proposal mentions, to the 'sterling area' which already existed. The third envisaged the issuing of a new currency, the 'Albanian lira', to be spent only on importing goods from Italy.

It was thought that the first proposal, the extension of the Italian lira to Albania, would be ineffective unless accompanied by the adoption in Albania of exchange and foreign trade systems similar to those used in Italy (and in the Italian colony of Ethiopia), and by adequate guarding of Albania's borders. Without these measures, simply extending the circulation of the Italian lira to Albania, apart from the international complications it would cause, would not be sufficient to prevent the transfer of lire from Italy to Albania being used to acquire goods and services from third countries,[23] which is what in fact was happening. The lack of rigorous controls at the Albanian borders would also encourage people to export Italian banknotes. The burden of transferring funds would not be lessened, the document concluded, unless a system to defend the Italian currency was created in Albania.

This proposal would have radically solved any exchange rate risk issue between the two countries, once the appropriate conversion rate of the Albanian franc (which was to disappear) into the Italian lira had been decided upon, but would have needed additional foreign exchange and trade controls.

The second proposal addressed the problem of the exchange rate directly, maintaining the Albanian franc in circulation and linking its rate to the lira at the level then prevailing on the market, around 6.20 lire per franc. More specifically, the project supported the less drastic alternative of a 'lira area', which, whilst allowing the monetary systems of the two countries to remain independent, would tie the value of the Albanian currency to the Italian lira, rather than to gold. In addition to the political advantage of establishing a closer link between the two states without the trauma of unification, two economic advantages were identified: eliminating the hazard of exchange rate fluctuations for entrepreneurs in Albania, and encouraging not only the National Bank (which already did this), but also other banks and companies to deposit their funds in Italy, where they would not be exposed to exchange rate risks. The procedures by which the two currencies were to be linked reveal a tacit but clear deflationary aim, which was to be brought about by means of a kind of 'monetary illusion': Albania would have to change its currency unit from the franc to the lek (which until then had been equal to 0.20 Albanian francs); keeping the exchange rate at the current market rate, the lek was to have an exchange rate of 1 lek to 1.25 lire. It was anticipated that using a smaller monetary unit would make it easier to reduce wages in lire terms, thus reducing the costs of investment for Italian business enterprises. For example, according to the document, it would have been more acceptable to change a wage of 3 francs (18.7 lire at the exchange rate of the time) to 10 leks (12.5 lire) rather than to 2 francs (also 12.5 lire).

The third proposal, which followed a few months after the other two, was that of the 'Albanian lira'. It was centred around the old problem of balancing Italian expenditure on investments in Albania with additional Albanian imports from Italy. The project envisaged the creation of a parallel currency, the 'Albanian lira': the National Bank would issue 'cash vouchers' in 'Albanian lire', 'for the forthcoming land reclamation investments, which will involve extremely large expenses' (an estimated billion lire, at the rate of about 100 million a year). The new money would only be valid for purchasing goods in Italy. Unused vouchers could be traded, provided that they were to be used for the same purpose (imports from Italy). It was recognized, however, that, in order for the scheme to work, the Albanian government would have to make it easier to import goods from Italy, exempting them from customs duty if necessary. It was envisaged that in the long run the 'Albanian lira' could be made legal tender, replacing the Albanian franc entirely. In this way, this project ultimately returned to the suggestion made in the first proposal, though integrating it with considerations of a commercial nature (the facilitation of imports from Italy), which would avoid its inconveniences.

There was also a fourth proposal,[24] which was more peripheral in relation to these three, and which was drawn up during the feverish days of the occupation (it is dated 7 April 1939), in anticipation of the 'imminent reopening for business of the National Bank of Albania, which has been closed *de facto* since Wednesday, the fifth of this month'. Compared with the others, this project was more concerned with the basic principles of the Albanian economy and therefore reached opposite conclusions to the previous ones. It noted that, without Italy's help in maintaining it, the value of the Albanian franc would be exposed to heavy devaluations, due to the poor performance of Albania's foreign accounts. The Albanian currency unit should therefore be devalued in relation to the lira. Albania would adopt a new currency, the lek, linked by a 1:1 ratio to the lira, which would involve a devaluation of approximately 25 per cent. According to the proposal, this would bring about a reduction in costs for Italian enterprises operating in Albania (note that, while the other proposals were wary of exchange rate risks, this one was content with a fixed exchange rate but was aiming to make Albanian currency less expensive for the Italian investor). The containment of costs for Italian investors in Albania was an important factor: a rise in costs within Albania was indeed foreseeable, in the light of the increased flow of Italian spending there. Finally, the proposal saw the upheaval of the annexation as the ideal time to carry out the devaluation. There was a draft monetary agreement between Italy and Albania,[25] which spoke explicitly in terms of transferring the gold and foreign currency belonging to the National Bank of Albania, to the Bank of Italy, which in turn would cover Albanian circulation 100 per cent with Italian banknotes.

In summary, the common purpose of these projects was to stabilize the exchange rate (even by simply abolishing the Albanian currency). Where they differed was in relation to the appropriate rate: whether to keep a high level for the Albanian currency with a view to making Italian exports more competitive; or to devalue the currency (or simply extend the lira to Albania) in an effort to facilitate Italian investments in Albania.

The new monetary regime

The actual legislative framework which was created after the 'union' of the two crowns to a large extent adopted the ideas expounded in the first three projects described above, though it avoided the more extreme proposals such as that of extending the lira circulation to Albanian territory or the formal transfers of the National Bank's reserves to the Bank of Italy. The idea of a cheaper Albanian currency to stimulate Italian investments there was rejected, as trade considerations prevailed.

The focal point within this framework was the 'economic, customs and currency Agreement', signed in Tiranë on 20 April 1939 (a few days after the occupation) by Francesco Jacomoni for Italy and Fejzi Alizotti, the Finance Minister, for Albania.[26]

At a commercial level, Italy and Albania were established as a customs union and therefore, in terms of the application of tariffs and other customs laws, they were taken to be a single territory, which conferred on both states reciprocal freedom of trade. The customs union meant that Italian import and export bans also applied in Albania. Italy would arrange for its own trade agreements with third countries to be extended to Albania, while Albania would be obliged to terminate its own. Customs management and the guarding of customs posts at the borders were taken over by the Italian administration. Italy would receive all proceeds from customs duties, and pledged to pay Albania the annual sum of 15 million Albanian francs, on the understanding that, if the net customs receipts exceeded 9 million francs in the year, the difference would be added to the 15 million.[27] Albania would however retain its fiscal autonomy.

At a monetary level, the idea of extending the circulation of the lira to Albania was not put into practice. The Albanian franc was kept as the currency unit but was debased and disconnected from gold, and was pegged by a fixed exchange rate to the Italian lira. The backing for the circulation in Albania would no longer be made up of gold and foreign currencies, but exclusively of Italian lire, in the form of banknotes or other credits to be drawn on the Bank of Italy. The Albanian franc would keep an indirect link to gold, equal to that of the Italian lira. In fact, Albanian francs, no longer redeemable with gold, would be freely convertible into lire. It could be seen as a sort of model of the gold exchange standard, bearing in mind that the lira was tied by a fixed parity to gold (1 lira having been equivalent to 0.04677 grams of fine gold since October 1936). It should be remembered, however, that the lira's own gold convertibility had been 'temporarily' suspended in July 1935 and so the wording of the Italo-Albanian Agreement, which speaks of gold cover for the franc, does not appear to reflect the reality of the situation. To a great extent, the system being applied in Albania was an outright 'lira standard'.

We have already seen in Chapter 6 that a large proportion of the Bank of Albania's reserves were held in lire, against which it had obtained a guarantee in gold from the Italian authorities. In 1936, 28.5 million lire had been transferred to the Bank in application of this guarantee. During this phase of weakness of the Italian lira, it was important to safeguard Italy from possible further demands by Albania to apply the 'gold clause'. For this reason, the arrangements established with the 1939 Agreement, by which the National Bank of Albania's reserves would be made up no longer of gold but only of Italian currency, aimed to forcibly solve the root of the problem by operating a 'standard' which, although in appearance it could be seen as a gold standard if taken to its logical extreme, was in practice, as we have said, a 'lira standard'. In this way, the 'lira area' advocated in the 1938 proposal came to be put into practice. One very important matter was that of deciding on the exchange rate between the franc and the lira, and it was set in the Agreement at 6.25 lire to the Albanian franc. The previous rate of the lira to the franc, since the 1936 devaluation of the lira, had been 6.22.[28] In December 1938, the average rate had been 6.22 and, in March 1939, 6.19.[29] The rate of 6.25 therefore highlighted a further slight drop in the value of the lira.[30] Therefore the idea of devaluing the franc in order to make the transfer of Italian capital to Albania cheaper was never put into practice. It was preferred instead to keep the franc at an overvalued level in relation to the lira, so as to smooth the way for a greater flow of Italian goods and services into Albania.

In this way, Italy was able to reap the political benefits of a customs union and the economic benefits of an overvalued Albanian currency.

Finally, the Agreement established a monopoly on foreign exchange transactions, assigning it to the National Bank of Albania, which was to exercise it in accordance with the regulations in force in Italy. A complex system of foreign exchange controls was set in motion, whose peculiarities lay not so much in the tightness of the regulations – fairly common for many years among European countries – as in the total inclusion of Albania within the Italian regulatory framework.

A confidential appendix attached to the Agreement established that no monopoly rights or duties of any sort would apply to oil products brought into Albania for use by the Italian and Albanian armed forces.[31]

In addition, a series of other regulations was introduced as a kind of technical supplement to the new institutional framework defined in the Agreement, which the National Bank of Albania quickly incorporated into its own Charter.[32] These regulations were contained in the Lieutenant General's Decree on the exchange monopoly, of 15 May 1939, and in a series of regulations issued by the Bank of Albania on 12 June.[33] The regulations provided for the following:

(a) A devolution of foreign exchange transactions to banks with branches in Albania, upon authorization by the monopoly holder, the Bank of Albania. These banks were to be designated as 'agent banks'.
(b) With respect to Albanian exports, a distinction was made between those destined for Italy, its possessions and Italian East Africa, and those destined for third countries. For the former, no currency constraints were introduced, except that payments were to be made exclusively in Albanian francs, whereas for the latter an approval was required from the Bank of Albania or one of the agent banks. In addition, any foreign currency received in payment of these exports had to be ceded to one of these agent banks. Delayed payments were allowed, within set time limits, but the option to keep the currency abroad in foreign accounts was not permitted.
(c) With respect to Albania's imports, whilst it was allowed complete freedom to import from Italy, its territories and Italian Africa, for imports from third countries the importer would have to apply to the National Bank of Albania for the appropriate amount of foreign currency as payment. The application had to be extremely detailed

and provision was made for the Bank to reject it 'at its sole and non-transferable discretion'.

(d) Regarding foreign exchange transactions relating to travel abroad, strict limits were imposed on the export of Italian and Albanian banknotes from Albania. However, whilst a tourist travelling from Albania to Italy or Italian Africa was able to take unlimited cheques and money orders in denominations of francs or lire without going through any formalities (and vice versa for an Italian tourist in Albania), Albanian tourists visiting third countries would only be able to take with them, in addition to the few banknotes allowed, those means of payment 'which the National Bank shall see fit to allocate to them'. Meanwhile, tourists from third countries entering Albania would be obliged to declare all the means of payments in their possession.[34]

(e) And finally, a strict system of conditions and permissions on the part of the National Bank of Albania was introduced with respect to the exporting (or importing) of banknotes, money orders, cheques, securities and other financial assets out of (or into) Albania, without altering the relative freedom of circulation between Italy and Albania and the freedom to bring any such financial assets into Albania if they were in the form of currencies other than Albanian francs or Italian lire.

In order to implement the legislation through the regulations of the National Bank, a Commission was established, to be composed of three officials from the Bank itself and three delegates from the Ministry of Finance, the Exchequer and Customs and Excise respectively. Corresponding legislation was introduced in Italy.[35]

CHAPTER 8

A short-lived 'lira area'

Financial and trade consequences of the union

The few years of the 'lira area' are as dense with important developments on the political and economic scene as they are lacking in adequate documentation which could allow us to follow these developments with some accuracy, especially in the area of statistics. With the union of Italy and Albania, Albania actually disappears from the League of Nations statistics. In the material published post-1939, accuracy and objectivity of information are sacrificed to an abundance of propaganda. Italian material published immediately after the Second World War, being mainly concerned with the dispute with Albania over the question of war reparations,[1] does not provide an exhaustive picture of the period of Italian occupation in Albania. Archive documents are certainly of assistance, though they are far from abundant, and as yet we do not have access to the archive of the Italian Under-Secretariat for Albanian Affairs, parts of which moreover are missing due to events during the war. It seems useful at this point, before embarking on a more detailed analysis of this phase, to quote certain extracts from a report found in the Bank of Italy's archives, 'Impressions on Albania'. It is undated and unofficial, but it is helpful in giving an overview of the economic situation in the country after the Italian occupation and of Italian 'moods' at the time, though we are not able to ascertain whether these moods are peculiar to the report's author or whether they were more or less shared at an official level (and here, also, we cannot say whether 'official' is in relation to the Bank of Italy or to the Italian government).[2] On the subject of inflation, the report notes:

> The cost of living in Albania is very high and overall seemed to me to be about twice as high as the cost we see in our own kingdom. To compensate for this however, it can be said that in terms of nutrition, they are not badly off and in fact I was surprised to find good quality pasta, good bread, mineral water, coffee, etc. . . . Owing to the sizeable

> bonuses which the [Italian] military and civilians over there receive and to the public works policy which has made our own working masses, and unfortunately the local ones also, accustomed to very high wages, a large supply of currency has come into circulation, with a resulting increase in prices, the latter however being also due to increased spending and to difficulties in transporting goods from Italy. Consequently the impression has spread, especially among the ignorant and mistrustful indigenous population, that the inflation of paper money is perhaps higher than it actually is.

Concerning the choice of economic strategy to pursue, the report's author puts forward an alternative. According to the grander choice:

> In order to fully resolve the Albanian question, as soon as a victorious peace has been reached of course, to my mind what would be needed is a constant flow of means and men. . . . This would involve, on our part, granting a much greater provision of means than in the past – such as 40–50 billion lire, spread over ten years, with a sufficient and suitable flow of immigration from Italy alongside the flow of capital. In this way, Albania could become self-sufficient in food production, could continue to develop its mineral industry and create new economically viable industries and, importantly from a political point of view, become a true Italian territory, because the Italian population would in the end prevail.

The less ambitious one follows straight after:

> However, if such means were not available, it would perhaps be more appropriate to allow a period of reflection, while confining our policies to ordinary administration, supporting the economic forces already in place and encouraging any others which show potential.

Moreover, in the author's words, in an 'Adriatic sea which will become ours from a totalitarian point of view, and with Greece as an integral part of our living space', the position of Albania would then take on a lesser importance for Italy. The report goes on to question whether it would not therefore be more useful to invest resources in developing Italy's Mezzogiorno instead of Albania.

The reason for dwelling on this document, in spite of its being unofficial, is that it highlights the fact that, even after the union between the two countries, the basic nature of the economic and financial problems which dogged their relationship had not changed. In spite of the Fascist regime's increased political, military and financial presence in Albania, discussions were still taking place as to whether it was really worth pursuing financial and human engagement in that country to the end (that is, until the territory became completely 'italianized') or whether it would not be better instead to divert the resources to Italy's own underdeveloped areas.

There is no doubting, however, that, especially after the end of the conflict between Italy, Greece and Yugoslavia, the reform of Albanian institutions on the corporative model went ahead briskly enough. In the economic field, once the structure of the Central Council for the Corporative Economy had been modified, with its members subdivided into the four sections of agriculture, industry, trade, and arts and crafts (Lieutenant's Decree no. 55, 18 April 1942), a Joint Ministerial Working Committee for Technical Advancement was created (Lieutenant's Decree no. 66, 18 April 1942), to promote professional training in the agriculture, industry and tertiary sectors. At the Ministry for the Economy, a Central Committee for Provisioning and Consumption was formed, to deal with product distribution and price regulation. Its chairman was the Permanent Secretary to the Ministry and it was made up of members with particular skills in the economic sectors which it was to regulate (Lieutenant's Decree no. 152, 21 July 1942). This same decree created a Provincial Economic Council for each prefecture, chaired by the local *federale* (a local representative of the Fascist Party), and provided for a District Economic Council for each sub-prefecture. These bodies were appointed to monitor the execution of orders from the Ministry for the Economy and kept the central bodies informed of the local food supply situations.[3]

In tandem with these institutional developments, there were two other features of the Italo-Albanian union: a further increase in the flow of financial resources into Albania and an expansion in trade, especially on the side of Italian exports into Albania, which served to create a marked surplus for Italy in the trade relationship which had deteriorated so badly during the 1930s. Nonetheless, the Fascist presence in Albania after the invasion did not last long enough to provide an accurate test of the effects of the conquest on the two countries' economies.[4] However, even in that short period, corruption and a lack of financial reliability prevented any worthwhile results from being achieved. Moreover, the war in the Balkans, which Mussolini had placed as his top priority in the early 1940s, undid everything that Benini, as Under-Secretary for Albanian Affairs, and Jacomoni, as the King's Lieutenant General in Albania, had sought to do.[5]

Attention has been drawn to the way in which Ciano considered Albania as a kind of 'family property'. The fact that he christened cities with names of his relatives was a typical example. In the 1950s press sources reported the deployment of sizeable secret funds in Albania, even after Zog's escape, as well as a network of corruption during Italy's occupation. We will not go into these aspects in detail, and in any case the sources consulted do not expand on them any further, but will try instead to look more closely at the question of financial reliability during the heightened Italian presence.

In relation to the programmes pursued by the regime following the occupation of Albania, we see the same reservations surfacing again that had been present before the events of 1925. Guarneri speaks of having acted as a restraining force on Ciano's projects, worried that Italy's already tightly squeezed economy would have to take on new pressures, though he apparently goes on to accept Ciano's frequent phone calls willingly enough, as Ciano described the regime's new initiatives 'as if giving so many victory bulletins', making a point of emphasizing that Guarneri's worries were unfounded, 'since even in the economic field, Albania was turning out to be a worthwhile affair after all'.[6] It was certainly worthwhile from the Italian exporters' point of view, thanks to the customs union between the two countries and the more favourable exchange rate. Unfortunately, there is no complete series of statistics on Albania's trade during the years following the occupation, either overall or in relation to Italy. However, the few data which are available are explicit enough. In 1939, excluding exceptional imports from Italy which were not recorded in the customs statistics (such as exports on behalf of the Italian government and those made by the military authority or by companies holding concessions), around 71 per cent of Albania's imports were coming from Italy, as against 36.3 per cent in the previous year. Meanwhile, Albanian exports into Italy were also strengthened, making up 90 per cent of the total in 1939, as opposed to 68.4 per cent in the previous year.[7]

Note that these percentages of the total apply to foreign trade figures, which were expanding greatly in relation to their pre-1939 levels. In fact, for the three years 1940–1942, we have the following figures:[8] (a) average yearly imports from Italy: 159.6 million Albanian francs; (b) average yearly exports to Italy: 17.3 million Albanian francs. These figures, although inflated because of huge increases in price levels (see later in this chapter), give an idea of the way in which trade between the two countries was expanding, if we bear in mind that, in the three years from 1928 to 1930, which was the most solid period for trade between the two countries before the occupation, the corresponding yearly averages were 16.6 million Albanian francs and 8.5 million Albanian francs respectively (see Chapter 5).

There is no doubt that the new customs arrangements played a part in this, as they altered the distribution of trade flows. The new foreign exchange regulations also contributed to boosting the figures, as they limited trade with other countries whilst free trade between Italy and Albania was further eased by the absence of currency restrictions.[9]

According to the publication *What Italy Has Done for Albania*,[10] a large part of Albania's imports from Italy were purchased at political prices, that is at lower than market prices. Another further advantage for Albania, according to the same publication, was that it was able to pay for its imports from Italy using its own national currency. This advantage must be appreciated if we consider the rule introduced by the Bank of Albania in 1939, mentioned in Chapter 7, which stated that, if an Albanian importer wanted to import from third countries, he would have to make a request for the necessary exchange to the Bank of Albania itself, a request which the Bank could reject 'at its sole and final discretion'!

There is no doubt that, as Borgatta observes,[11] the impetus for the increase in import activity from Italy came from the increased transfers of financial resources into Albania.

With Laws 1064 and 1065 of 1939, the Italian government set out a vast programme of public works. In the first Law, 800 million lire were earmarked for road works, to be spread over eight financial years, starting from the year 1939–1940. In the second, another 1,200 million were earmarked for land reclamation works.[12] Guarneri notes that, in the space of a few months, the works were 'making good progress', transforming the appearance of the urban centres. This contributed to 'the impression that Albania was on the point of becoming an important complementary element in Italy's economy'.[13]

The public works other than those in the urban centres mainly involved the road and rail networks. In 1941, 1,167 kilometres of roads were repaired and another 290 kilometres of new roads were built, while the rail works were primarily on the Durrës–Elbasan line.[14]

Overall, if we are to rely to some extent, in the absence of other sources, on the above-quoted post-war publication *What Italy Has Done for Albania*, the amount spent by Italy on public works after 1939 came to a total of around 6.5 billion lire,[15] or 1,045 million Albanian francs.

Given that: (a) during the period 1940–1942, the annual average deficit in Albania's balance of trade with Italy is reported in the above-mentioned statistics as being 142.3 million Albanian francs; and that (b) the disbursements for post-1939 public works alone were 1,045 million Albanian francs, and assuming trade deficit figures for 1939 and 1943 roughly in the region of those under (a), we can deduce that the total deficit in Albania's trade with Italy for the period 1939–1943 can be estimated at approximately 700 million Albanian francs, which is lower than the total of thc financial resources transferred for public works. This is keeping in mind that the figures available cannot be checked against other sources and therefore are not completely reliable. In other words, Italy's exports into Albania, although thriving, were not sufficient to close the gap on the capital account side.

Banking structure, payment services, circulation and prices

Italy's increased presence in Albania also raised new problems in several areas:

(a) the adequacy of the banking structure;
(b) the management of the payment services between Italy and Albania, taking into account that the transfer of funds to Albania was by then reaching considerable proportions; and
(c) changes in the circulation and prices.

The second and third issues were largely affected by Italy's heightened military activity and later, from October 1940 onwards, by the beginning of hostilities against Greece, which were drawn out until spring 1941, and for a short time consolidated Italy's presence in Albania.

(a) On the first point we see how, in 1939, Albania's unusual constitutional position caused some confusion for the Italian authorities, in terms of where certain responsibilities lay. In April 1939, immediately after the invasion, the Governor of the Bank of Italy, Azzolini, expressed the opinion to Thaon di Revel, the Finance Minister, Guarneri, the Minister for Currency and Exchange, and Ciano, the Foreign Minister, that Albania's existing banking structure (the National Bank, with eight branches, and the Banco di Napoli, with four) would be adequate for the time being to cope with the country's credit needs, and he suggested that the Joint Ministerial Committee[16] should postpone the opening of any new bank branches in Albania for a year.

Di Revel responded by referring him to the Under-Secretary for Albanian Affairs for an opinion. Guarneri, who as we have seen was baffled by the regime's latest initiatives in the country, declared that the question was outside his remit, 'as it is now a matter of an internal nature'.

Ciano, however, was of a different mind. He replied to Azzolini that a general postponement was inappropriate and that, instead, each case should be taken on its own merits. A month later, Ciano's position became clearer. Reopening the dialogue with Azzolini, he reiterated the politico-economic programme he intended to carry out in Albania and recommended the Banca Nazionale del Lavoro (BNL) as being suitable for the task. 'It has therefore been submitted to the Duce, on the seventh of this month, that it would be beneficial to authorize the BNL to open a branch in Tiranë.' The Duce approved and, as Ciano was keen for the bank to start business as soon as possible, he asked

Azzolini to make arrangements 'with the utmost haste', for the formal deeds to be drawn up in order for the BNL to start its business there. The Joint Ministerial Committee gave its approval.[17]

Only at that point was the Bank of Albania asked to submit proposals, for a division of work between itself, the Banco di Napoli and the BNL, in order to prevent any prejudicial competition.[18] The Bank of Albania proposed to reserve for itself, in addition to its issuing activities, the role of intermediary on behalf of the Italian and Albanian governments for Italian payments into Albania, and for short-term credit activities. The Banco di Napoli would be entrusted with the land credit (including taking on the activities of the Albanian Agricultural Bank, following its takeover in 1939),[19] and the BNL with mortgage credit.[20]

The anonymous author of the report quoted at the beginning of this chapter reports some time later, clearly echoing the opinion expressed by the Bank of Italy, that the number of banks open was already 'more than necessary'. He complains of excessive competition between the Banco di Napoli and the BNL which was 'harmful to both', and remarks that the numerous branches opened by the former in smaller towns had, considering the small size of the country's economy, 'the sole purpose of cornering the market for an indefinitely distant future'. The same report refers to the interest in the Ionian Islands shown by some managers at the Bank of Albania and Greece, which was however judged as being unsuitable, partly out of a wish not to damage the Italian banks already operating there.

In 1942, then, the country's basic banking structure looked like this: the Bank of Albania with 13 branches (and around 450 employees); the Banco di Napoli, present since 1937 with 12 branches; and the BNL, present, as we have just seen, since 1939.[21]

(b) Italy's increased financial commitment following the occupation of Albania raised the question for the Italian authorities of how to set up an efficient Treasury service in Tiranë to act on behalf of the Italian state.

It is interesting to see how, in a modern view of the payments system, the National Bank of Albania connected this issue to an efficient monetary management. The problem was raised very soon, immediately after the occupation.[22]

The main concerns were: the handling of sums generated by Albanian customs, which according to the Agreement of 1939 were to be administered by the Italian government; payments to the military units stationed in Albania; receipts and payments on behalf of the Lieutenant General of Albania's office; payments to agencies and to Italian residents in Albania. The idea of a new Treasury service was floated, which could eventually incorporate even the Albanian government's own Treasury functions. The new Treasury could be based at the Bank of Albania, but managed by staff provided by the Bank of Italy: an arrangement similar to that already in force in Italy.

In practice the service continued to be managed by the National Bank of Albania, which in 1942 was still outspoken in claiming the exclusive right to handle this function, faced with the prospect that it might be transferred to the Italian banks operating in Albania (the Banco di Napoli and the Banca Nazionale del Lavoro).[23]

In a memo, the Bank defended its exclusive right to handle the service both in terms of monetary policy ('the remittances of funds from the Italian state are the fundamental element in regulating the circulation of the Albanian franc in Albania, its backing being made up of lire, after the Agreement of 20 April 1939') and of money supply control ('it seems inconceivable to remove from the institute, which has taken on the responsibility for the movement of funds for abroad, the main source of this movement'). According to the Bank of Albania, the consequences of handing this function over to other bodies could be very serious. The Bank would be exposed to a reduction in the backing for the circulation and hence obliged to withdraw the investment of its own reserves in Italian Treasury bills. The Bank pointed out that until then it had discharged its function without charging any commission and, if the service were to be even partially devolved to other institutions, it intended to ask the Italian state for a contribution to its administration costs.

Here also, the archive documentation is incomplete and does not allow us to formulate a reliable picture of the outcome. We do know, however, that already by July 1942, which is when the memorandum was written, the Bank of Albania's investment in Italian Treasury bills had clearly been drastically reduced, from an equivalent of 96.5 million francs in December 1941 to 71.6 million in July 1942.

(c) The last question to consider in relation to this final phase of the Italian presence is the central bank's ownership, its monetary policy and price trends.

We have already seen in Chapter 4 that, in practice, in spite of a large part of the Bank's capital being registered in the names of the 'Italian financial group' or its dummies, it was INCE (an Italian government agency) which had taken on the actual payment of the capital. As time went on, this state of affairs was to become enshrined in law. Royal Decree Law no. 1614 of 28 August 1935 made it obligatory to sign over to INCE, 'on behalf of and in the interest of the State Treasury', all foreign assets owned by Italian citizens or organizations. This meant that the National Bank of Albania's shares, which until then had formally been held by Italian banks and individuals, were now all concentrated in one place, in the hands of the Istituto dei Cambi, in other words the Italian state. Moreover, between 1935 and 1941, the foreign banks which were shareholders of the Bank of Albania ceded their shares, totalling 15 per cent of the capital, to the Italian government, so that in 1941 around 90 per cent of the capital itself belonged to the Italian government.[24]

In September 1943, the Bank's capital was divided up as follows:[25]

100,000	founding shares, held by INCE
325,000	ordinary shares, held by INCE
112,805	ordinary shares, held by SVEA (which in turn was wholly owned by the Italian Finance Ministry)[26]
50,000	ordinary shares, held by the Banque Zadrouga of Belgrade
7,195	ordinary shares, held by various Albanian names
595,000	

Overall therefore, only 57,195 shares, or less than 10 per cent of the voting power, were not Italian owned.[27]

There was no subsequent change in the division of the shares, so that during the final period of the Bank's life it was formally owned almost entirely by the Italian government.

In these final years, the ex-Finance Minister, Antonio Mosconi, was at the helm at the Bank, while its technical management was still largely in the hands of the Managing Director, Amedeo Gambino.

If we scan the institution's financial statements and read journalists' accounts of the Bank's activities, particularly at the time of its annual general meetings,[28] the salient features in the Bank's statements are, on the liabilities side, the continuing steady increases in the circulation and, on the assets side, the backing in lire for that circulation.

It is worth pointing out here that, with the Italo-Albanian economic, customs and currency Agreement of 1939, gold coins disappeared from circulation, which then came to be made up entirely of banknotes and token coins. However, the disappearance of the gold circulation (1,589,000 Albanian francs by 30 April 1939, which was the last month when the gold circulation was recorded) did not lead to an increase in the Bank's metal reserve.

The gold coins in circulation were privately stockpiled. Table 8.1 shows, in the composition of the reserves, that the Bank concentrated on building up its lire stocks in preference to the gold component, which actually saw a small decrease. The gold did stay in the reserves, however, meaning that it was not sold or transferred. What is also clear from Table 8.1 is the ever-increasing proportion of the reserves made up by Italian Treasury bills. In a perfect 'lira standard' situation, with the gold component of the reserves remaining more or less constant in absolute terms, the remainder of the reserve, made up of lire, served increasingly as a direct funding of the Italian state. By 1943, Treasury bills, which in December 1938 were 21.3 per cent of the lira reserve and barely 12.7 per cent of the total reserve, had come to represent 88.9 per cent and 45.3 per cent respectively.

The Bank was not alone in absorbing Italian Treasury securities.[29] Thanks to the complete freedom of capital movements within the 'union', the Italian press carried triumphant announcements about the encouraging number of subscriptions to long-term Italian Treasury bonds by the Albanian public. The first of these issues took place in 1940: 1,200 subscribers absorbed Italian state bonds maturing in 1949 worth 9 million lire (around 1.5 million Albanian francs).[30] Referring to two further issues of Treasury bonds, for which no actual figures are available, Agenzia Stefani announced, on 13 April 1942, that they had had 'most pleasing success, far greater than that of the 1940 issue'.

The expansion in money circulation, primarily as a result of transfers from Italy on behalf of the state, caused problems for price levels. In spite of the relatively reassuring tone of official communications, an

Table 8.1 Circulation and backing, 1938–1943 (in thousands of Albanian francs)

	Circulation				Backing			
	Bank notes	Gold	Fractional currency	Total	Gold	Lire	Italian Treasury bills	Total
Dec. 1938	10,529	1,583	1,958	14,070	7,574	8,912	2,408	18,894
Dec. 1939	26,316		3,511	29,827	7,567	40,149	5,280	52,996
Dec. 1940	80,178		4,454	84,632	7,567	81,852	33,600	123,019
Dec. 1941	108,417		4,429	112,846	7,567	62,084	96,480	166,131
Dec. 1942	141,897		4,438	146,335	7,567	76,722	80,480	164,769
Jul. 1943	182,915		4,454	187,369	7,567	102,195	90,880	200,642

Source: Financial statements of the National Bank of Albania, in ASBI, Baffi papers.

unpublished study of March 1941, found in the Bank of Italy's archives, highlights the strong increase in prices and attempts to identify possible reasons for it.[31] This study is interesting given that, as mentioned previously, Albanian statistics disappeared from the international records immediately after the union with Italy. According to the author, between March 1939, the brink of the Italian occupation, and December 1940 both wholesale and retail prices increased by 170–175 per cent, compared with a 420 per cent increase in the circulation during the period January 1939 to September 1940.[32]

The author of the study, De Toma, having pointed out that, based on an observation of the monthly figures, the growth in price levels followed three months after the growth in circulation, goes on to identify the causes of inflation not only in the increase in circulation, but also in its increased velocity, brought about by heightened economic activity and a reduction in the geographical area of the Albanian franc's circulation because of the war (late 1940 and early 1941 were the months of the Greek campaign). Another factor in the price increases, according to De Toma, was that certain goods were increasingly in short supply.

On the other hand, he identifies restraining factors on price levels as being the system for controlling prices itself, the growth in imports from Italy, and the creation of small savings deposits by soldiers and manual workers. Finally, he advocates even greater levels of imports from Italy and more effective controls to prevent further price rises, and gives a pessimistic forecast for the following months, based on an analysis of the increased circulation in the previous ones.

An analysis by the Bank of Italy confirmed in fact that wholesale and retail prices in 1941 were still showing an extremely high increase, with their yearly average registering a 95 per cent increase 'because of the war needs and the presence in Albanian territory of [Italian] workers and troops'.[33]

This statistic for 1941 is the last piece of information on prices in Albania which comes from a direct source, but the growth of the circulation, as detailed above, would suggest that in 1942 and 1943 the price increases would not have been any less accentuated. Thus, in his work *Albania*, Skendi cites a table which gives the increase in wholesale prices as follows:[34]

January 1939: 100
December 1939: 147.4
December 1940: 272.5
December 1941: 559.3
December 1943: 1,096.9

CHAPTER 9

Some observations on Albania's income and the economic aspects of the Italian presence

A stagnant economy

Throughout this study, one important aspect of Italy's economic penetration into Albania which has not been dealt with is the influence which Italy's massive financial engagement had on the country's economic development. While one of the reasons for this gap is that the main aim of this research has been to analyse the economic and financial relations between the two countries, rather than to look in depth at their effect on Albania's economy, the gap is also a result once again of the almost total lack of statistics on Albania's national accounts and more generally on macro-economic data. Nonetheless, it is worth making a few brief observations.

We have few estimates of Albanian national income, and they refer to two years only, 1927 and 1938. The reasons for the choice of these years are unclear. However, these are interesting years, coming at the beginning of the Italian economic involvement and almost at the end of Albania's independence.

All these estimates, with one exception, are pre-war. The fact that even relatively recent research has been obliged to use these estimates indirectly confirms their uniqueness, and also means that they are isolated figures and as such cannot be relied upon for a view of national income trends in Albania.

For the year 1927, we have an estimate by Albania's representative at the League of Nations and subsequent Prime Minister, Mehdi Frashëri.

According to this estimate, the national income was around 102 million Albanian francs (about 60 per cent of which was from agriculture and fisheries, 30 per cent from livestock and the remaining 10 per cent from forestry and mining); the Italian economist Borgatta observed that the figure was too low and corrected it to 120 million francs.[1] But even Borgatta's correction falls short of another estimate by a certain Elvepidi (1930), who substantially raised the national income for 1927 to 172 million francs: a number which was again revised by Pano – in 1982 – to 177 million Albanian francs.[2] In 1940, even Demaria, another Italian economist, considered the Frashëri/Borgatta estimate to be incorrect by a wide margin, due to revenues which 'had escaped the eye of the investigator'.[3]

For 1938, Demaria – pointing implicitly to a substantial stagnation of the Albanian national income – gave an estimate, in real terms, of 175 million francs. According to his research, even for the year 1938 the agricultural and livestock sectors of the economy were predominant, but less than in 1927: 51.4 per cent, against 90 per cent; Demaria gives the following breakdown for the other sectors: 8.6 per cent forestry, 5.7 per cent mining, 11.4 per cent small industrial concerns, 11.4 per cent services and 11.4 per cent property.[4]

This continuing agricultural bias stands out clearly from the structural composition of Albania's exports, in which agricultural and livestock produce generally made up over 50 per cent of their total.[5] The above percentages also emphasize the still minimal importance given to the exploitation of mineral resources on the eve of the Italian occupation, in spite of the fact that extensive explorations had been going on since the early 1920s.

Pano returned, in the post-war period, to the Albanian national income of 1938: on the basis of a series of observations, also focused on the size of the prevailing agricultural sector, he estimated the nominal income, i.e. at current prices, for 1938 at 110 million francs. Taking into account that, from 1927 to 1938, the general wholesale price index fell from 100 to around 63, and the agricultural price index fell further, to around 53, that nominal income of 110 translates into a real income, i.e. at constant 1927 prices, of 198 million francs. This is a real growth for the period of around 12 per cent, equivalent to an average yearly growth of approximately 1 per cent.[6]

In conclusion, we can envisage, for the period in question, a range of growth of the Albanian economy between zero and 12 per cent.

We have already said that no trend can seriously be made out from these few data. But, if we are tentatively aiming to see if Albania's population was better off at the end of this period of time, a comparison of these estimates may be attempted. Assuming, with the more favourable estimate by Pano, a real growth of 12 per cent between 1927 and 1938, it was certainly insufficient to substantially raise the Albanians' standard of living and was not able to bring Albania out of its underdeveloped state: the more so, if we consider the per capita income.

With a population estimated at around 830,000 for the previous year, 1926,[7] the plausible figure of a national income of 177 million Albanian francs for 1927 gives an annual per capita income of 213 francs. For 1938, the national income estimate of 198 million francs at constant prices, and a population of 1,050,000,[8] give a per capita income of 188: an actual decrease in real terms. In other words, the almost stagnant income (+12 per cent in that period) was unable to match the increase in population (+26 per cent), resulting in an impoverishment of an already under-developed country.

This backward economic situation was most keenly felt towards the mid-1930s, when the effects of the Great Depression were added to those of the temporary interruption to the flow of Italian capital.[9]

A comparison with Italy shows that in 1927 there was quite a large gap in per capita incomes. At the average exchange rate, the Albanian per capita income would be equivalent to around 740 lire, compared with an Italian income of 3,183 lire: more than four times greater[10] (even though this comparison does not take the price level and hence purchasing power into account).

An estimate for 1938 does indeed widen the gap. At current prices, the Albanian per capita income (relying on Pano's estimate) of 104 francs gives an amount of 647 lire, vis-à-vis 3,175 for Italy: five times greater.[11] Moreover, this comparison is strongly biased by the huge devaluation of the lira in 1936 (around 49 per cent), which of course immediately raised the Italian lira equivalent of any franc-denominated figure.

It has been observed that Italy's economic policy towards Albania was oriented more towards stability than development. In Pernack's opinion, for example, the very monetary and credit policies pursued by the National Bank of Albania show that it was not so much interested in a policy for sustaining growth as in stability in the value of the currency and in an entrepreneurial approach to management aimed at increasing the Bank's profitability. The issuing bank's prudential approach, according to Pernack, deliberately restrained the growth of an adequate credit system for the country's capital needs, whilst on the fiscal side the tax burden on the agricultural sector was aimed, in an indiscriminate and almost exploitative way, at increasing revenues, with the effect of reducing disposable income and impeding investment.[12]

In Chapter 6 on monetary policy, we dwelt on the fact that the Bank's management criteria were more like those of the private sector and its board members very 'prudent' in their approach. We also pointed out that the monetary policy could not be qualified as entirely restrictive and could be divided into different phases, while the fiscal policy, as we saw in the same chapter, cannot be properly understood without considering the expansive influence exerted by Italy's loans, which were often aimed at funding Albania's budget deficit.

In support of his thesis that the Albanian economy was stagnating, Pernack also cites the sluggishness of imports as indirect evidence of the lack of growth in the national income.[13] During the period 1927–1938, imports actually show quite varied trends, not only in value, but also in volume (bearing in mind the drop in import costs in the first half of the 1930s). Table 9.1 constructs the value and volume indices relating to Albanian imports. Considering that Italy was Albania's main trade partner, the only variables we have taken in our working hypothesis to arrive at a series of data on quantity have been the wholesale price index in Italy and the exchange rate of the Albanian franc to the lira.

Italian exchange rate and price trends push up the quantitative import index, but this index should be viewed with a good deal of caution since a more complete study would have involved all the countries exporting into Albania and not only the main one. Overall, the import trends seem to be cyclical in nature, without any clear pattern of growth. We can assume that the national income followed a similar pattern: according to the information in our table, it saw a very deep slump in the mid-1930s, with the turning point coming in 1934.

This picture of an underdeveloped economy does not appear to undergo radical changes during the brief period of the Italian occupation, even

Table 9.1 Albanian imports, 1927–1938: value and volume indices

	A	B	C	D	E	F	G
1927	24.7	3.84	94.848	100.00	94.848	100.0	100.0
1928	32.1	3.67	117.807	96.33	122.295	129.9	128.9
1929	38.6	3.66	141.276	91.75	153.979	156.2	162.3
1930	33.3	3.68	122.544	82.58	148.394	134.8	156.4
1931	29.5	3.79	111.805	71.56	156.240	119.4	164.7
1932	22.8	3.78	86.184	66.97	128.690	92.3	135.7
1933	15.9	3.65	58.035	61.47	94.412	64.3	99.5
1934	12.3	3.78	46.494	59.64	77.958	49.8	82.2
1935	13.7	4.00	54.800	66.06	82.955	55.5	87.5
1936	16.8	6.22	104.496	73.39	142.385	68.0	150.1
1937	18.9	6.22	117.558	86.25	136.299	76.5	143.7
1938	23.0	6.22	143.060	91.75	155.924	93.1	164.4

Key:
A: imports in millions of francs;
B: lira/Albanian franc exchange rate;
C: lira equivalent, in millions, of column A;
D: wholesale price index in Italy;
E: imports adjusted on the basis of the Italian price index and the lira/franc exchange rate;
F: import index (value) (from column A);
G: import index (volume) (from column E).

Source: See Tables 5.2 and 5.9.

though Italy undoubtedly redoubled its exploitation of raw materials, in relation to its own requirements, particularly for military purposes.[14] Shortly before the war, a suggestion to work the extracted minerals in Albania itself was put forward and plans were drawn up in Italian quarters to install a steelworks by 1941.[15] Industrial initiatives remained few and far between, however, rather than being part of an overall programme, and their aim was to exploit existing potential. The actual 'concept of industrialization' was lacking.[16] According to Skendi, a short-lived period of prosperity occurred after the occupation, benefiting the merchant class in particular, as it prospered by re-exporting goods bought in Italy to Greece and Yugoslavia. One can assume that the profits must have been due, at least in part, to the political prices of many imports from Italy.[17]

The war halted the Italian initiatives, with the exception of those that were closely connected with the war effort. This was particularly noticeable in the case of the exploitation of mineral resources. As Demaria observed, 'from a political point of view, the problem of exploiting Albania's mineral resources was clearly affected by Italian autarchic policies and by the intention to produce as much as possible of the nation's industrial mineral requirements in Italy itself'. He adds, 'The needs of the war, most dominant in our times [he was writing in 1940], have acted as an extremely effective correction to those plans, in that they have indefinitely accelerated the exploitation of the mineral fields beyond the limits which the vital force of an industry would naturally permit.'[18] The same author explicitly states that only 'once the war has been won' could a rationalization of the mineral resources be implemented, in other words a policy which was more conscious of the 'cost/profit dynamic', all economic considerations at that time being subordinated to the demands of the war.[19] The impression we draw from this is that the most intense financial engagement was not equalled by an optimal allocation approach aimed at productively channelling the resources invested.

Ultimately, the insufficiency of available information, especially statistical data, prevents us from drawing accurate conclusions and leaves a wide margin for different opinions. At one extreme, there is the radical opinion of Marxist Albanian historiography, which paints a totally negative picture of the Italian presence; at the other, we have historians who somewhat overemphasize Albania's economic and overall progress between the wars. In the middle we have Pernack, and more recently Tomes, who feel that the development policies had little success to speak of: in spite of Italy's financial and technical investment, no transformation took place in Albania's production structure. However, definitive appraisals are best avoided, since the period in question is too brief to give us an understanding of Italy's real intentions and possibilities. All in all, the Italian presence in Albania, though not to be underestimated in terms of works carried out, did not set in motion any widespread process to industrialize the country's economy or any consistent flow of revenue for the local population. In effect, Italy's penetration focused essentially on the areas of public works (mainly through SVEA), land reclamation and a few fundamental industrial sectors (especially mining). The only drawback was that, as has been said of Italy's Mezzogiorno, 'public works do not create a permanent flow of income, and base industries, instead of producing large masses of wages, produce returns on capital and profits which do not always stay in the area'.[20] These comments could just as well be applied to the Albanian economy in the inter-war period.

It is therefore safe to say that the Fascist regime had little interest in starting a process of industrialization. There are various motives which can explain this lack of interest. One motive is that, in acting thus, the regime was in large part moving in the very direction which the League of Nations had advocated through the Calmès Report, which, as we have seen, had identified as priority initiatives the areas of public works (roads), reclamation of the marshes, agricultural development and mining, explicitly setting industrialization aside for a subsequent phase of interventions.[21]

A second motive, which is interesting because it brings us back to one of the fundamental aspects of the Fascist phenomenon, is that, according to an authoritative body of opinion, one of the regime's economic policy objectives was precisely to contain industrial development, while extolling the virtues of the rural life, within a conservative political framework designed to shield society from the major shocks of a disorderly development of the urban working class, who were notoriously dismissive of the regime. Through this policy, rightly termed 'archaic', Mussolini was aiming, on a social level, to discourage urban development and, on an economic level, to improve the balance of trade by means of increased agricultural output.[22] The 'wheat battle' and land reclamation works are well-known expressions of this 'rural vocation' of the regime (intensive land reclamation also being carried out in Albania), which Mussolini adroitly exploited for propaganda purposes.[23]

We have every reason to believe, therefore, that the same philosophy was behind the Fascist regime's economic interventions in Albania, with aims not unlike those pursued in the motherland, in other words to avoid the birth of an industrial working class which in a country beset with social troubles and still tied to a semi-feudal production structure would have been in a position to present a conscious opposition in the first instance to Zog and then to his Italian ally.[24]

Another motive not to be underestimated is that, in terms of trade, it was in Italy's interest to maintain a closely complementary relationship between the two economies, which meant having Albania firmly rooted in a development model based exclusively on agriculture and raw materials:

> the absence [in Albania] of any industries similar [to those in Italy] meant that Italian industries posed no threat of competition. On the other side, the relative scarcity [in Italy] of agricultural products in relation to our dense population meant that there was no competition from Italian agricultural exports to Albania, while an inflow of exports of agricultural produce and raw materials from Albania was desirable.[25]

In short, despite the Fascist intention to favour agriculture at home and abroad, Italy remained incomparably more industrialized and it was convenient for it to export industrial products to Albania, in exchange for imports of agricultural produce and raw materials.

But there is another point, which is understandably de-emphasized in the Italian quasi-official documentation prepared in the aftermath of the world conflict, to put in a better light Italy's policy before the Allied powers: the military aims of the Fascist financial intervention in Albania were strong, and may have prevented an alternative, industrially oriented use of the available resources. In 1927, meetings were held between SVEA and General Alberto Pariani, the head of the Italian Military Mission to Albania, and it was decided to push for the funds of the SVEA loan to be employed in public works of 'outstanding interest' from the military and political point of view, even if this might have caused a negative reaction in the Albanian public opinion and press.[26]

A list of accomplishments

This is a suitable point at which to summarize the concrete results of the Italian presence, by briefly listing the main activities carried out in Albania.[27]

It is worth remembering that industrial activity in Albania had to start from scratch. In 1922 there were just 85 industrial establishments (35 in 1912). Only the bitumen plant in Selenicë had around 500 workers, the others being mainly micro-firms, with two to five workers. The first joint-stock company was only created in 1921, in Vlorë.[28]

In the area of public works, we need to mention SVEA's activities, of course, which we have already dealt with from a financial point of view. A statement of its activities was drawn up in 1936, in a special publication.[29] We have already seen that, thanks to the SVEA loan, Albania had a fund of around 62.7 million Albanian francs at its disposal, minus an initial sum which was paid out immediately for works already completed and for the first two half-yearly loan and interest repayments, leaving a total of 57.8 million. As at December 1935, 55.9 million of this sum had effectively been paid out. The payment of the loan was therefore almost complete and the summary of works carried out can be considered sufficiently exhaustive to give a complete picture of how the loan was used. Basically, the categories of works were as follows:

(a) Ports (mainly the port at Durrës, as well as the wharfs at Vlorë, Sarandë and Shëngjin).
(b) Roads (275 kilometres, at a cost of 19.5 million francs, compared with an initial plan for 965 kilometres and an estimated cost of 6.2 million) and bridges (at a cost of 14 million, as against an initial forecast of 4 million). The works relating to the Durrës–Tiranë route (38 kilometres) should be added to the list. Originally planned as a railway, it was later converted to a road.
(c) Public buildings, at an actual cost of 11 million, compared with a forecast of 3.4 million.
(d) Land reclamation involving embankments and canals, and here the expenditure was much less than had been planned, at least as far as the SVEA loan was concerned: only 1.5 million as opposed to the 15.5 million forecast.[30]

Overall, the uses to which the 62.7 million loan was put can be broken down to the following percentages:[31]

New roads	31
Bridges	23
Public works	17
Ports	14
Two half-yearly repayments	6
Studies and supervision	3
Works prior to 1926	2
Embankments and canals	2
Residual item	2
	100 per cent

It is interesting to note that, under the heading of building expenses, a good 45 per cent of the total was spent on royal residences and ministerial palaces, and a further 30 per cent on military buildings. Hospitals accounted for 14 per cent and schools for 4 per cent.[32] This breakdown is significant as it demonstrates what low priority was given to the education and health of the Albanian population, and the high priority given to exploiting the country for war purposes. The expenditure on royal residences is also an indication of the Fascists' desire to gain Zog's sympathies. Another point of interest is the nationality of the companies who won the contracts for the works: 69.6 per cent of the total costs went on works carried out by Italian companies, 21.8 per cent on those by Albanian firms and 5.1 per cent on those by firms from other countries.[33]

In the same publication, we learn that for carrying out similar works the costs were higher in Albania than in Italy, because of the need to import specialized labour and many of the construction materials, and the higher general costs such as sickness, insurance and transport.[34]

Another relevant area of intervention was mining. We have already seen how a battle had taken place between the Italians and the British, with significant political implications, over the question of exploiting the oil fields, and how on the whole the matter had first been settled in favour of the British. However, they did not have a monopoly on oil drilling and gradually lost ground to the Italians, nor did the return on the fields live up to expectations. Even by 1930, it was admitted that the annual output of oil (2,492 tonnes) was consumed in the drilling plants themselves and that it had not yet been possible to begin exporting.[35] In 1937, it was recognized that the returns were lower than had been foreseen.[36]

The Italian state had intervened in the Albanian oil initiatives with various legal provisions. With Royal Legislative Decree no. 1301 of 8 July 1925, AIPA (Azienda Italiana Petroli Albania), the Italian agency for Albanian oil, had been set up as an independent agency within the Ferrovie dello Stato (the Italian state railways), for the exploitation of the Albanian oil fields; other provisions were aimed at carrying out explorations and providing AIPA with suitable financial backing.[37] By 1932, the Albanian government had granted five concessions on its territory:

(a) To D'Arcy Exploration & Co. Ltd., a branch of the Anglo-Persian Oil Co., in Berat and Durrës (33,642 hectares).
(b) To the Ferrovie dello Stato, in Vlorë and Berat (47,213 hectares).
(c) To SIMSA (Società Italiana Miniere di Selenizza), in Vlorë (2,140 hectares). It is worth remembering that SIMSA, originally operating in the field of bitumen, was among the few companies which had been the object of Italian diplomatic intervention at the time of the first negotiations with Zog, as part of the 'package' of proposals presented to him in early 1925.[38]
(d) To the Ferrovie dello Stato again, in Berat, Durrës and Vlorë (116,825 hectares for exploration, on the completion of which the concession was not to exceed 25,000 hectares).
(e) Then there was the French presence through a French–Albanian syndicate (Crédit Général du Pétrole), with an area of 118,193 hectares allocated for prospecting, to be reduced to 30,000 on completion of the searches.[39] In 1936, the Albanian government came to an agreement with the Société Française Industrielle et Commerciale des Pétroles, which took the place of the previous syndicate.[40]

In 1933, the number of concessions had risen to around 15.[41] The oil fields in which drilling plants were developed, especially after the annexation, were those of Devoll (where the 'delightful town' created next to the oil field was named Costanzo, after Galeazzo Ciano's father[42]) and Patos (which had been used by the British, who had by then abandoned it). But it was only in 1936 that imports of crude oil from Albania became a separate item in Italian import statistics. In that year, 407 tons of Italy's imported oil came from Albania, out of a total of 3,008 (in that year, Iraq, the United States and Colombia were still ahead of Albania in terms of volume).[43] From the start of drilling activities until September 1943, total Italian output was 970,000 tons.[44]

Still in the area of mining industries, after bitumen which has already been mentioned, there was also coal and lignite production (the Azienda Carboni Italiani began exploiting the mines at Priske, near Tiranë, in 1939, and its output in 1942 was around 50 tons per day). As for metal mines, Italy had a presence in the form of SAMIA (Società Anonima Mineraria Italo-Albanese), prospecting for copper in Delvinë since 1939, and AMMI (Azienda Minerali Metallici Italiani). This was expected, in 1942, to be able to meet Italy's requirements for chrome. In 1939 again, Ferralba (Ferro Albania) was formed for iron production, and was taken over a year later by Finsider, which however did not go beyond the geological exploration stage.[45]

Mussolini looked to Albania as a plentiful outlet for Italy's excess labour force; it was expected to absorb 2 or 3 million people. The first 300 colonists arrived in 1926 and started to conquer the fertile but uncultivated southern lowland.[46] In 1940, a commissariat for emigration and colonization was established to oversee the transfer of labourers from Italy.[47] The initial, and effectively the only, take-up, however, was not encouraging. According to a generous estimate for the mining industries, excluding the oil industry for which we have no data, no more than 3,000 people arrived in Albania to work. We do not have a breakdown of the figures by nationality, but certain estimates point to the fact that the Italian element was mainly confined to specialized labour. The estimated figures for labour employed for the public works is higher, but here also the majority were Albanian (10,000 to 15,000 people). The greatest employment level reached in the sector was a remarkable 70,000, of whom around 20,000 were Italian.[48]

As previously stated, the regime devoted particular attention to the agricultural sector.[49] In the early 1930s, two-thirds of the 300,000 hectares of land which were most suitable for cultivation belonged to the major landowners, and one-third to the state. Very small properties were only to be found close to towns and villages and in minor valleys. But large properties did not correspond to large farms, which were very rare: most of the large properties were broken up into small concerns leased on a profit-sharing or piecework basis. One instrument of the Italian presence was EIAA (Ente Industrie Agrarie Albanesi), an offshoot of the Opera Nazionale Combattenti (the national ex-servicemen's association), created in 1926, which carried out extensive land reclamation works (around 5,000 hectares), employing around 300 Italians in 1939, out of a total of 1,300 people.[50] Other companies to operate subsequently in the agricultural area were Italba (Impresa di trasformazione agraria e lavori di bonifica albanese), from 1940 onwards, and SIAA (Società Industriale Agricola Albanese).[51]

As mentioned earlier,[52] measures for agrarian reform had been adopted in most of the Balkan countries after the First World War, involving the expropriation and redistribution of land and the abolition of feudal structures. This occurred in Greece from 1917 onwards, in Romania from 1918, in Yugoslavia from 1921 and in Bulgaria immediately after the war.[53] Albania was well behind. Only in 1928, as an element in the preparation of the land reform, was a land registry introduced.[54] In 1930, with the collaboration of Lorenzoni, an Italian expert, a Land Reform Law was passed (Law of 3 May 1930). The Law provided for an 'untouchable' area of 40 hectares for each property; of the remainder, one-third was to be compulsorily expropriated immediately and the other two-thirds left to the owner for 15 years, provided that, on penalty of future expropriation, he carried out the necessary improvements on his land. The parts which were expropriated were to be redistributed to citizens who did not own any land, or whose land was not large enough to meet their families' needs. The price to be paid for the expropriation was 20 francs per hectare.

Within the framework of the reforms, the Law also provided for the creation of an Albanian Agricultural Bank, with a capital of 5 million Albanian francs, part to be provided by the state and part by Albanian citizens. Subscriptions to the capital would be organized so as to allocate shares to the landowners who had had land expropriated, at a nominal value equal to the sum owed to them for the expropriation. The Bank's loans were to be under two years. In practice, the Bank was only created in 1936, partly with finance supplied by Italy.[55]

It should be noted that, while in the early 1930s the other Balkan countries were adopting measures to aid farmers hit by the Great Depression and struggling with heavy debts,[56] no steps of this kind were taken in Albania. The Land Reform Law itself, as Italy's diplomatic representative in Albania wrote to his Ministry, had been intended by Zog more to scare the large landowning beys than as a real vehicle of social reform, and in practice nothing was done to enforce it.[57] In the words of the Albanian historiography, the reform was a 'mystifying farce' and the only people who took advantage of it were a few families who had fled to Albania from Kosovo to escape the attacks of the Yugoslavs.[58] As Berend points out, only little more than 4,000 hectares of land were distributed.[59]

Finally, it is worth mentioning the services sector. In 1940, ETA (Ente Turistico alberghiero Albania) was created to develop the tourist industry. The initiative was devised by the Under-Secretary for Albanian Affairs, and finance was provided by the Ministry of Finance and the Ministry of Popular Culture. It was responsible for managing several hotels in Tiranë, Durrës, Berat, Lezhë and Gjirokastër, which were highly publicized by the regime.[60] Some attention was also devoted to transport by sea (with the Società Adriatica) and by air, with services linking the country to Italy, Greece, Bulgaria and Romania.[61]

CHAPTER 10

The question of the 'Albanian gold'

The looting of gold

We have already had occasion to mention the fact that the vast majority of the gold belonging to the National Bank of Albania was held in Rome. In the Bank's balance sheet at 31 December 1942, the value of the gold was entered as 7,567,717 Albanian francs, corresponding to 2,196.9 kilograms at the original parity of 0.290322 grams of fine gold to the franc, which was still in force. Since a small gold stock of 64.4 kilograms was held at the Bank's branches in Tiranë and Durrës, the total held in Rome was actually 2,132.5 kilograms. In addition to this gold, another amount of 208.3 kilograms was deposited in Rome and entered on the balance sheet as backing for other liabilities of the institution, the largest of which was towards the Bank for International Settlements in Basel, of which the National Bank of Albania had been a member since 1931.[1]

On 16 September 1943, the 2,340.8 kilograms of gold[2] were removed from the vaults in which they were kept in various proportions at the Bank's Rome headquarters, the Mint and the Bank of Italy, on the orders of SS Major Herbert Kappler and the Chancellor of the German Embassy in Rome, Joseph Ortmann.[3] The gold was transported to Germany[4] and deposited at the Reichsbank. Two confidential agreements were signed on 6 April 1944, the first between the German and Albanian governments and the second between representatives of the Bank of Albania, the Reichsbank and the German Foreign Ministry. Clearly aimed at covering the theft in legal terms, they established that the gold should remain in Berlin and that only the management of the Bank of Albania in Tiranë had the right to use it, subject to written authorization from the pro-Nazi Albanian government. The agreements also physically identified the gold as bearing the seal of the Bank of Albania.[5]

On 17 November 1944, however, the German occupation in Tiranë ended. The city was liberated by the National Liberation Army led by General Mehmet Shehu,[6] and a new Albanian government was formed. Many Italian employees of the Bank were arrested and the Bank was closed.[7] At the start of the new year, on 13 January 1945, the anti-Fascist Albanian government passed two laws. The first annulled the Agreement of 1925 with the 'Italian financial group' and declared void all shares in the Bank of Albania. The second transferred all its assets and liabilities to a new State Bank (Banka e Shtetit). Furthermore, Italian personnel were barred from working at the new institution, and on 20 September 1945 the handover procedures took place between the Italian managers and the new State Bank.[8] In September and December 1945 respectively, the Banca Nazionale del Lavoro and the Banco di Napoli, having already been obliged to close their branches in November 1944, were likewise confiscated by the Albanian government.[9]

At the end of the war with Germany's unconditional surrender, the Allies found a large quantity of gold in Germany, which had been hidden by the Nazis in a potassium mine in Merkers. Even though it was estimated as representing only 20 per cent of the gold which the Germans had actually looted, the discovery formed the main nucleus of this gold. The majority of it was subsequently transferred to London, to be held at the Bank of England, while a smaller amount was sent to the Federal Reserve Bank of New York.

It was debated whether any gold whose country of origin could clearly be identified should be restored to that country, as advocated by the British. The opinion which prevailed, however, was the view, held by the Americans and French, that because of problems with identification all the gold found in Germany should be divided between the looted countries entitled to restitution, in proportion to their respective losses. The problems in identifying the gold were due at least in part to the fact that it had been the practice of the Reichsbank to remelt the bars coming in, thus making it impossible to identify their original owners.[10]

On 14 January 1946, Part III of the Final Agreement of the Paris Conference on Germany's reparations, signed by 18 countries including the United States, France, the United Kingdom and Albania, contained a solution to the problem of restoring the gold looted from various countries by Nazi Germany along those lines. It stated that all the monetary gold which the Allies had found in Germany and which was to be restored to one of the countries from which gold had been taken should be 'pooled for distribution' amongst the countries participating in the pool, in proportion to their respective losses.[11]

Since the Paris Agreement asked that the American, French and British governments should take 'the appropriate steps' to carry out this process of distribution, a Tripartite Commission based in Brussels was formed by the three governments on 27 September 1946 for that purpose.

A large area of German territory was occupied at the time by Soviet troops. Whilst the Soviet Union renounced any claim to the gold found in the zone occupied by the Western Allies, the latter, for their part, did not attempt to find out whether any monetary gold had been found by the Soviet Union in their zone or elsewhere.[12] The Soviet Union aside, Albania and other countries behind the Iron Curtain, such as Czechoslovakia and Poland, submitted claims on the gold pool. Claims were also raised by Western or neutral countries such as Austria, Belgium, Greece, Italy, Luxembourg, the Netherlands and Yugoslavia. The claims made by these countries came to a total of 23.6 million ounces of fine gold, and far outstripped the gold stock available, which was equivalent to approximately 9.8 million ounces.[13] Although the Tripartite Commission only recognized approximately 16.5 million ounces' (around 514 tonnes) worth of these claims, which brought the total down, the discrepancy between the amount in the pool and the amount of the claims was clear: hence the need to proceed with the restitution on a pro rata basis.[14] Moreover, the Commission decided that the responsibility for restoring the gold taken by the Nazis from victims of the concentration camps was outside its remit. In accordance with the Paris Agreement, gold of this nature found in Germany was handed over to the Intergovernmental Committee on Refugees, to be restored to the victims.[15]

The Commission carried out the restitution in three phases, the 'preliminary' phase corresponding to the start of its activities. During this phase, which was concluded in November 1950, around 80 per cent of the total gold stock was distributed.[16] A second, 'quasi-final' phase took place between June 1958 and June 1959. This phase did not succeed in completing the distribution because, in the words of the Tripartite Commission, certain countries 'presented problems'. Most of these belonged, not surprisingly, to the Communist bloc: other than the Netherlands, they were Poland, Czechoslovakia and Albania. In the end, as we shall see in more detail, only the 'Albanian case' was left. The Commission, which had not met between May 1988 and June 1995, resumed its task in the wake of the reopening of Western relations with the Albanian government after the death of Enver Hoxha on 11 April 1985, and the subsequent fall of the Communist regime a few years later. In 1996 the Commission proceeded with the pro rata restitution of Albania's share. Once the Albanian case had been settled, the third and 'final' phase concerned the distribution of the residual gold stock of around 180,000 ounces, and took place between April and July 1998. The claims concerned were by that stage relatively small, which made it practically impossible to allocate gold bars to all the claimants. The restitution involved all the countries mentioned above including Albania and, for the reason just mentioned, was made partly in gold and partly in currency (sterling).

Other problems arose at this stage in connection with the transfer of the gold to Jewish organizations by those countries benefiting from the final distribution, as well as with the fact that, at the time of the final distribution, Yugoslavia no longer existed as a country and the states which succeeded it all presented separate claims on the remaining gold stock. But that is another story and is not relevant to our present discussion. The Tripartite Commission declared the gold pool closed on 13 July 1998 and the formal closure of the Commission itself took place on 9 September of the same year.[17]

Against this wider background, our interest now is in how the specific case of the Albanian gold unfolded in various international forums during the course of the post-war period, giving rise to an extremely complex international dispute.

The Tripartite Gold Commission, the Corfu incident and the arbitrator's decision

The Commission began its work by distributing a questionnaire about the gold in March 1947 to the countries of the pool and three other countries including Italy which had not been represented in Paris. On it, each country was asked to give details of its own claim on the gold pool.[18]

As for the Italian government's position, it had already made its claim in September 1944 and in April 1945, not only for the gold belonging to the Bank of Italy, but also for that of the National Bank of Albania.[19] The attention of the Italian government had also been drawn to the problem by the persistent and impassioned involvement of the Bank's management, especially Amedeo Gambino. The latter's concerns related not only to the financial side of the question, but also to the human interests of its staff:

> The Italian staff – so we read in the copy of a memorandum of 1945 – have found themselves in a very difficult situation . . . due emphasis should be given to the tragic fate of two Italian employees. In late December (or very early January), the Central Manager Dr Ettore Melis himself was arrested. In his role as the person entrusted with ultimate managerial responsibility at the Bank in Albania and because of his striking personality (his anti-Fascist and anti-German sentiments were well known), he had come to represent the highest exponent among civilians of the Italian community in Albania.[20]

Again, on 4 April 1946, while presenting the Rome headquarters' separate operations for 1945 to the Treasury Minister, Epicarmo Corbino, Gambino recalled that '[The Albanians] had turned a deaf ear to certain approaches we made towards the [Communist] Albanian mission in Bari in the early part of 1945, the main purpose of which was to bring some assistance to the staff who had remained in Albania in conditions which were as critical as ever'. At the same time, he presented the problem of the Albanian claim on the gold belonging to the National Bank and reminded the Minister that, in successive memoranda of February, March and June 1945, he had called upon the Foreign Ministry to press for the recognition through diplomatic channels of the Bank's own right to the restitution of the gold.[21]

On 21 May 1947 the Italian government presented its claim to the Tripartite Commission for the above-mentioned amount of 2,340.8 kilograms, even though Italy had yet to be admitted to the gold pool.[22]

On 15 September 1947, the Albanian government made its request for the restitution of the gold belonging to the Bank of Albania, a total of 2,463.8 kilograms, plus another 116.1 kilograms which it said had been taken from Tiranë, making a total of 2,579.9 kilograms.[23] On the same day, the Peace Treaty between the Allies and Italy came into force and a few months later, on 16 December, the British, French, American and Italian governments signed an agreement in London giving Italy the right to join the gold pool on the same terms as the other participating countries.[24]

Meanwhile, on 1 October 1947, the Tripartite Commission, under the leadership of its first General Secretary, Michel Hirigoyen, had made a preliminary assessment of the Albanian claim. Regarding the gold removed from Rome, it noted a difference between the Albanian claim, for 2,463.8 kilograms and the Italian claim, for 2,340.8 kilograms. It observed that the discrepancy was in the coins: 'It appears to simmer down to 21 bags of francs and 1 bag of crowns and rubles, the fine gold contents of which are not stated in the German–Albanian lists.'[25] The Commission asked Albania to produce copies of the original documents in support of its claim and asked Italy to give a more precise figure for the gold stock removed from Rome. The Commission believed that in any event at least the smaller part of the Albanian claim which had been specified by Italy should be admitted, whereas the claim for 116 kilograms removed from Tiranë was seen as 'highly doubtful', there being little evidence to support it. Until further information was forthcoming, it decided therefore not to admit the latter.[26]

On 14 February and 30 June 1948, the Commission, having in the end validated the Albanian claim up to 2,454.9 kilograms, decided to make two preliminary allocations to Albania, totalling 1,121.4 kilograms.[27] In the event, however, the gold was not handed over. There were some quibbles over procedures, but more importantly, on a political level, it emerged that the Italian government had strong objections to the gold being handed over to Albania. The Italian claim for 2,340.8 kilograms was presented for a second time in March 1949 (by then, as we have seen, Italy had been admitted to the pool with the London Agreement of 16 December 1947), after the Commission had already decided on the two preliminary allocations to Albania. The Commission found that the Italian claim did not have sufficient substance to justify overturning its previous decisions of 1948 in which it assigned part of the gold to Albania. The Italian government, however, presented its formal opposition to the transfer of the gold to Albania, and on 11 July 1949 the Commission decided to suspend the delivery. Albania in turn voiced its protest, citing the Peace Treaty in support of its claim.[28]

In order to put this decision of the Commission's in the appropriate context, we need to consider that these developments were influenced more and more by the British government's policies. In this regard, we need to step back a few years. The fact that Albania was now definitively lost to Western influence and, to an even greater extent, the Corfu incident of October 1946 in which two British destroyers had been seriously damaged by mines in Albanian waters[29] were beginning to exert a strong influence on British policy and inclining the British to support the Italian claim.

Two months after the Corfu incident, the Bank of England came out in favour of allocating the gold to Italy. It wrote to the Treasury stating that, 'in principle', the gold should go to the 'Italian' National Bank of Albania. However, since the Tripartite Gold Commission only dealt with governments and therefore the Bank of Albania could not address itself directly to the Commission, the onus for pressing the claim was on the Italian government. The alternative would have been to remove the Albanian gold from the pool. The Bank of England considered the Albanian claim 'extremely dubious', stating that 'Since the use which they would make of the gold if they got it would also be highly dubious there may well be every political reason to give them no assistance.'[30]

The Treasury, on the other hand, observed that, since the National Bank of Albania's gold 'cannot be considered to form part of the monetary reserve of Italy, it will be necessary to produce some convincing argument if this gold is not to be awarded to Albania'. However, the matter did not require an immediate decision, in the Treasury's view, as long as no interim payments were made to Albania.[31] Uncertainty prevailed, between the Bank of England, the Treasury and the Foreign Office, over what to do. On the one hand, there was the weight of the Corfu incident and, on the other, Italy's 'Atlantic' policy. 'Sir Otto Niemeyer [a member of the Court of Directors of the Bank of England]', reads a memorandum from the Foreign Division of the Bank of England, 'felt the help should not be extended to Albania'; and the draft of a letter from Arthur Gunston, an Assistant Adviser at the Bank of England, to the Treasury states explicitly that 'the proper claimant for gold belonging to the National Bank of Albania (an Italian, never an Albanian concern) is Italy'. Sir Otto jotted on the draft, 'No, I am afraid I can't fight this way longer, though I am sure the present Albanian [State] Bank will misuse this windfall.' In Gunston's reply to Bielinky of the Treasury he admitted having been in favour of the Italians' reasoning, but added, 'if however after considering all the facts you feel it right to give this gold to the Albanians I do not wish to oppose this course, although it still seems to me a pity to provide Albania with the means for blowing up more of our ships'.[32]

The Corfu Channel incident was destined therefore to be of prime importance in the matter. Enver Hoxha described it as an 'unprecedented provocation towards our country'[33] and, after many years, responsibility for the incident is still disputed.[34]

The matter in question was actually a series of incidents involving British warships in the Corfu Channel in 1946. Immediately after the war, Albania was one of the territories of the Balkan peninsula contested between East and West. The British and Americans had backed the Albanians' struggle against the German occupation with military missions, directing their support towards pro-Western or openly Zogist movements, who in turn were engaged in a domestic battle with the Communist movements. As we know, the latter prevailed, but the Allies did not give up their attempts to extract Albania from the orbit of the socialist countries.[35] However, this is not the place for discussing this chapter of recent European history. Suffice it to say that, in this context of increasing attrition, especially with the British, the matter of clearing the mines from Albania's territorial waters arose. According to Hoxha, British warships had repeatedly approached the Albanian coast in provocation until, on 22 October 1946, 'four British warships emerged from the Corfu Channel, sailing towards the north. They left the international waters on the portside and again, without informing us, entered our waters. It was clear that Britain was seeking a pretext for an international conflict. . . . When the warships approached the coast, there was a sudden explosion and two of them went on fire.'[36] The account is not unlike the one given by Leslie Gardiner in his book devoted to the incident. On 24 October 1946, the British Admiralty announced, 'His Majesty's destroyers *Saumarez* (Captain V. H. Selby) and *Volage* (Commander R. R. Paul) were damaged by mines in the channel north-east of the island of Corfu. Both ships are now proceeding to Corfu. Some casualties were sustained.' The casualties of the incident were around 40 killed and as many injured. The channel had been searched by mine-sweeping forces in the previous months without any mine having being found.[37] A second minor incident took place on 12 and 13 November.

The British government drew from these events the conclusion that the Albanian government had mined the Corfu Channel, or had allowed it to be mined. They demanded reparations, including a payment equivalent to the value of the two destroyers (one lost and the other damaged) and compensation for the relatives of the sailors who had been killed or wounded.[38] Hoxha refused and, at the beginning of 1947, the British government took the dispute to the United Nations. The majority of votes in the Security Council laid the blame on Albania, but the Soviet Union used its veto, leading Britain to seek another path, which it found in the International Court of Justice at The Hague. On 9 April 1949 the Court ruled, by 11 votes to 5, that Albania was responsible, as it must have been aware that its waters were mined, and in December of that year it set the damages to be paid by Albania at £843,947 (approximately £20 million at today's value). The Tripartite Commission's decision to suspend delivery of the gold to Albania, dated 11 July, as previously mentioned, falls exactly between the two rulings of the Court.

Even before the Court of Justice had ruled on the case, the British government had begun considering how to obtain payment for the damages. The Treasury had brought to the attention of the Foreign Office that one valuable amount to consider was the allocation by the Tripartite Gold Commission of 1,121 kilograms of gold, which was only the first of other possible payments to be decided in the future. They also mentioned the Italian claim on the gold, considering it to be 'admittedly, a complicating factor . . . [but] a very weak one'.[39] Whilst the sterling value of this first allocation was decidedly lower than the damages claimed by the British, the total value of the Albanian claim on the gold was higher. They observed that the figure of £843,947 set by The Hague would be amply covered by the full amount of the Albanian gold claim, which was then equivalent to over £900,000.

Britain therefore began to distance itself from the Italian claim, which had initially been favoured as a means of opposing Albania, and instead began to see a connection between the Albanian gold and its own request for damages for the Corfu incident.

While Italy was going to great lengths diplomatically, mainly through Ugo Sola, the Chairman of the Management Committee of the National Bank of Albania in Rome, the Tripartite Commission decided to withdraw from the dispute for the time being, having observed on 17 November 1950 that, since Albania's claim on the gold was based on the Peace Treaty, it was outside its own remit. The Commission revoked its previous allocation of gold to the Albanian government.[40]

For this reason, the matter fell once again to the three governments which had created the Tripartite Commission. With the Washington Agreement of 25 April 1951, they decided that the question of whether the National Bank of Albania's gold belonged to Italy, to Albania or in fact to neither should be submitted to an arbitrator, to be appointed by the President of the International Court of Justice at The Hague, the same court that had decided in favour of Britain in the Corfu Channel case.[41]

The arbitrator chosen was the Swiss Georges Sauser-Hall, a professor of law at the University of Geneva and Neuchâtel and member of the Permanent Arbitration Court. Submissions on the matter were presented by the French government (in February and June 1952), the British government (in February) and the Italian government (in February and June),[42] via the intermediary of the Tripartite Commission. Sauser-Hall's decision, given in Brussels on 20 February 1953, established that the gold belonged to Albania within the meaning of the Paris Act of 1946.[43]

It will be useful to take a closer look at the text of the arbitration, in terms of the legal arguments, but more importantly in terms of the new claims put forward during the preliminary stage, which complicated the matter from a political point of view and made the conclusions of the arbitration themselves pointless.

The arguments in the submissions presented by the different countries were as follows:

(a) The British argued that the gold had constituted Albania's monetary reserve until April 1939 (the date of the Italo-Albanian union), and that either the Italo-Albanian Agreement of that year did not alter its status or, alternatively, this Agreement itself should be considered void.
(b) The Italians argued that the gold belonged to Italy, having been accumulated as a result of regular purchases made by the National Bank on the markets.
(c) The French argued that the gold could not be considered to be monetary gold as defined in the Paris Agreement, and therefore belonged neither to Italy nor to Albania.[44]

In reality, new elements were behind the standpoints adopted, especially where Italy and Britain were concerned. Britain asserted that it was entitled to receive the gold in settlement of the £843,947 which Albania had been ordered to pay by the International Court of Justice in damages for the Corfu incident. It was therefore in Britain's interests to support Albania's claim for the gold, with this aim in mind. Italy on the other hand took as a premise that the Albanian law confiscating the National Bank was not effective outside Albania and consequently the Bank's gold should go to Italy towards compensation for the confiscation, on the basis of the Peace Treaty of 1947.[45] The United States had only one priority and that was that the gold should not go beyond the Iron Curtain.[46]

All this meant that, if it should be established that Albania was entitled to the gold, it should not be made available to Albania.

The three governments of the Tripartite Commission, in handing the matter over for arbitration, agreed that, if the arbitrator should allocate the gold to Albania, it should actually pass to the United Kingdom in partial settlement of the damages relating to the Corfu incident, unless Albania or Italy appealed to the International Court of Justice within 90 days of the arbitrator's decision.

As for Sauser-Hall, the arguments he put forward in his ruling were as follows:

(a) that, at the time of its removal from Rome in September 1943, the gold still constituted the metal backing for Albania's circulation and should therefore be defined as Albanian 'monetary gold';
(b) that, under the terms of article 31 of the Italian Peace Treaty, the Italo-Albanian economic, customs and currency Agreement of 20 April 1939 was null and void;
(c) that, under the terms of the Paris Agreement, the restitution of a pro rata portion of the pooled monetary gold was not subject to proof of ownership of the gold by the claimant state;
(d) that the claimant state was only obliged to demonstrate that the gold was backing for its circulation at the time of the removal;
(e) that it had been demonstrated that the gold in question was the property of the National Bank of Albania, which constituted a legal entity under Albanian law, and that it constituted the backing for the Albanian state's circulation.

For these reasons, Sauser-Hall ruled that the gold belonged to Albania, under the terms of the Paris Agreement.[47]

In view of the various arguments mentioned above, however, needless to say the matter was far from settled. In response to the decision, the Italian government appealed to the International Court of Justice, bringing two separate proceedings on two different grounds. On 19 May 1953, Italy submitted a claim for the gold as partial compensation for the damage it had suffered as a result of the Albanian confiscation law of 13 January 1945, and claimed priority over satisfaction of the British claim relating to the Corfu incident. But on 30 October the Italian government raised the preliminary question as to whether the Court of The Hague had the appropriate jurisdiction to consider the merits in the claim on the monetary gold within the framework of the Paris Agreement of 14 January 1946.[48] Albania, like Italy, had not had a part in drawing up the declaration with which the three governments had handed the dispute over to the arbitrator. It did not however submit an appeal to the Court. The case presented itself with some unusual characteristics, among them being the fact that the challenge to the Court's jurisdiction was raised by the same party which had invoked the Court, and the fact that Albania, one of the main parties in the case, was not involved in the proceedings and was not summoned by the Court. Even the United Kingdom, which for understandable reasons had declared itself satisfied with the Court's jurisdiction, had done so with arguments which were so tortuous that, if accepted, were more likely to lead to the same result that Italy was aiming for, and that was to deny the Court's jurisdiction over the merits of the case.[49] The change in direction in the Italian proceedings, probably brought about by the feeling that the Court's decision on the merits of the case would probably be akin to that of Sauser-Hall, turned out to be a success. In its ruling of 15 June 1954, the Court noted that, in order to judge whether Italy had suffered damage as a result of the Albanian confiscation law, it would be necessary to establish whether Albania had committed an offence against Italy in international law and if so whether this merited compensation. This would entail examining the merits of a dispute between Italy and Albania, which would be impossible 'without Albania's consent'. Ultimately, Albania's absence from the proceedings constituted, in the eyes of the Court, a fundamental obstacle to a decision on the merits of the case of ownership of the gold and by *force majeure* the case of whether Italy's claim had priority over that of Britain.[50]

In 1956, an extraordinary general meeting of the National Bank of Albania in Rome put the Bank into liquidation.[51] The liquidation was completed on 28 February 1957.

Cold War developments

For several years, the question of the Albanian gold disappeared from the public limelight. The extremely poor relations between Hoxha's Albania and Western countries, in particular the absence of diplomatic relations between the United Kingdom and Albania, contributed to making any solution to the dispute impracticable. There was also another motive for not publicly adopting positions on the matter – a topic such as the nation's gold reserve, to which public opinion was very sensitive, could have aroused heated arguments along party-political lines. This did not mean however that the respective foreign offices did not revisit the question, albeit in secrecy.

In the mid-1950s a compromise was considered, though it never materialized, which provided for a 50:50 split between the United Kingdom and Italy, leaving Albania out, so long as Italy established its claim before an independent judicial tribunal. Italy's reaction was unfavourable. Its government observed that the matter could be brought to a tribunal, but only according to its own terms of reference. Different variations on the proposed split were discussed at later dates. According to one of these, put forward in 1957, Italy, on receiving its 50 per cent, would be obliged to indemnify the three countries of the Tripartite Commission against any possible claim by Albania and would have to accept the jurisdiction of the Court of The Hague should Albania decide to invoke it.[52]

As mentioned earlier, in 1958 the Tripartite Commission implemented a further important phase in the restitution of the gold to the looted countries, the so-called 'quasi-final' phase. Several countries received allocations, including Italy for its own gold, and Albania. On 9 June the Commission made its adjudication for around 1,574.4 kilograms on the basis of the Albanian claim for 2,454.9 kilograms of gold, which had been recognized as valid in 1948, and in the context declared, 'The claim of the government of the Republic of Italy, 2,340.8 kilograms, therefore fails.'[53] The gold was not actually delivered to Albania, however, because of the concomitant British claim in connection with the Corfu incident (as mentioned above, delivery was also delayed in the case of the Netherlands, Poland and Czechoslovakia).[54] During the 1960s, France played an active role, proposing that Italy should renounce the gold, which should be allocated to the United Kingdom and then half of it transferred to Italy by private arrangement. In 1964, the Italian Embassy in London put forward a similar plan.[55] It was clearly necessary to rethink the subject as a whole, as it had become fragmented into a series of bilateral proposals. Picking up again on an idea which had already been aired in Britain in 1956,[56] a four-nation conference was held in London in 1965, between the powers of the Commission and Italy. France proposed an extra-legal split between the United Kingdom, Italy and Albania. But apart from this idea, which was not taken up, the conference was uneventful. The only development was in the position of the United States which, having always been firmly opposed to the gold travelling beyond the Iron Curtain, raised, for the first time it seems, a claim of its own in partial settlement of its unadjudicated nationalization and property claim of 37 million dollars against Albania.[57] Meanwhile, Italy's position was losing political ground: 'Our impression here is that the British, French and American governments were not disposed to take this Italian intervention very seriously.'[58]

In the early 1980s, two developments took place which have a bearing on our subject. First, in 1982 after years of painstaking negotiations, the discussions on the restitution of monetary gold to Czechoslovakia ended favourably, which created an important technical precedent for channelling the Albanian gold in the same way. Second, the political scene in Albania was changing. The country was by that time isolated both from Russia and from China and was becoming more and more in need of outside economic support. Moreover, now that the head of state, Enver Hoxha, was ageing, the feeling grew that a change of leadership would provide the opportunity for a rapprochement between Albania and the West.

However, while awaiting negotiations with Albania, the British were aware of the potentially troublesome Italian claim on the gold. An important turning point came on 5 November 1982. The Foreign Office sent the following message to all the British Embassies concerned:

> Italian counsellor [of the Embassy in London] called yesterday and read out the following statement: 'In consideration of the political

importance that the envisaged agreement could have on relations between Albania and the West, we will not put procedural obstacles in the way of activities of the Tripartite Commission, nor would we undertake actions against allied governments who will be acting in their capacity as members of the Commission.'

It was made clear that the statement represented the formal position of the Italian government.[59]

Although the British government was unsure whether such a verbal declaration could be considered binding, it felt that to request written confirmation would be counter-productive. A step-by-step plan was formulated by the British, according to which the French government, which already had diplomatic relations with Albania, would approach the Albanians and propose that the Tripartite Commission should lift the block on the 1958 allocation of gold to Albania of around 1,574.4 kilograms; that Albania should issue a waiver renouncing all other claims; and that it should pay minor sums both to the United Kingdom in respect of the Corfu incident and to the United States for the reparations mentioned above. In each case, the sum would be lower than 2 million dollars, while the value of the gold to be handed over was around 20 to 25 million.[60]

In reply, Albania requested the interest on the gold entitlement, and a waiver on the part of the British for any residual claim relating to the Corfu incident. Documentation to support the American claim was also requested.[61]

For its part, the Italian government actively supported this approach, in keeping with its declaration (it was from the Italian Embassy in Tiranë that the British learnt that the French had made the above-mentioned démarche towards the Albanians). The British considered whether it might not be better to hold the meetings with the Albanians in Rome, recognizing Italy's role, which was extremely significant since it meant not having to deal with the obstacle of the Italian claim. However, it seemed that the Italian government itself was afraid of leaks to the press if the meeting were held in Rome (all the governments were worried about possible adverse public reactions to the negotiations) and that, as well as the Foreign Ministry, other Italian ministries might become involved and the question of the Italian claim resurrected.[62]

In the absence of a written undertaking to renounce their claim, the British remained cautious towards the Italians' position. The Bank of England was expressing concerns over the negotiations as a whole, both because of the question of the payment of the interest on the gold requested by Albania (a technical problem in which the Bank feared the Foreign Office did not have specific experience) and because of the reimbursement in connection with the Corfu incident. Also, according to the Bank, Italy's attitude was 'still far from clear and the risk of attachment from that quarter cannot be ruled out'.[63]

In fact, it seems that the Italian government's policy was based on the criterion that Italy felt able to renounce its claim in so far as the other two claimants against Albania, the United Kingdom and, more recently, the United States, were also renouncing the substance of their claims – 'as long as the UK and USA settle for "token" sums'. The Foreign Office therefore felt that it was important to stress that the British and American claims would be reduced to minimal sums, representing a 'political' settlement. If the British had pressed for full satisfaction of their original claim, the Italians would no longer have supported them. In the words of the Foreign Office, 'The lower the compensation paid to the UK and USA, the less inclined the Italians were likely to be to pursue their own dormant claim on gold.'[64]

Final restoration

On 15 March 1985, the first meeting for 35 years between representatives of the British and Albanian governments took place in Paris. The Albanians were informed that the block on the delivery of the gold already assigned to Albania by the Tripartite Commission would be removed; that the United Kingdom and the United States would settle for minimal sums – 1.9 million dollars each – for the respective damages; but that no interest would be paid on the gold.[65] Other meetings in Paris followed the first. Albania shifted its position and claimed generically a profit on the gold instead of a precise interest, thus demonstrating greater flexibility. It did not budge on the question of documentary evidence for the American claim, but did not rule out the possibility of making symbolic payments to the United Kingdom and the United States.[66]

Hoxha's death on 11 April, instead of speeding up the negotiations, slowed them down, as the new leadership, understandably, needed time to reflect on the situation. Meanwhile, the talks remained in deadlock because the Albanians were insisting on full restitution of the gold prior to discussing the counter-claims.[67]

Only at the beginning of 1988 did the Albanian government show a willingness to enter into discussions again. The British government took care to inform the Italian government of the new developments.[68]

The Tripartite Commission did not meet between May 1988 and June 1995. Meanwhile, on 8 May 1992, with the Communist regime having fallen and diplomatic relations between Albania and the United Kingdom having been re-established, a memorandum of understanding was signed in Rome between the two countries, on the basis of which Britain would approve the delivery of around 1,574 kilograms of gold to Albania, the quantity which was previously set to be returned to Albania but which, as we have seen, was never actually delivered. At the same time, Albania would pay the United Kingdom 2 million dollars. The Americans withdrew their veto on the delivery to Albania in 1995 and the French did likewise the following year. Thus, the Tripartite Commission was able to restart the process of restoring the gold to Albania.[69]

Negotiations with Albania were started once again.[70] On 29 October 1996, 1,574.3 kilograms of gold were delivered to Albania, which in turn conceded 2 million dollars each to the United Kingdom and the United States.[71]

The rest is very recent history. A new problem emerged in the same year, when a British member of parliament requested of the Foreign Secretary, Malcolm Rifkind, that the residual gold still to be distributed by the Tripartite Gold Commission after the consignment to Albania should be handed over to the American-based World Jewish Restitution Organization, as compensation for the private Jewish victims of the Nazi regime.[72] Various options were put forward, one being simply to proceed with the final distribution to the looted countries, another being to approach the claimant countries and encourage them to give priority to Jewish organizations, and another to actively support the Jewish organizations in the claims. The deliberations were influenced of course by the extent to which the pool contained only monetary gold. The original certainty of the British that 'no non-monetary gold originating in the British Zone [of Germany] had been placed with the Tripartite Gold Commission gold pool' was now mingled with doubts that perhaps this gold was tainted with gold taken from private individuals.[73]

An international conference was held in London at the end of 1997, at which a generally sympathetic attitude towards the Jewish requests prevailed, with some exceptions.[74] The final distribution of gold to the looted countries, from the remainder left in the pool, was made in 1998. The beneficiaries, other than Albania, were Austria, Poland, the Czech Republic, Italy, Greece, Slovenia and Luxembourg. The portion destined for Albania on 13 July 1998 was 1,571.543 troy ounces (around 48.9 kilograms) of gold, plus £2,106.24.[75] The individual countries were to make their own decisions on the devolution of their gold to Jewish organizations.[76]

Fifty-five years after its theft from Rome, the question of the Albanian gold was finally closed. Out of a validated claim of around 2,454.9 kilograms of gold, Albania actually received a total amount of 1,623.2 kilograms plus £2,106.24, in other words 66.1 per cent of the claim (see Table 10.1).

Table 10.1 Tripartite Gold Commission: 'Albanian gold' restitutions (kilograms, rounded to one decimal place)

Albanian claim (1947)	2,579.9	Italian claim (1947)	2,340.8
TGC validation, for gold removed from Rome (1948)	2,454.9		2,340.8
Preliminary allocation (1948)	+ 1,121.4		
Suspended (1949)			
Revoked (1950)	– 1,121.4		
Preliminary and quasi-final allocation (1958)	+ 1,574.4	'Fails'	
Suspended	– 1,574.4		
Distributed (1996)	+ 1,574.3		
Final (1998)	+ 48.9		
Total distributed (1998)* (around 22.6 million US dollars, at today's gold price of 434 dollars per ounce)	1,623.2		

* plus £2,106.24

Source: PRO, DG9/16, DG9/18, DG9/45.

CHAPTER 11

Summary and conclusions

As a conclusion to this research, we may try to summarize the main themes as follows:

1 In the early 1900s, the Albanian question was gradually emerging on the European political scene. Several factors contributed to putting Albania in the focus of the great powers' attention: the nationalist unrest fermenting among the peoples of the Balkan nations; the gradual dissolution of the Ottoman Empire, of which the two Balkan Wars and the Libyan War were significant indications; the attempts by Austria-Hungary to counter the expansion southwards of Slavic nationalism; and Italy's growing cultural, economic and political interest in the territory of Albania. Albania thus became, as a contemporary historian put it, 'the crucial southern meeting-place of Austro-Italian collaboration and rivalry'.

   With Albania's new-found independence and the defeat of the central empires in the First World War, Italy was able to consolidate its special relationship with Albania. Despite vacillations in Italian foreign policy, this relationship was sanctioned on an international level by the resolution of the Ambassadors' Conference of November 1921, recognizing that Italy had a special politico-strategic interest in Albania.

2 From an economic point of view, the Albanian question should be seen, at the beginning of the twentieth century, in the context of the attitude of Italian industry and finance towards the Balkan peninsula as a whole. While Italian business initiatives in Albania were still modest and involved only private concerns, the marked increase in trade between the two countries in the first two decades of the century, and in particular the growth in Italian exports, was a clear forerunner of Albania's entry into the Italian sphere of influence. Austria gradually withdrew and the very failure of the first serious attempt to create a central bank in Albania using Italian and Austrian capital clearly demonstrates the unease around joint ventures in an area in which the

interests of the two great powers were too far apart to come together in any stable way.

3 After the First World War, the power vacuum produced by the collapse of the central empires in the Balkan region explains why Fascist revisionist policy, which had grown out of existing nationalist tendencies, came to focus on the countries of that region, and on Albania in particular. The close link which Mussolini established with Ahmet Bey Zogu, later King Zog, represented a compromise between the more openly imperialistic Fascist movements and the tendencies inside the Foreign Ministry which had greater respect for Albania's political independence. Against this background, Italy undertook a large-scale financial engagement in Albania. The Italian financial community, though apparently accepting the directives of the regime's foreign policy with good grace, seems to have been a led rather than a leading force, which was true not only of Albanian affairs, but also of those of the Balkans as a whole. For this reason, the Italian state was always present, as an 'invisible' but major partner, behind the Italian ventures for the creation of an issuing bank and for the concession of a loan, initiatives which were taken forward primarily by the Central Director of the Credito Italiano, Mario Alberti. At this time, Italy's policy developed at two different levels: on the one hand, with Tiranë; and, on the other, with a 'third party', that is, with the League of Nations at first, and later, the League having stepped aside, with the United Kingdom, which competed with the Fascist government for Zogu's favour.

4 The institutional framework of Albania's monetary system, as created on Italy's initiative, was a gold exchange standard regime, as defined in essence by the Genoa Conference of 1922; the system also fulfilled the recommendations drawn up by the League of Nations in the Calmès Report of the same year. The essence of this framework – established in 1925 – was the recognized independence of the central bank from the government, and the granting to the Albanian government of the large SVEA loan, which, although earmarked for the carrying out of public works, took on a role of currency stabilization, not unlike that of other foreign loans granted in the post-war period, especially under the aegis of the League of Nations. As has been said, the financial burden of the loan fell to the public purse, as it proved impossible to place the bonds issued to fund the loan either among private Italian investors or abroad.

5 The period from 1925 (the creation of the central bank and the SVEA loan) to 1939 (the end of Albanian independence) was characterized on a political level by a difficult and troubled Italo-Albanian alliance. Zog proved to be an awkward ally who, especially from the early 1930s onwards, tried to avoid the ever firmer embrace sought by the Fascist

regime. Financial events need constantly to be viewed against this background, since political strings were always attached to the pouring of financial resources into Albania. But international financial circumstances did not favour Zog, as his attempt to achieve political independence through financial independence, abandoning Italian support in his search for that of other European partners or of the League of Nations, took place just as the Great Depression of the early 1930s was causing the loans to the Balkans as a whole to dry up.

6 A closer look at Albania's currency from the point of view of the balance of payments shows that the Albanian gold franc remained pegged constantly to its original gold content, which was that of the Latin Union, and to its gold convertibility. This supposed strength, at a time when all the main currencies were having to abandon the gold standard, either officially or unofficially, held out in spite of a balance of trade which was heavily in deficit and never offset by the other parts of the current account. The overall deficit on the current side was counterbalanced only by the inflow of capital from Italy.

However, the Fascist regime did not have enough political weight to impose tied loan conditions on Zog, by which the granting of loans would be counterbalanced by a flow of Italian goods and services in return. In fact, although Italy continued to be Albania's principal trade partner, the balance of trade between the two began on the plus side for Italy but then went into the red. An attempt to create a customs union, pursued by Italy for political reasons, and by Albania in order to increase exports to Italy and thus rebalance its trade, failed: a further sign of strained relations between the two countries.

7 These are the circumstances in which the economic premises for the politico-military events of 1939 developed. On the one hand, Zog was seeking greater independence from Italy, via attempts to increase exports, which would also make servicing the foreign debt more manageable, and to free himself from the Italian loans, searching in vain for other suitable lenders. On the other hand, Italy saw no tangible return for its own investments, either at a political or an economic level. What did serve Italy's interests, however, was maintaining the Albanian franc's long-standing gold parity. 'Realigning' it, although justified by fundamentals of Albania's economy and foreign accounts, would have put Italy's trade in an even worse situation. Moreover, if we examine the Albanian franc/lira exchange rate, on the basis of real exchange rate movements, we find that, at least until the 1936 devaluation of the lira, the franc could not be considered to be overvalued in relation to the lira itself.

8 Moving on to consider the National Bank of Albania's monetary policy, the research tries to identify certain controversial points, such as:

(a) Its relative tightness. According to a widespread criticism, evidence of the restrictive stance of its monetary policy is that the Bank did not provide the necessary support to Albania's economic development. This criticism must be qualified on the basis of the available data. Monetary policy was actually expansive until the early 1930s, heavily restrictive from then until 1934, for the duration of the Great Depression, and then again moderately expansive. As is to be expected given the role of the external loans, the foreign component of the money supply played a decisive role, first promoting expansion, then aggravating the restrictive phase with the suspension of the loans and then again holding back the reflation attempted via the internal component of the money supply until 1936, when Italy decided to restart the loans. The foreign component also served to finance the Albanian state's budget deficit, given the latter's inability to obtain credit from the central bank under the terms of its Charter and to implement any form of public debt management policy within the country.

(b) The gold convertibility of Albanian banknotes as an instrument for despoiling the Albanians of their gold. This is another criticism which was immediately voiced at the time and later taken up by historians. The balance of payments was continuously in surplus throughout the period in question and the main reason for the formation of a gold reserve seems to have been this accumulated surplus on the foreign account side, which, as has been said, essentially arose from the influx of funds from Italy, via services and grants and via the movement of capital. It is a fact, however, that the very creation of the National Bank and the new monetary system was aimed at centralizing the gold coins already in circulation at the Bank, in exchange for paper currency.

(c) The degree of independence of the National Bank of Albania. While the idea of a management completely disconnected from the political scene of the time in Italy is impossible, the case of the National Bank appears to confirm the thesis of Mussolini's tendency to entrust the running of large sections of the public administration, especially public bodies, to 'technocrats'. This thesis is borne out if we consider certain areas such as the reserve management policy, the question of bimetallism and, more generally, the prudential approach of its operations. The National Bank wanted to avoid being locked up in long-term loans, incompatible with the necessary liquidity of its balance sheet. The real issue for Albania, a backward economy without the necessary credit support, was not the central bank's unwillingness to expand its range of activities (in this, Alberti was technically right), but rather the virtual non-existence of a network of commercial banks. The choice was made to leave the financing of infrastructures and industrial ventures to other institutions: in practice, this choice was insufficient, and largely influenced by military goals.

As regards the Bank of Italy, it seems to have acted as mediator between the National Bank of Albania and the Italian government, defending the National Bank in its technical bias.

9 The union between Italy and Albania brought about by the military action of April 1939 led to the establishment of a single area, from a commercial and monetary point of view. On the commercial side, Italy and Albania formed a customs union, with mutual freedom of trade and the extension to Albania of the import and export bans and trade agreements with third parties which were in force in Italy. On the monetary side, more 'totalitarian' ideas of a simple extension of the circulation of the Italian lira to Albanian territory having been abandoned, a true 'lira standard' was created. The Albanian franc broke its link with gold and was linked to the Italian lira at a fixed exchange rate. The exchange rate decided upon was based on the market rate prevailing at the time of the occupation (with a further small slide in the lira value), and hence the franc was kept at an overvalued level, which smoothed the way for an increased flow of Italian goods into Albania. To complete the picture, the National Bank of Albania was entrusted with the exchange monopoly. It was empowered to employ other banks as its agents for this purpose. Currency legislation was introduced, aimed at greatly limiting the availability of foreign currency for imports into Albania and imposing clearance conditions on exports to third countries.

On the whole, the term 'lira area' was widely used to refer to this system, in a deliberate imitation of the much larger and more established 'sterling area'.

10 During the few years of the lira area, the flow of financial resources into Albania was intensified, partly because of wartime events, while trade between the two countries expanded, especially on the side of exports from Italy, thus bringing the trade relationship back into a marked surplus for Italy, after its heavy deterioration in the 1930s. Nonetheless, in this short period, the scant statistics we possess lead us to the conclusion that, although strong, Italian exports into Albania did not succeed in redressing the imbalance present on the capital account side. During this final phase, the exploitation of mineral resources became more intensive, but – owing to the presence of wartime requirements – had no regard for the profitability of the investment.

The huge expansion of the circulation, caused mainly by the transfers of capital from Italy and free from the restraints of the currency's gold convertibility, produced strong upward pressure on prices.

This period also saw the Fascist regime being more heavy-handed in its control of the banking system in Albania. Against the advice of the National Bank of Albania and the Bank of Italy, there was an increase in the number of bank branches open, presumably motivated more by political imperatives than by economic considerations. In fact, in this phase too, an effective banking structure was still missing.

11 Although peripheral to the main body of the research, I have included a chapter which touches on the influence of Italy's huge financial engagement on the development of Albania's economy. The Italian presence, occupied mainly with the areas of public works, land reclamation and a few base industry sectors (notably mining), did not actually initiate any process of industrialization and development. A military intent seems to have been behind several of the initiatives. Education and health care remained a rather neglected field of action. Tentative estimates of the Albanian income confirm that no improvement in the standard of living followed the Italian involvement, possibly the reverse being true.

Several possible reasons are suggested for the regime's lack of interest in starting a serious process of industrialization. One initial motive is that, in substance, the regime was moving in the direction dictated straight after the First World War by the League of Nations itself, which had identified priorities as being initiatives in the areas of public works and agriculture, postponing industrialization in the country for a later stage. A second motive can be identified in the regime's more general aim to contain industrial development, within the framework of a conservative policy intended to prevent society from being subjected to major upheavals through the growth, both numerical and political, of the urban working class. A third can be found in the wish to keep the Albanian economy in a position complementary to that of Italy, hence assigning to Albania the role of provider of agricultural produce and raw materials and preventing the competition which would have arisen from a 'duplication' of industrial structures.

12 A final chapter of the research is dedicated to the question of the 'Albanian gold' in the post-Second World War period. It is, strictly speaking, somewhat unrelated to the main theme, but worthy of consideration as a singular 'by-product' of the Italian financial presence in Albania. Again, in a singular way, we see a renewal of the political confrontation between Britain and Italy that characterized the very beginning of their involvement in the new Albanian state.

> The gold of the National Bank of Albania's reserve was the object of a long-standing controversy, due to the conflicting claims of Albania (who claimed the gold as the country's reserve), Italy (who had an equal claim, the National Bank being an Italian-owned institution) and the United Kingdom (whose claim was based on the damage suffered as a consequence of two British warships having been blown up in Albanian territorial waters immediately after the Second World War).
>
> After international debates which lasted 50 years, the disputed gold has finally been returned to Albania.

Even if this book deals with the specific theme of the relations of Fascist Italy with Albania from a financial perspective, its purpose could not be fulfilled without looking, on one side, at developments that go back to the very independence of Albania (1912–1913) and, on the other, at a chain of events that unfolded during the entire Cold War period, ending only after the fall of Communism in Albania (1992). In this wider context, the whole story of this book seems to be a fitting example of Hobsbawm's view of the past century as 'The Short Twentieth Century', a kind of projection, on a local level, of the shadow cast by the great dictatorships of our era.

Appendix

The following three documents express three very different points of view on the politico-economic situation in Albania in the 1930s: the Albanian, the Italian and the British.

The first document is an interview given in May 1933 to an Italian anti-Fascist newspaper in Paris, *La Libertà*, by an Albanian academic, Dr Ali Klissura. As relations between King Zog and Mussolini entered a very difficult phase, Klissura gave a perceptive account of their ambivalent relationship: both as allies and as adversaries, each was exploiting Italy's huge financial engagement in Albania to put pressure on the other. Klissura hoped that in the end not only would Italian designs on Albania cease, but also the Zog regime would fall, 'to the jubilation of all Albanians'.

The second document reproduces a report on the socio-economic situation in Albania in the mid-1930s, drawn up in 1934 by the Italian Legation in Tiranë and addressed to the Foreign Ministry. It is interesting in that, given the lack of statistical data on the Albanian economy as emphasized in this research, it provides a very vivid picture of the population's living conditions during the period of greatest depression in the country's economy, caused by the world crisis and the interruption of the Italian loans. Note how this document emphasizes Albania's attempts to draw close to the League of Nations and Yugoslavia again, and the Zog government's anti-Italian feeling at the time.

The third document shows the viewpoint of the third major player in the Albanian question, the United Kingdom, as expressed in an internal memorandum of the Foreign and Overseas Department of the Bank of England written in 1939, immediately after Italy's occupation of Albania. It traces the history of Italian penetration in the country and its general tone is clear enough from the very beginning: 'The story of the Italian penetration over the past fifteen years centres around the financial exigencies of a king whose personal expenditure and ideas for the development of his country were quite out of keeping with the poor resources at his command.'

Sources:
La Libertà, 3 May 1933 (courtesy of Dr Tanush Frashëri);
ASMAE 31–45;
BoE, OV 116/1.

DOCUMENT 1

La Libertà, 3 May 1933
The Troubled Situation in Albania

Fascist policy failing – Zogu's resistance – the Alliance is compromised –Mussolini's prestige takes a blow

For some time now, Albania's internal situation has been attracting attention in international political circles. Among the Albanian population, a growing unrest has been fermenting against the Italian Fascists' interference in the life of the country, and under pressure from public opinion even King Zog has been obliged to adopt an attitude of reserve, which may soon turn to hostility, against the Rome government. For several years, Mussolini has been pursuing a policy of economic, political and military penetration into Albania. He has been attempting to turn the country into an Italian colony. The Treaty of Tiranë, drawn up with the acquiescence of the British and against the rules which underpin the League of Nations, had, in 1927, placed Albania in Mussolini's hands (it was on this occasion that Senator De Jouvenel, then a member of the French delegation, resigned with vehement protests against international tolerance of this arrogant act of the Fascists'). But major changes are now being reported. In Rome, Fascist circles are beginning to be afraid of the hostile murmurings against the blackshirts spreading amongst Albanians, and of Zog's change of attitude, and they are wondering whether it was worth spending those enormous sums (more than a billion) that the regime has poured into the Albanian venture, only to reap worries and unpleasant surprises. We decided to interview an eminent representative of Albanian political emigrants on the subject. Dr Klissura, an ex-member of the Tiranë parliament and political adversary of the Zog regime, speaks for a large part of the Albanian population.

He told us that the information published in the British press about a serious conflict taking place between Zog and the Fascist regime is perfectly correct. This is no surprise to us, as there has been latent disagreement for a long time. In fact, it was present from the very beginning, and the current events are the result of the opposing aspirations of these two accomplices, united by the same desire to gain supremacy over the free will of the Albanian people. You know how Zog, Yugoslavia's instrument for gaining power, turned next to the Fascists, who gave him greater support and assured his position in power. In 1926, in order to put down the revolt of the Malissori, Zog threw himself at Mussolini's feet, and with the Treaty of Tiranë he tightened the chains binding the Albanian people. The

Fascists, however, have not played their cards right. First and foremost, they have not taken Albanian nationalist feeling into account. Secondly, they did not realize that by securing Zog his power with their grants they were at the same time empowering our despot to gain independence from Rome's impositions. It must be recognized that Zog has made some very clever manoeuvres. He has seduced the regime with infinite promises, in order to get economic and financial aid; but when it came to the absolute and definitive military occupation of Albania which the blackshirts wanted, in order to transform it into an Italian colony, he has always played for time and avoided the issue. The Fascists have been arrogant and spread corruption. But they have gradually earned themselves the deepest hatred of the Albanian population, in whose midst such ill feeling is brewing that it could explode at any moment in open acts of revolt.

From using sly tactics, Zog has recently shifted towards an aggressive stance. It seems now that he wants to demolish the Fascist edifice that he had allowed to grow up. The Treaty of Tiranë has not been renewed, despite Mussolini's lively insistence. The trade treaty, which is about to expire, will suffer the same fate. The regime had attempted to create a customs union between Italy and Albania, but Zog disclosed the Fascists' manoeuvres to the British, who opposed the move. The authorities in Rome were extremely annoyed by this trick. Furthermore, the Albanian press has begun a lively campaign for a review of the legislation concerning the Italian bank [the National Bank of Albania] aimed at keeping the Fascist regime's financial and economic hegemony in our country.

– Do you know anything about reprisals by the Fascist regime?

– Yes. Mussolini has decided to cut off Zog's supplies. He has in fact blocked the payment of the annual subsidy of 10 million gold francs which the Fascist regime gives Albania. It is this sum which maintains Zog's regime and now, having received nothing, it is experiencing very serious difficulties. Public employees have not been paid for six months. The Minister in Paris himself, having been unable to pay the rent for the Legation, has been threatened with eviction and has had to go to Tiranë to ask for money. Mussolini has also pressed SVEA to ask Zog to pay the annual instalments of the loan SVEA granted when he first came to power. Until now, there has been a moratorium. One annual payment alone constitutes half of Albania's national budget. The SVEA representatives have arrived in Tiranë in the last few days. Zog has asked for the loan to be cancelled, claiming that the whole sum received was spent on strategic works which the Fascist regime had wanted. The negotiations have failed and the conflict is at an acute stage.

What is more, Zog has now moved on to the counter-attack. He has threatened to scale down the army and to throw out the Fascist officials and leaders who have been taking over the country. As a warning shot to the regime, he has already closed down the Italian schools in Albania, some of which were very old, and has also closed the Catholic seminaries, subsidized by the Rome government, in which lessons were taught mainly in Italian. Generally speaking, Zog's attitude is one of rebellion against Fascism. If the latter does not keep its promises and does not pay the money, Zog will knock down the whole architecture built by Mussolini up to now for his hegemonic and militaristic ends.

– In your opinion, what will be the consequences of this aggressive attitude of Zog's?

– It is difficult to predict what they will be. It depends on how the Fascist regime reacts. Zog's agents state that under no circumstances can he or will he give up his defence of the national interests. This seems to be borne out by the measures he has taken regarding the schools. It is possible however that, as on previous occasions, these measures have only been adopted to calm the Albanian population's annoyance at major new concessions made to the Fascists. Now if Zog does not give up on these tactics, the Fascists will face a dilemma: either come to terms with a humiliating position, making do with certain superficial concessions in order to fool Italian public opinion and to hide the failure of Mussolini's policies in Albania; or abandon Zog to his fate, completely cutting off his means and leaving him in the difficulties he is in now. In the latter case, it will speed the demise of the present regime, to the jubilation of all Albanians. The Fascists could even try to replace Zog with a new despot, but after a period of time such a person would have to follow the same course, and the situation would be unchanged.

– Do you think that if Fascism refuses to give way to Zog's demands he will throw himself into the arms of Yugoslavia?

– I don't think so, for these reasons: first and foremost, because Zog is afraid of the Fascists' revenge. Indeed, if the Albanian tyrant, after having received arms, millions of lire and the Albanian crown from Rome, were to go over to the opponent's side with all this baggage, it would be too serious a blow to Mussolini's prestige and the latter would spare no pains in seeking revenge. Zog knows this, so he is cautious. Besides, I do not believe that Yugoslavia is willing to take over Italy's role in this mission to protect Zog. It is certainly in Yugoslavia's interests to draw the Albanian government into the circle of the Little Entente, but it knows Zog and knows what his word is worth. The Yugoslavs know that Zog is only after money and strength in order to oppress the Albanian people and he will side with whoever pays the most. Besides, it is not in Belgrade's interests to consolidate Zog's dictatorship, as this would set them against the entire

Albanian population, in its aspirations to independence and freedom. This people, hostile now towards Fascism, would turn against Yugoslavia, which would entail serious consequences for the situation in the Adriatic and the Balkans. To conclude, the people of my country are no longer disposed to tolerate foreign interference, especially when it is a cover to hide aims of nationalistic or strategic predominance. This does not mean that Albania wants to be isolated – far from it. It will still seek to collaborate with the Italian people, with whom it is linked by converging interests and sincere goodwill.

These statements by Dr Klissura demonstrate the gravity of the situation in Albania. The Fascist regime is about to pay for its mistakes and arrogant behaviour in pursuing a troubled dream of supremacy and tyranny on the other shore of the Adriatic.

DOCUMENT 2

The Situation in Southern Albania (1934)

Royal Italian Legation

Telegram No. 453/144
Addressed to the Royal Ministry for Foreign Affairs, Rome
Tirana,* 8 February 1934, XII

Position: A.1

Re: Bulletin from our agent on the situation in Southern Albania.

Text:

One of our agents, who has recently made a journey to the Southern Albanian interior, has sent me a report, a copy of which I attach herewith, in which he relates facts and impressions from his journey.

It brings to light above all the serious difficulties with which the population is struggling and while here and there it strays into exaggeration of the seriousness of the situation it gives an accurate enough picture of the harsh conditions in which the country has found itself since, because of the attitude assumed by its central government towards the government in Rome, the latter has had to suspend its assistance to the country.

The resignation shown by this people, who are accustomed to suffering, is an infinite resource, but the situation has become so critical that it is not difficult for them to realize the need for Italian help and they have little faith in those attempts at improvement based on a reconciliation with Yugoslavia. The informing agent refers to the efforts being made by the local authorities to extol the recent pact and to demonstrate the new spirit animating their dealings with the citizens of the neighbouring state, and reports how the population shows no sign of being convinced by this and treats such displays coldly, even scornfully. And in fact this is the general feeling among the population at the present time.

Koch

Santi Quaranta [Sarandë], 29 January 1934, XII

In various memoranda of mine, I have always spoken at length about the economic circumstances of the Albanian population, which continue to be as serious as ever. To have an idea of the utter wretchedness afflicting the population, one needs to look not in the cities, and the more populated

* The spelling of geographical names follows the original Italian version of the document (Author's note).

areas, but among the villages and in the countryside. People are feeding themselves on nothing but tiny amounts of buckwheat they manage to scrape together, or off the charity of some rich person, or from petty thefts they made last October in the fields. The labourers are so weakened by hunger that they cannot stand up for long and so cannot go into the fields to sow or to gather wood.

On the 25th, which is bazaar day in Tepeleni where I arrived around midday on my way from Valona [Vlorë], one hundred or so Albanians, ragged, barefoot and barely able to stand up, were crowding round the 'Baskija' house to ask for help. The armed forces were obliged to intervene, consisting of 6 soldiers from the local recruitment centre. They dispersed those poor people who were incapable of even a single shout or oath.

These last four days, I have made a tour of Himara, Valona, Fieri, Tepeleni, Premeti, Argirocastro [Gjirokastër] and Delvino. The terrible wretchedness was the same everywhere: men almost naked, women a spectre of their former selves, children naked, crying and hungry.

Pictures of desolation and brutalization.

I am convinced that they cannot go on any longer and that the days of blood are in store for Albania in the spring.

In the cities there is now talk of Yugoslav loans and intervention by the League of Nations. These rumours are being spread by civil servants and employees who are closely allied to the present regime, but they are not given any credence and everyone now believes that it is all a cynical farce which the Albanian government has been playing out for several months, in order to deceive the people and keep them at bay. It is also confirmed that many civil servants have not been paid since September. They are all in debt. There will be trouble for those small traders in the interior if they stop giving credit to officials and employees high up in the government departments.

The roads are terrible and the bridges perilous. Lorries are a rare sight on public roads. The various carriage companies compete for passengers and a few goods, at prices that are truly ridiculously low. Many shops have closed down. Since 1 January, goods have not been arriving from Greece, or only in the smallest quantities. Even those goods arriving in Albania from Japan are very few. Some shopkeepers I spoke to during my short trip reported that there is little use in importing goods, even at very low prices, because it is too difficult to sell them on.

The people of the villages along the route from Santi Quaranta to Valona, via Himara, had relied greatly on exporting their olives to Italy but then the embargo was imposed and the olives were either left to rot on the trees and the ground because the landowners did not have the money to pay their labourers, or were bought up by opportunists at ridiculously low prices. Many Albanians saw a glimpse of hope when a foreigner turned up to buy olives in the Province of Himara. The price he paid was far higher than the cost of oil in Yugoslavia and someone pointed out that no doubt the Gravosa and Antivari Chamber of Commerce must have been paying the difference.

A real propaganda campaign favouring Yugoslavia has started lately throughout almost the whole of Albania and it is being made easier by the fact that the Albanian officials and civil servants themselves, being natives of countries which were under Yugoslav rule, speak the Slav language extremely well.

On Tuesday, for example, four Albanians from the Province of Argirocastro were due to depart from Santi Quaranta to work in France. They were all keen to leave on a motor ship belonging to the Compagnia Adriatica, but at the last minute the sub-prefect for Santi Quaranta found some fault with their passports and suggested that the passengers come to his office the next day, when they would be able to leave on board a 'big, comfortable and clean' Yugoslav steamer.

It may be a small example, but it amply demonstrates the current approach of Albanian employees and especially the sub-prefect for Santi Quaranta, who has always been a prime anti-Italian and has always found every possible excuse for fighting with our Royal Consular Agent Cav. Conte.

One Mr Vasil Papas, who owns car and tyre shops in Santi Quaranta and Durazzo [Durrës], has for some years been a close friend of Mr Koço Kota* and has also shared with him the profits of certain business ventures. Today, Papas told me:

> The day before yesterday I was in Tirana and as usual I was Kota's guest. Naturally our conversation included the current situation between Italy and Albania and the business situation. Because Kota has been to Rome several times over the last few months, he no longer enjoys the king's confidence or the sympathies of certain ministers, especially Abdurraman Dibra. Kota does not approve of the Tirana government's behaviour towards Italy. He believes that Italy has every reason to demand of Albania the full recognition of certain rights. Italy has given money and wants respect in return. I can assure you that Albania will not find credit anywhere in Europe. Maximos, the Greek Foreign Minister, will certainly have talked to Mussolini about the Albanian question. Mussolini voiced his opposition to Albania becoming party

* K. Kota: exponent of the right wing of the Zog regime. Having been Prime Minister after Zog was pronounced king, he was to fill the office again in November 1936, on Zog's reconciliation with Italy (Author's note).

> to the Balkan Pact. One only has to read the statements made by President Tsaldaris in the last few days to see what is happening.

There is talk now of a Yugoslav–Albanian Bank and two delegates have already arrived in Tirana, one Belgian and one Yugoslav. Setting aside the need to combat our own National Bank of Albania's systems, which are damaging to our businesses and our population, in my opinion it will be very difficult to form a new bank headed by Belgrade. Another grave error being made by our men in government is to seek a reconciliation with Yugoslavia. Is Yugoslavia really fit to help Albania at this time, when everyone knows what a sorry state it is in politically and economically?

DOCUMENT 3

Albania

The story of Italian penetration over the past fifteen years centres around the financial exigencies of a king whose personal expenditure and ideas for the development of his country were quite out of keeping with the poor resources at his command. King Zog, although not proclaimed king until 1st September 1928 has in fact been in control of Albania since the Spring of 1922. There was, however, a short interval in 1924 during which his position was usurped by a revolutionary government under Mgr. Fan Noli, but reinstated with the assistance of Yugoslavia, he became President of the 'Albanian Republic' on 31st January 1925. His friendly relations with Yugoslavia were nevertheless of very short duration. Lured by the prospect of financial aid from Italy he used the occasion of a revolt among the mountain tribes of the North as a pretext for severing his old attachment and in November 1926 signed the Pact of Tirana, whereby Albania came under Italian protection. A year later, in November 1927, the two countries entered a treaty of Alliance.

By this time Italian interests were already getting a hold over the economic life of the nation. In May 1925 the SVEA (Società per lo sviluppo economico dell'Albania) had granted a 7½% Public Works Loan of Lire 248 mn. and as part of the bargain had secured for Italy the exclusive right to set up a national bank of issue. With the stabilization of the lira this loan had been consolidated a few months later at A.F. 50 mn., representing a capital reduction of about A.F. 15 mn. But the service even of this loan was apparently beyond the capacity of the country. The first annuity had been deducted from the proceeds of the loan; that for 1926 (the first to be paid from ordinary revenue) was not forthcoming. An adjustment of the loan service had to be secured, and this was affected by an agreement of 28th February 1928, under which a complete moratorium was granted for the period 1926 to 1929 (inclusive) and regular service was to be resumed in 1930 on a rising scale commencing at A.F. 1 mn. Only A.F. 9 mn. of the 1930 annuity was actually paid, and immediately after the service again went into complete default. The loan remained in this state for some years, no claim being made on the secured revenues (which consisted of Customs duties and the revenue from salt, matches and cigarette paper monopolies) but in April 1938 the Italians agreed to a new settlement which treated Albania very favourably.

Encouraged by Italian assistance the government paid little attention to the rapid fall in ordinary revenue between 1929/30 and 1932/3 and maintained expenditure at over A.F. 30 mn. a year, in which Defence figured for between 45% and 50%. The king seems to have thought that as long as he remained on good terms with Italy all would be well. It is difficult to tell how much assistance was received from the Italian government direct, as a considerable amount was apparently given in the form of secret subsidies, but in June 1931 Italy openly agreed to advance up to A.F. 10 mn. a year for a period of 10 years, i.e. A.F. 100 mn. in all. This loan was non-interest bearing and was not repayable until State receipts reached more than A.F. 50 mn. a year. A.F. 17 mn. was received from Italy in 1931 and 1932, but in 1933 the agreement lapsed owing to strained relations. To his cost King Zog discovered that Mussolini was beginning to want a good deal for his money. The latter's demands, in fact, went so far as the placing of administration in Italian hands and the opening of the country to Italian colonization. This King Zog could not tolerate. Circumstances therefore seemed to favour the attempts which were being made about this time to get Albania into the Balkan Entente. King Zog's precarious position, however, made him stand out for guarantees and indemnities which the other members were not prepared to grant, and he was thrown back on his own resources. With the cessation of Italian subsidies, and the almost complete exhaustion of the 1925 S.V.E.A. loan, the financial difficulties became acute and from 1933/4 expenditure was drastically curtailed even though it meant the abandonment of many schemes in a half-finished condition.

Reconciliation with Italy began in the early part of 1935 and by March 1936 Albania was able to secure renewed assistance at the price of fresh concessions and increased political intervention. Italy promised to make substantial gifts and lend on extremely easy terms, and in return Albania agreed to accept Italian advice on the general development of the country. Two important institutions which benefited under these agreements were the Agricultural Bank (which opened on 1st August 1937 and to which Italy subscribed an initial capital of A.F. 2.8 mn.) and the E.I.A.A. (Ente Industria Agraria Albania) which now occupies a preponderant and to some extent monopolistic position in the country's trade. Such institutions have naturally helped to accelerate the process of economic penetration. The Italians have also seized upon the country's large adverse balance of trade* in order to influence commercial policy. In 1933/4 Albania experimented with the quota system, but this was abandoned in 1936 in favour of preferential treatment to those countries (including Italy) which take a certain proportion of Albanian exports. In practice this means that Albania is being forced to buy more and more Italian goods, and the system has become very unpopular with the local merchants, especially after the further tightening up which took place in March 1938.

* (Aggravated by the fall in emigrant remittances from A.F. 10 mn. to about A.F. 1 mn. a year).

Anti-Italian feeling undoubtedly had its roots very much deeper than was apparent from the so-called student demonstrations of recent weeks. A significant political change occurred last May when Dr. Toci, the strongly pro-Italian Minister of National Economy, was replaced by a member of the younger school with somewhat different leanings. Italy's own increasing financial difficulties, moreover, led to severer criticism of Albanian extravagance during the past twelve months, and it appears that the Italians actually went back on some of their promises much to the displeasure of the king, who is said to have courted the idea of seeking help elsewhere. Whether the Italians had come to distrust the king, or whether they regarded his administration as inefficient and an impediment to the rapid realization of their programme, it is impossible to say.

The idea that Italy, in occupying the country, merely acted in defence of her own legitimate interests can be dismissed. Even had they been threatened, there were plenty of less drastic weapons available by which the country could easily have been brought to book. There can be no doubt that what has been done has been done as part of a deliberate plan, even though precipitated perhaps by the fear that developments in other countries might upset calculations.

The vital question, of course, is whether Albania could possibly be considered an end it itself. At present the standard of life is extremely low and poverty on the increase everywhere except in the towns. But the country can certainly be made to support a much larger population that the existing 1,000,000. Only about 12% of the land is cultivated, and the agricultural methods employed are usually of the most primitive kind. The cultivated area could be appreciably extended and modern technique introduced to give a greater yield per acre. Italy already absorbs over 75% of Albania's exports, which consist of a narrow range of pastoral and agricultural products such as raw wool (18%),* skins (15%), cheese (9%), eggs (7%) and maize and olives (according to the harvest). It is naturally to Italy's advantage that more attention should be given to the development of cereals, but efforts during recent years have concentrated on the output of crude petroleum. Since 1935, when this product began to be exploited on a commercial basis, the output has increased rapidly though not to the extent that had been hoped. Annual production does not amount to much more than 100,000 tons, against an estimated maximum yield of 300,000 tons. Even if the latter figure is realized it would amount to only a small fraction of Italy's peace time requirements and the oil, being of inferior quality, is only suitable for a limited range of use. About 80% is already absorbed by Italy, and no doubt an additional quantity is taken direct by the Italian navy. Other natural resources include timber, lignite, copper,

* 1937 figures (value).

iron and other minerals, but they are little worked at present owing to inaccessibility.

Taken all in all Albania is no great economic prize, and any country without railways or good roads needs a large expenditure of capital (which Italy can ill afford) to bring it into profitable employment. It must be remembered, moreover, that the expenditure which Italy has already made in the country has been directed more by strategic than economic considerations. Roads are few and have been designed for military traffic, and much effort has been expended on the fortification of passes. Such works have clearly served Italian aims rather than Albania's, and the transformation of Durazzo into a naval base was obviously not carried out to provide accommodation for the Albanian navy (which consists of four small motor boats!). The immediate strategic advantages of Albania clearly overshadow the economic assets (or probable liabilities), and the fact that Italy has suddenly decided to place herself in supreme control of those advantages by forceful means may well cause consternation to the rest of the Balkan peninsula.

The political implications being therefore of paramount importance, the small economic interests at stake in Albania itself need not be dealt with in any great detail. They are, of course, predominantly Italian. There is now no internal long-term public debt, and although Albania is in principle responsible for a small part of the old Ottoman Debt that obligation has never in fact been discharged. The two main loans from Italy have already been mentioned. There are probably further large amounts due to the Italian government for arms, etc., and to various Italian companies. The floating domestic debt is unknown, but must in any case be very small.

Beside the National Bank* and the Agricultural Bank already referred to, the only other banks established in the country are the Yugoslav Banque d'Exportation (with a branch in Tirana), the Banco di Napoli, and two small local banks.

At one time petroleum concessions were held by five or six foreign companies, but those of the Anglo-Iranian Oil Co., the Standard Oil Co., and Mr. Rushton have been abandoned, leaving those of a French concern – 'Société Française Industrielle et Commerciale des Pétroles (Group Malopolska)' – a small Italian company – 'Società Italiana delle Miniere di Selenizza' – and the Italian State Railways. The last named interest is by far the most important, and is said to have invested about Lire 200 million in the development of its various fields, the most successful of which is that in the Devoli basin now connected with Valona by a pipe line. No

* The National Bank has a gold reserve of A.F. 7.5 million (£1/2 million), A.F. 9.6 million in Foreign Exchange, and A.F. 8.5 million in Foreign Government Securities (the last two probably being mainly lire).

up-to-date information is available on other concessions but some years ago it was reported that Italians had secured the right to work copper and asphalt deposits, Germans to exploit certain forest areas, and Americans and Swiss to undertake estate development. More recent concessions, e.g., the fishery and mineral concessions of 1938, seem to have gone exclusively to the Italians.

Overseas & Foreign Department [Bank of England],
12th April, 1939

Notes

Preface

1 M. Kaser, 'Economic Continuities in Albania's Turbulent History', in *Europe–Asia Studies*, vol. 53, 4, 2001, p. 627.
2 United Nations, National Accounts Main Aggregates Database, unstats.un.org.
3 *Corriere della Sera*, as quoted in R. Morozzo della Rocca, *Albania. Le radici della crisi* (Milano, Guerini e Associati, 1997), p. 99.
4 See Morozzo della Rocca, *Albania*, p. 88.
5 The 'economic goals' which Fascist Italy set itself in Albania are summed up well in an unsigned note from the Foreign Ministry of June 1932, in ASMAE 31–45, 'Albania', 11: 'To create potential outlets in Albania for our industrial produce and to get our hands on resources which are of use to us.'
6 'If European affairs had been in the hands of men of good sense, they would have entrusted the running of Albania to the League of Nations for a period of twenty-five or even fifty years': G. Salvemini, *Mussolini diplomatico* (Bari, Laterza, 1952), p. 192.
7 ASBI, Azzolini, 97, Guarneri to Governor Azzolini, 16 May 1939.

Chapter 1

1 On tribal organization and social structure in Albania before its independence, see C. Chekrezi, *Albania Past and Present* (New York, Macmillan, 1919), ch. XVI; J. Swire, *Albania: The Rise of a Kingdom* (London, Williams & Norgate, 1929), ch. I; S. Skendi, *Albania* (New York, Praeger, 1956), part I; S. Pollo and A. Puto, *The History of Albania, from Its Origins to the Present Day* (London, Routledge & Kegan Paul, 1981), ch. V. The latter offers an interesting Marxist perspective on Albanian history. For geographical and population estimates, see J. R. Lampe and M. R. Jackson, *Balkan Economic History, 1550–1950: From Imperial Borderlands to Developing Nations* (Bloomington, Indiana University Press, 1982), p. 332: this is a vast work which, however, overlooks the case of Albania (as Berend points out in his very thorough 'Balkan Economic Development', in *The Economic History Review*, May 1984). For estimates on the different religions, see M. Boldrini, 'Sull'antropologia e la demografia degli albanesi', in *Principii di economia albanese* (Padua, Cedam, 1940), pp. 27–29, and, more recently, R. Morozzo della Rocca, *Nazione e religione in Albania (1920–1944)* (Bologna, Il Mulino, 1990).

2 See Swire, *Albania*, p. 22.
3 For Toptani, see notes 17 and 19. For the Vrioni ownership, see I. Berend, 'Agriculture', in M. Kaser and E. A. Radice (eds), *The Economic History of Eastern Europe 1919–1975* (Oxford, Clarendon Press, 1985), vol. I, p. 204.
4 Chekrezi, *Albania Past and Present*, pp. 193f.
5 E. Maserati, 'L'Albania nella politica estera italiana degli anni 1896–1901', in *Clio*, January–June 1977, p. 51. On the rise in Italy of a lively interest in Albanian politics, culture and economics, see also Gioacchino Volpe's neat synopsis in *L'Italia moderna* (Florence, Sansoni, 1949), vol. II, pp. 101–106 and by the same author, *Formazione storica dell'Albania* (Rome, Reale Accademia d'Italia, 1939). It is worth remembering that several decades before that, in 1878, Crispi had refused Bismarck's offer at the Congress of Berlin to renounce Italy's irredentist claims on Austria in return for territorial gains in Albania. Italy believed that its interests in the Adriatic would be sufficiently protected as long as Albania remained part of the Ottoman Empire: see L. Albertini, *The Origins of the War of 1914* (London, Oxford University Press, 1952–1957), vol. I, p. 29; see also ASMAE 31–45, 'Albania', 81.
6 Lampe and Jackson, *Balkan Economic History*, p. 228.
7 Ibid.
8 R. A. Webster, *Industrial Imperialism in Italy, 1908–1915* (Berkeley, University of California Press, 1975). See pp. 358, 360, 363 of the Italian edition: *L'imperialismo industriale italiano, 1908–1915* (Turin, Einaudi, 1974).
9 Ibid., pp. 554–557; R. Bosworth, 'The Albanian Forests of Signor Giacomo Vismara: A Case Study of Italian Economic Imperialism during the Foreign Ministry of Antonino Di San Giuliano', in *Historical Journal*, XVIII, 1975.
10 On Italian rail projects of this period, see Filippo Tajani's essay 'Le comunicazioni albanesi', in *Principii di economia albanese* (Padua, Cedam, 1940). More recently: S. Romano, *Giuseppe Volpi: industria e finanza fra Giolitti e Mussolini* (Milan, Bompiani, 1979), especially ch. V. For an overview of railway construction in the Balkan states and its funding, in the period following independence, see Lampe and Jackson, *Balkan Economic History*, pp. 208–212.
11 Maserati, 'L'Albania', p. 65.
12 *L'Albania economica*, published by the Camera di Commercio Italo-Orientale (Italo-Oriental Chamber of Commerce) of Bari (Bari, SET, 1928).
13 Other statistics, quoted by Bosworth ('The Albanian Forests'), however, would seem to show that, in 1910, Austria had still not lost its advantage over Italy as principal trade partner with Albania (see p. 575).
14 *L'Albania economica*, pp. 105–106.
15 28 November 1912: The National Congress of Albania declared its independence and formed a government; 29 July 1913: The Ambassadors' Conference of the six great powers (Great Britain, France, Germany, Austria-Hungary, Russia and Italy, the last three having, as we have seen, a more direct interest in Albania's affairs) meeting in London for a complete review of the problems in the Balkans following Turkey's defeat by the 'Balkan League', recognized Albanian independence, proclaiming Albania a 'hereditary principality' and confirming its neutrality. It entrusted control of the administration and finances of the new state to an international commission of the six powers, with an Albanian delegate (see Swire, *Albania*, ch. IV; Pollo and Puto, *The History of Albania*, ch. VII; Skendi, *Albania*, Introduction; Skendi, *The Albanian National Awakening 1878–1912* (Princeton, NJ, Princeton University Press,

1967), ch. XVIII; M. Vickers, *The Albanians: A Modern History* (London and New York, I. B. Tauris, 1995), ch. 3.

16 See P. Pastorelli, *L'Albania nella politica estera italiana 1914–1920* (Naples, Jovene, 1970), p. 407, for an in-depth look at this period, in particular at the negotiations for the Treaty of London, the so-called 'Gjirokastër Proclamation' and the negotiations for the Conference of Paris. For Italo-Austrian relations on the Albanian problem immediately after its independence, see M. Mazzetti, 'L'Italia e la crisi albanese del marzo-maggio 1913', in *Storia Contemporanea*, June 1973. There are also interesting passages in the following works: I. Bonomi, *La politica italiana da Porta Pia a Vittorio Veneto* (Turin, Einaudi, 1944); Albertini, *The Origins of the War of 1914*; R. Bosworth, *Italy and the Approach of the First World War* (London, Macmillan, 1983); C. Seton-Watson, *Italy from Liberalism to Fascism 1870–1925* (London, Methuen, 1967); G. Giolitti, *Memorie della mia vita* (Milan, Garzanti, 1945).

17 Ismail Qemal headed the provisional government of Albania formed on its independence. Basically he tried to achieve a social model in Albania based on Western societies. Fears of agrarian reform aroused opposition from the Muslim beys and led to a separatist movement led by Esat Pasha Toptani, who established a 'senate' in Durrës. Ismail Qemal's attempts to govern independently set him at odds with the international controlling commission. He was obliged to leave Albania in January 1914 (see Pollo and Puto, *The History of Albania*, pp. 153–157; Swire, *Albania*, pp. 180–183).

18 Swire, *Albania*, p. 182.

19 The Prussian prince, Wilhelm Von Wied, was the choice of the six powers. It was a difficult choice which in the end turned out to be an unfortunate one. He accepted the crown on 22 February 1914 and arrived in Albania on 7 March. He was not lacking in good will, but did not have sufficient knowledge of the country and was influenced by the German Kaiser. He also made the mistake of giving the home affairs and defence portfolios to Esat Pasha Toptani, who had his own designs, as we have mentioned. A revolt broke out in Durrës, instigated by Esat, and another in the south, supported by the Greeks. In addition, this was happening during the months in which the First World War was brewing, and the disagreements between the members of the international control commission were becoming more marked. In the end, they 'advised' the prince to leave the country, which he did on 3 September 1914 (see Skendi, *Albania*, pp. 11–12; Pollo and Puto, *The History of Albania*, pp. 157–163; Swire, *Albania*, ch. V; see also, for an interesting and 'partisan' view of events, I. Sulliotti, *In Albania. Sei mesi di regno* (Milan, Treves, 1914).

20 Swire, *Albania*, pp. 194 and 229.

21 See ASMAE 31–45, 'Albania', 66. Note Swire: 'Austria-Hungary and Italy appear to have recovered by taxation during the war the amounts advanced upon the credit they had accorded to Prince William's Government' (p. 315). The problem was, in fact, more complex. In the accords of Tiranë of 1920, which put an end to the Italian occupation, it was agreed that the materials ceded to the Albanian government on the exit of the Italian troops were given on loan and that this loan (of an unspecified amount) should be added to the 5.5 million loaned to the prince. However, on that occasion, a sum of around 6 million lire (approximately 5.6 million euros, at current values – it should not be forgotten that the current Italian GDP is, in real terms, 10 times higher than the GDP of that time) was brought into Italy, belonging to the administration of Gjirokastër and Vlorë and therefore constituting an Italian 'debt'. In 1936,

when the loan to Wied was 'rediscovered', it was felt that the Albanians could justifiably refuse to repay it on the grounds of the 6 million credit just mentioned. Italy therefore decided that Wied's old debt should be definitively cancelled (see correspondence in folder 66, quoted above). Edith Durham says that, out of the 10 million francs loan, 6.7 million were spent mostly for military purposes and 3 million were committed for payment to Italian and Austrian companies. In the end, the Albanian Treasury under Wied had just 300,000 francs as available cash. See E. Durham, 'Notes from Albania', in *The Near East*, 18 September 1914. The article is reprinted in E. Durham, *Albania and the Albanians*, ed. B. Destani (London, Centre for Albanian Studies, 2001).

22 Société des Nations, Commission Economique et Financière, Comité Financier, *La Situation Economique et Financière de l'Albanie, Rapport présenté par le professeur Albert Calmès (Luxembourg) à la suite de la mission d'études en Albanie* [Calmès Report], Geneva, September 1922.

23 For Italy's evolving policy, see Pastorelli, *L'Albania nella politica estera italiana*, especially ch. VIII. Giolitti notes in his *Memorie* that the waning of the Habsburg Empire had calmed fears that 'it would penetrate Albanian territory and thus create an even more difficult situation for us, by having control over the entrance to that sea [the Adriatic]'. Hence his willingness to let go of Vlorë (*Memorie della mia vita*, pp. 568–571). In reality, Giolitti seems to have deliberated long and hard before accepting this solution (see Pastorelli).

24 See Pollo and Puto, *The History of Albania*, p. 182; see also Skendi, *Albania*, p. 174, and Swire, *Albania*, pp. 339 and 412. The contract was not ratified by the Albanian parliament, however, due to opposition by competitors from other countries.

25 Swire, *Albania*, p. 339.

26 Cassels believes this action amounted to an international sanction for Italy to turn Albania into a protectorate. See A. Cassels, *Mussolini's Early Diplomacy* (Princeton, NJ, Princeton University Press, 1971), pp. 241–242. Note that, in July 1921, Bonomi had succeeded Giolitti as Prime Minister of Italy.

27 Pollo and Puto, *The History of Albania*, p. 184.

28 Swire, *Albania*, pp. 386–389.

29 Ibid., pp. 394–395.

30 See I. Fishta and V. Toci, *Ekonomia e Shqipërisë në vitet e para të ndërtimit socialist, 1944–1948* [The Albanian Economy in the First Years of Socialist State Building] (Tiranë, Akd. e Shkencave e RPS të Shqipërisë, 1984), p. 433; Pollo and Puto, *The History of Albania*, p. 188.

31 See Skendi, *Albania*, p. 96.

32 We will consider these efforts towards effective independence from an economic and financial standpoint later in the book.

33 J. Tomes, *King Zog: Self-made Monarch of Albania* (Stroud, Sutton Publishing, 2003).

34 See Swire, *Albania*, p. 412; Skendi, *Albania*, p. 174.

Chapter 2

1 See *The Balkan States* (Royal Institute of International Affairs, London, Oxford University Press, 1936). For a broad comparative economic history of the Balkan nations, see Lampe and Jackson, *Balkan Economic History*.

2 The percentage of agricultural land expropriated after the war varied from

50 per cent in Greece and 30 per cent in Romania to barely 10 per cent in Yugoslavia and even less in Bulgaria and Albania.

3 On the coexistence of dinars and crowns in Yugoslavia and the problems of their relative exchange rate, see Lampe and Jackson, *Balkan Economic History*, pp. 378–379.

4 By deflating nominal values in local currencies, Lampe and Jackson place the role of foreign loans in the post-war efforts at stabilization in a lesser perspective and emphasize instead the importance of the restrictive budget policies pursued by the Balkan countries (*Balkan Economic History*, pp. 382–394).

5 See the 'Relazione dei delegati italiani alle riunioni di esperti preliminari alla Conferenza di Genova, tenutesi a Londra dal 20 al 28 marzo 1922', in ASBI, Azzolini, 111.

6 See H.G. Grubel, *The International Monetary System: Efficiency and Practical Alternatives* (Harmondsworth, Penguin, 1969), p. 132; R. Harrod, *Money* (London, Macmillan, 1969), pp. 99–100; B. Eichengreen, *Globalizing Capital: A History of the International Monetary System* (Princeton, NJ, Princeton University Press, 1996). See also Resolution no. 11 in the 'Rapporto della Commissione Finanziaria alla Conferenza di Genova', April 1922, in ASBI, Azzolini, 111. For an account of the Genoa Conference, see the chapter 'International Relations: To and from Genoa', in R. S. Sayers, *The Bank of England 1891–1944* (Cambridge, Cambridge University Press, 1976), vol. I.

7 See Resolution no. 2, Resolution no. 7 and the previously quoted Resolution no. 11 of the above-mentioned 'Rapporto della Commissione Finanziaria'.

8 M. Alberti, *La guerra delle monete* (Como, Cavalleri, 1937), vol. I, p. 32.

9 Fascist 'philosophy' on this point is summed up well by Spinedi: 'While on balance we are opposed to the idea of a London-led gold exchange standard which amounts to entrusting the management of a country's own gold to larger financial centres, we realize that it is not always possible in every case to "manage on one's own". There is a minimum level of structural development which needs to be reached before a country can stand on its own feet and it seems that for the present this is not the case in Albania.' F. Spinedi, 'La Banca Nazionale d'Albania nel mercato finanziario mondiale', in *Rassegna Monetaria*, 1936.

10 See Chapter 1.

11 Calmès Report, p. 29.

12 Ibid., p. 20.

13 Ibid., pp. 22–28.

14 G. Di Nardi, 'Le finanze pubbliche dell'Albania', in *Principii di economia albanese* (Padua, Cedam, 1940), p. 245.

15 Foreign banks were present in the country, but only in border areas: the Serbo-Albanian Bank in Shkodër and the Bank of Athens in Korça and Durrës. See G. Borgatta, 'Moneta e credito in Albania', in *Principii di economia albanese* (Padua, Cedam, 1940), p. 191.

16 Calmès Report, pp. 20–22.

17 Ibid., pp. 29–31.

Chapter 3

1 An anonymous handwritten account in the archives of the Italian Foreign Ministry, apparently of 1932, which to all intents and purposes rewrites the whole history of Italo-Albanian relations after the advent of Fascism, states in

fact that 'we must not forget that our policy in Albania always followed two separate lines, one which reflected the exclusive relationship between Rome and Tiranë, and one which reflected Rome's relationship with all the other European governments, who were not disposed to give our expansion into Albania free reign' (ASMAE 31–45, 'Albania', 11).

2 It is a widely held opinion among current historians that Fascism's rise to power did not constitute a change of direction in Italian foreign policy. Mussolini's foreign policy was in keeping with the tendency towards nationalism which had already been strong in Italian political tradition even before the First World War, though this war certainly fuelled it further through the myth of a 'mutilated victory'. The claims related not only to the 'unredeemed territories' of the Italian peninsula but also, more generally, to Italy having a wider and more active role in European affairs. The political situation created in Europe by the First World War was a determining factor in focusing the Fascists' revisionist aims and economic expansionism on the Balkans, where the rule of the fallen Austro-Hungarian Empire had been replaced by a collection of barely viable states, in which ethnic unrest and revanchist movements were brewing. Their instability generated a power vacuum. Of the states which had been accustomed to supremacy in the region, the Habsburg Empire had disintegrated, Germany had been reduced to impotence by military disarmament, and Russia had retreated into diplomatic isolation. As has been observed, the 'pendulum of power had clearly swung towards the West'. On the first phase of Fascist foreign policy, see R. De Felice, *Mussolini il duce: gli anni del consenso 1929–1936* (Turin, Einaudi, 1974); Seton-Watson, *Italy from Liberalism to Fascism*; Bosworth, *Italy and the Approach of the First World War*; R. De Felice, 'Alcune osservazioni sulla politica estera mussoliniana', in *Il regime fascista* (Bologna, il Mulino, 1974); Cassels, *Mussolini's Early Diplomacy*; E. M. Robertson, *Mussolini as Empire-Builder* (New York, St Martin's Press, 1977); G. Rumi, 'Revisionismo fascista ed espansione coloniale', in *Il regime fascista* (Bologna, Il Mulino, 1974); A. Lyttelton, *The Seizure of Power: Fascism in Italy 1919–1929* (London, Weidenfeld & Nicolson, 1973); M. Donosti (pseudonym of Mario Luciolli), *Mussolini e l'Europa: la politica estera fascista* (Rome, Leonardo, 1945); D. Mack Smith, *Mussolini's Roman Empire* (Harmondsworth, Penguin, 1977); H. J. Burgwin, *Il revisionismo fascista* (Milan, Feltrinelli, 1979); E. Di Nolfo, *Mussolini e la politica estera italiana 1919–1933* (Padua, Cedam, 1960); G. Carocci, *La politica estera dell'Italia fascista* (Bari, Laterza, 1969).

3 The Hunger Report of 31 August 1923: Société des Nations, Premier rapport du Conseiller financier après du gouvernement albanais, *Journal Officiel*, January 1924.

4 A copy of the plan, drawn up in Geneva, is in the Bank of Italy's archives (ASBI Studi, 'Albania').

5 BoE, OV116/1, undated internal memorandum.

6 See the previously cited account in ASMAE.

7 PRO, FO 371/9639, Eyres to FO, 20 February 1924.

8 See PRO, FO 371/9642: Eyres to FO, 9 and 10 March 1924; 4th Hunger Report to the League, 14 March 1924; Drummond to Miles Lampson (Lampson was a Counsellor at the Foreign Office), 26 March 1924; Eyres to Lampson, 21 April 1924; Albanian government to the League's Secretary-General, 22 April 1924.

9 PRO, FO 371/9643, Eyres to MacDonald, 2 April 1924.

10 PRO, FO 371/0642, Lampson to Drummond, 9 June 1924.
11 PRO, FO 371/9642, Niemeyer to the Council, 10 June 1924.
12 PRO, FO 371/9641, Eyres to FO, 18 December 1924; FO to Eyres, 20 December 1924.
13 PRO, FO 371/9643, Chamberlain to Eyres, 28 March 1925.
14 See Alberti, in his inaugural speech for the Bank in Rome, 2 September 1925 (the minutes of the inaugural meeting are in ASBI, Baffi papers) and in *La guerra delle monete*, vol. II, p. 301. See also: L. Amoroso, 'Il contributo italiano allo sviluppo economico dell'Albania negli ultimi quindici anni', in *Rivista italiana di scienze economiche*, April 1939; 'Balcanicus', 'L'opera economica e finanziaria dell'Italia in Albania', in *Sud*, May–June 1927; P. Formentini, 'La Banca Nazionale d'Albania e il riordinamento monetario albanese', in *Rivista Bancaria*, 1927; A. Gulinelli, 'L'Albania e il suo riordinamento monetario', in *Giornale degli Economisti e Rivista di Statistica*, September 1927, and 'L'azione italiana in Albania', in *Rivista di politica economica*, VII–VIII, 1927; F. Nobili Massuero, 'La rinascita economica dell'Albania', in *Rivista di politica economica*, 1927; R. Martino, 'La Banca Nazionale d'Albania', in *L'Italia d'oltremare*, August 1942.
15 The events linked to Zogu's relationships with foreign powers, in particular Yugoslavia, Italy and the United Kingdom, and his increasing closeness to Italy, have been brought to light both by a substantial output of memoirs and by thorough historical studies. These can be referred to for a more in-depth discussion of political and diplomatic developments. In addition to the works of Swire, Pollo and Puto, Skendi, Cassels, Burgwin, Di Nolfo, Carocci, and more recently Vickers and Tomes, quoted above, see also, A. Lessona, *Memorie* (Florence, Sansoni, 1958); F. Jacomoni di San Savino, *La politica dell'Italia in Albania* (Bologna, Cappelli, 1965); P. Pastorelli, *Italia e Albania 1924–1927. Origini diplomatiche del Trattato di Tirana del 22 novembre 1927* (Florence, Biblioteca della Rivista di studi politici internazionali, 1967).
16 See the account in ASMAE quoted in note 1.
17 Which he reports as 300,000 lire.
18 PRO, FO 371/9639, Eyres to FO, 15 and 20 February 1924.
19 PRO, FO 371/9642, Hunger to the League, 13 May 1924.
20 There is a description of the treaty in *L'Albania economica*, ch. VIII. Albanian historiography considers this agreement as the beginning of the disastrous open-door policy towards Italy. It was only ratified after Zogu regained power from Fan Noli in the spring of 1925 (Pollo and Puto, *The History of Albania*, p. 191; Swire, *Albania*, p. 424) – see later. From Italy's point of view, entering into this trade agreement and others like it can be seen in the context of its re-entering into international economic arrangements after the First World War. As F. Guarneri writes in *Battaglie economiche* (Milan, Garzanti, 1953), vol. I, pp. 95 *et seq.*, in the post-war years and up to the end of 1922 Italy was carrying on commercial relations with other countries amidst a situation which was inherently precarious, given the almost total lack of any policy for making trade agreements with those countries, and this made getting its exports off the ground again extremely difficult. Under pressure from Confindustria and Assonime, the trade associations of manufacturers and of joint-stock companies, it came round to intergovernmental negotiations, which resulted in numerous trade agreements, dealing mainly with the subjects of reducing import duties and barriers.

21 The text of the letter is reproduced in ASMAE 19–30, 'Albania', 726. Two days before, Alberti had written to Janssen in order to have a better understanding of the other members' attitude – within the Finance Committee – towards the Italian initiative of creating a bank of issue in Albania. See LON, box 375/10/29441/19892.

22 The title of the head of the Bank was Director-General until 1928, when it was changed to Governor.

23 See PRO, FO 371/9644: Robert Graham, the British Ambassador in Rome, to FO, 16 April 1924; Harold Nicolson (FO) to Niemeyer (Treasury), 24 April 1924; Niemeyer to Nicolson, 26 April 1924.

24 Marxist Albanian historiography (see Pollo and Puto, *The History of Albania*, pp. 192–196) exalts the government of Fan Noli (dubbed the 'red bishop'), as a revolutionary experience which was both anti-feudal and anti-imperialist, contrasting it with the dark years of Zogu's reign, and cites as an example of his decidedly leftist approach his recognition of the Soviet Union, an 'unheard-of step', which caused outrage in Europe: see p. 213; see also J. Myrdal and G. Kessle, *Albania Defiant* (New York and London, Monthly Review Press, 1976), p. 112. It is worth recalling that similar recognition had in fact already come from the British Labour government (6 August 1924) and, moreover, the Italian government, right-wing though it was, was among the first to recognize the Soviet Union. The fact remains, however, that even Swire, whose interpretation of Albanian politics is far from Marxist, stresses that the intentions of the Fan Noli government were honest, even if his programmes were not totally new (Swire, *Albania*, p. 444).

25 See Cassels, *Mussolini's Early Diplomacy*, pp. 243–244, and Pollo and Puto, *The History of Albania*, p. 194, for an opposite view.

26 Pastorelli, *Italia e Albania*, p. 57.

27 See Lessona, *Memorie*, p. 28.

28 Cassels, *Mussolini's Early Diplomacy*, p. 247.

29 Pastorelli, *Italia e Albania*, p. 99.

30 Di Nolfo, *Mussolini e la politica estera italiana*, p. 183.

31 PRO, FO 371/9643, Parr to FO, 15 August 1925.

32 Pastorelli, for example, gives a different interpretation of his role in the economic treaty with Zogu (*Italia e Albania*, p. 130).

33 An expression used by Cassels in *Mussolini's Early Diplomacy*, p. 246.

34 The text is reproduced in Pastorelli, *Italia e Albania*, p. 104.

35 PRO, FO 371/10658, Eyres to FO, 5 February 1925; Parr to FO, 8 February 1925; FO to Eyres, 9 and 16 February 1925; FO to Eyres, 25 February 1925; the Ethelburg Syndicate to FO, 27 May 1925; FO to Sir Francis Voules of the Ethelburg Syndicate, 2 June 1925. The Italians assumed, probably wrongly, that the Midland Bank was behind the initiative: see a telegram to Mussolini of 22 February 1925 from the Italian Chargé d'affaires in Albania, Ugo Sola (ASMAE 19–30, 'Albania', 726). As for Gottlieb, a telegram to Mussolini of 26 February (see same folder) from the Ambassador to London, Della Torretta, states, 'it is unlikely that the Midland would take seriously any proposals . . . by the person in question'.

36 The offer is detailed in the telegram of 24 February from Sola to the Italian Foreign Ministry (ASMAE 19–30, 'Albania', 726).

37 The concession was granted on 2 March 1925, for 37,000 hectares, in the Patos oil field.

38 See, for example, the telegram of 3 March 1924 from Italy's Foreign Ministry to the Italian Legation in Durrës (ASMAE 19–30, 'Albania', 726), and the telegram of 24 February 1925 from Mussolini to the Legation (same folder).
39 That this payment was related to the 1923 sale of the Mat woods is confirmed in the 'Preliminary summary of expenses and works carried out in Albania', in ASMAE 31–45, 'Albania', 81, on which we will dwell more fully later on. The oil concession was for 47,213 hectares: see C. Alimenti, *La questione petrolifera italiana* (Turin, Einaudi, 1937), p. 94.
40 Lessona adds that the 'pay-off' for Zogu did not end with the sale of the Mat woods. Shortly afterwards, another 6 million lire were hastily scraped together, with Mussolini's personal intervention, and handed over to Zogu in great secret. Zogu said he needed the money to pay his army, who would otherwise have mutinied (Lessona, *Memorie*, pp. 100–106). According to the summary quoted in note 39, the payment, which was written off, was for 5 million lire.
41 Alberti, *La guerra delle monete*, vol. II, pp. 308–309. It is worth remembering that Swire reports Zogu as having said to Eyres, after signing the contract for the foundation of the Bank, 'Never will I fall into the arms of Italy' (*Albania*, p. 460).
42 Professor Sauser-Hall, who, as we shall see later on, took on the task of arbitrating the opposite claims of Italy and Albania on the National Bank of Albania's gold after the Second World War, observed that the League of Nations did not in fact confer a mandate on Italy. Its approval was at the most a 'moral' one and could be linked to the special recognition of Italy's interests in Albania sanctioned by the Conference of the Ambassadors in Paris in 1921.
43 See the table below:

Italian exports into certain countries 1918–1925 (in millions of Italian lire)

	Total	France	Germany	UK	USA	Switzerland
1918	3,305	1,207		727	169	410
1919	6,004	1,403	85	773	630	786
1920	11,628	1,696	574	1,379	939	1,505
1921	8,043	967	814	795	1,084	831
1922	9,160	1,365	972	1,117	1,018	1,208
1923	10,950	1,581	697	1,211	1,523	1,201
1924	14,270	1,823	1,565	1,493	1,239	1,612
1925	18,170	2,024	2,025	1,852	1,896	1,635

Source: ISTAT, *Sommario di statistiche storiche dell'Italia 1861–1975* (Rome, 1976).

NB: In terms of the percentage breakdown of the exports total, we see that exports to France, the main destination for Italian exports, drop from 23.4 per cent of the total in 1919 to 14.9 per cent in 1922 and 11.1 per cent in 1925. The corresponding percentages for Great Britain are 12.9 per cent, 12.2 per cent and 10.2 per cent, and for Switzerland, another of Italy's major export markets, 13 per cent, 13.1 per cent and 8.9 per cent. The figures for the USA, however, remain pretty stable, at 10.5 per cent, 11.1 per cent and 10.4 per cent.

44 G. Carocci, 'Appunti sull'imperialismo fascista degli anni 20', in *Il regime fascista* (Bologna, Il Mulino, 1974), pp. 426–427 and 433.

45 Ibid., p. 417; see also Lyttleton, *The Seizure of Power*, see p. 685 of the Italian edition: *La conquista del potere: Il Fascismo dal 1919 al 1929* (Rome and Bari, Laterza, 1974).
46 N. La Marca, *Italia e Balcani fra le due guerre. Saggio di una ricerca sui tentativi italiani di espansione economica nel Sud Est europeo fra le due guerre* (Rome, Bulzoni, 1979).
47 Ibid., p. 50.
48 Ibid., p. 78.
49 This was for loans to Bulgaria, Greece and Romania.
50 Figures drawn from Royal Institute of International Affairs, *The Balkan States*, pp. 142–145.
51 See pp. 14–19 of La Marca's study, *Italia e Balcani*, for more details.
52 Ibid., p. 24.
53 Carocci, *La politica estera dell'Italia fascista*, p. 37. See also Cassels, *Mussolini's Early Diplomacy*, p. 248. A note in the Italian Foreign Ministry's archives fully confirms this thesis. Alberti pointed out that the draft agreement being negotiated with the Albanian government entailed conditions which for Italy were 'neither sufficiently advantageous nor such as to augur an easy conclusion of the affair' (ASMAE 19–30, 'Albania', 726). After the agreement had been finalized, the Managing Director of the Bank, Amedeo Gambino, in a memo of 1926 to the Chairman of the SVEA, observed that it had been plain from the start that the ties being formed in Albania did not entail any financial benefit whatsoever, only enormous burdens, which could only be counterbalanced by advantages of a political nature (ASMAE 19–30, 'Albania', 734).
54 As we shall shortly see in more detail, the burden of the operation fell, in fact, upon the Italian Treasury from the start.
55 Carocci, *La politica estera dell'Italia fascista*, p. 264. In his *Taccuini*, Alberto Pirelli makes explicit reference to the lack of enthusiasm for economic penetration into Albania. See *Taccuini 1922–1943* (Bologna, Il Mulino, 1984), p. 66.

Chapter 4

1 The complete documentation covering the Bank's formation and the introduction of the new currency system can be found in the Bank of Italy's historical archives.
2 PRO, FO 371/10658; see Eyres to FO, 18 March 1925, and FO's comments.
3 On this point, see ASMAE 19–30, 'Albania', 726. It contains the minutes of Alberti's meeting with Antonievič.
4 Telegram in ASMAE 19–30, 'Albania', 726.
5 The details of the allocation and the pressure exerted by 'third party' countries are in a confidential memo of 1 May 1925, held in ASMAE 19–30, 'Albania', 726.
6 PRO, FO 371/10658, Parr to Austen Chamberlain, 29 August 1925. In the archives of the Bank of Italy, this position appears as unfilled. It is probable that, following the scandal, Eqerem Libohova had to resign.
7 See the handwritten memorandum of 1932 in ASMAE 31–45, 'Albania', 11. Note the radical assessment by Pollo and Puto: 'The great Italian banks succeeded in practice in securing almost all the title-deeds through fraud and corruption' (*The History of Albania*, p. 201). Swire also speaks of Libohova in terms of corruption (*Albania*, p. 466).

8 PRO, FO 371/10658, Eyres to FO, 16 November and 14 December 1925.
9 PRO, FO 371/10658, Parr to Nicolson, 15 August 1925. On this point see also Tomes, *King Zog*, p. 81.
10 Letter in ASMAE 19–30, 'Albania', 726. In a Bank of Albania memo of 5 February 1945, we read that 'It was political expedience which motivated this concealment' (i.e. purchasing shares under the name of the Italian financial group). See ASBI, Einaudi, 92.
11 See the 'Initial estimate of expenses and works carried out in Albania from 1925 to the present day', June 1938, in ASMAE 31–45, 'Albania', 81. The amount would be equivalent to 9.4 million euros in today's money.
12 The first board of directors appointed at the Bank's foundation was made up as follows:
Chairman: Mario Alberti (of the Credito Italiano, appointed honorary minister plenipotentiary by the Italian government);
Vice-chairmen: Federico Brunner (Banque Commerciale de Bâle), E. de Wouters d'Oplinter (Banque Belge pour l'Etranger);
Board members: Pietro Fenoglio (Banca Commerciale Italiana), Giuseppe Bianchini (other Italian banks), Ugo Viali (in reality, a dummy for the Italian group), Lalé Zuber (Yugoslav banks);
Secretary: Amedeo Gambino;
(The post of board member to be designated by the Albanian government was left temporarily unfilled and was filled at a later date by Stefano Zurani)
Auditors: Vincenzo Azzolini, Ajet Bey Libohova, Franco Marmont;
Substitute auditors: Giuseppe Marino, Massimo Aureli.
13 ASBI, Azzolini, 97.
14 On this point, see Skendi, *Albania*, p. 211.
15 The Albanian state would also receive 10 per cent of the Bank's profits (point 16 of the Agreement, article 54 of the Law and the Charter). On the subject of Alberti's views, see an undated handwritten memo in ASMAE 19–30, 'Albania', 726.
16 In the major countries, the exchange rate after the war was well below pre-war parity. In Italy, depreciation reached its worst level in 1920, with a devaluation of 82 per cent; in France, it was in 1926, with a 90 per cent devaluation; in Great Britain, it was in 1920, with a depreciation of 34 per cent in relation to gold parity before the war; and in the USA the worst was in 1917, with a 42 per cent devaluation. See R. Sédillot, *Toutes les monnaies du monde* (Paris, Recueil Sirey, 1955).
17 Named after Alexander the Great. In the Albanian popular tradition he is named Leka I Madh (Leka the Great, Leka being a nickname for Alexander).
18 The profits arising from the minting and note-issuing rights were to be divided equally between the Bank and the Albanian government (see above).
19 See the handwritten memorandum quoted above: ASMAE 31–45, 'Albania', 11.
20 See the somewhat irritated letter from Mussolini to de' Stefani of 17 June 1925, i.e. shortly before de' Stefani was replaced by Volpi: ASBI, de' Stefani, 200.
21 On Alberti's mission to New York to negotiate the $50 million loan, see Romano, *Giuseppe Volpi*, pp. 132–133.
22 See two memoranda from Morgan's of 15 and 23 June 1925 in ASBI, de' Stefani, 200.
23 See the account in ASMAE quoted in note 1 of Chapter 3. On the attempt to place the bonds for the loan with Italian state-controlled bodies, see the

telegram of 25 January 1929 from Mussolini to the National Bank of Albania, in ACS, BNA-SVEA, folder 39.1 (provisional), and letter of 19 August 1929 from Stringher to Paolo Grassi, Director-General of the Treasury, in ASBI, Introna, 19.

24 On the granting of the SVEA loan and the details of it, see A. Gambino, 'Le relazioni economiche fra l'Italia e l'Albania', in *Rivista internazionale di scienze sociali*, 1940, pp. 408–423; *Un decennio di vita della SVEA* (Rome, La Libreria dello Stato, 1936), especially pp. 19–20; 'Note esplicative sulla convenzione per il prestito per i lavori pubblici dell'Albania', in ASBI, Beneduce, reel 87.

25 See the undated handwritten memorandum quoted in note 15.

26 S. Homer and R. Sylla, *A History of Interest Rates*, New Brunswick and London, Rutgers University Press, 1991. See chapters XIX and XX.

27 Royal Institute of International Affairs, *The Problem of International Investment*, London, Oxford University Press, 1937, p. 135.

28 See Swire, *Albania*, p. 462.

29 See Chapter 9.

30 In today's terms, we would think of a loan of approximately 2 billion euros.

31 See an undated memorandum from Gambino to the Chairman of the SVEA, in ASMAE 19–30, 'Albania', 734.

32 See Gambino, 'Le relazioni economiche fra l'Italia e l'Albania', pp. 408–409.

33 On this point, see Di Nolfo, *Mussolini e la politica estera italiana*, p. 184. The provisions of the treaty, which had no deadline, covered the type of military aid to be given to Albania; the action to be taken in the event of war; the scenario of an attack on Italy by one of the Balkan countries; and territorial rewards in the event of a victory. Furthermore, Albania undertook not to make any military pacts without Italy's participation. See ASMAE 31–45, 'Albania', 81.

34 M. H. H. McCartney and P. Cremona, Italy's Foreign and Colonial Policy (London, Oxford University Press, 1928), p. 111.

35 The text of the pact can be found in Swire, *Albania*, pp. 478–479.

36 Burgwin, *Il revisionismo fascista*, p. 117.

37 See Cassels, *Mussolini's Early Diplomacy*, p. 332; Burgwin, *Il revisionismo fascista*, p. 118.

38 For the text of the treaty, again see Swire, *Albania*, pp. 509–512.

39 Thus Sola, as quoted by Swire in *Albania*, p. 512.

40 On Mussolini's intention to respect Albania's independence with the Treaty of Tiranë, Pastorelli is categorical: 'If we looked at Italo-Albanian relations in the light of that event [the Italian occupation], and thrown off track by current interpretations, we would find it hard to believe Mussolini's plans of 1927, were it not for the solidity of the documentation. It is without doubt one of the greatest surprises kept preserved in our sources' (*Italia e Albania*, p. 508).

41 G. Zamboni, *Mussolini Expansionpolitik auf dem Balkan* (Hamburg, H. Buske, 1970), as quoted by De Felice in *Mussolini il duce: gli anni del consenso*, p. 347. On this line of interpretation, see also Pollo and Puto, *The History of Albania*, pp. 203–204.

42 Burgwin, *Il revisionismo fascista*, p. 137.

43 Swire, *Albania*, p. 521.

Chapter 5

1 'The Albanian Lek', in *International Currency Review*, July 1977.

2 See ASBI, Azzolini, 111.

3 See Sédillot, *Toutes les monnaies du monde.*
4 Calmès Report, p. 20.
5 Ibid., p. 6.
6 Ibid., p. 21.
7 Ibid., p. 19.
8 This political aspect should be kept in mind with respect to the events of the following years also. The words of Mario Alberti, the 'founder' of the bank, are quite telling: 'One might consider the example of currency stability in Albania too small to prove the point. What does prove the point however, is the different manner in which Britain and Italy, as principal benefactors, conceived their duties. The Bank of England mobilized the full force of its influence and pressure in making certain that the peripheral currencies should go the same way as the pound. The Bank of Italy (since it is from there that the Italian group of the Bank of Albania ultimately takes its lead) has made it a point of honour to defend the integrity of the gold base with which Albania's currency began. Two different policies, two different methods, two different moral standards' (*La guerra delle monete*, vol. II, p. 302).
9 See P. Frasca Polara, 'Il commercio estero e la politica degli scambi in Albania', in *Rivista di politica economica*, 1932, for a detailed analysis of Albania's imports and exports.
10 BoE, OV 116/1, Memorandum of the Overseas and Foreign Department, 12 April 1939.
11 Frasca Polara, 'Il commercio estero e la politica degli scambi in Albania', p. 962.
12 The following observations are largely drawn from Royal Institute of International Affairs, *The Balkan States*, part II. See also Lampe and Jackson, *Balkan Economic History*, ch. XII.
13 The formation of public bodies for purchasing agricultural produce at state-subsidized prices signalled an important turning point in the economic policies of the Balkan countries, so much so that it was defined by Lampe and Jackson as 'The genesis of statism in South-Eastern Europe' (see *Balkan Economic History*, p. 435).
14 See an undated memorandum, probably of 1926, in ASMAE 19–30, 'Albania', 734. The arrangement for servicing the SVEA loan stipulated a yearly payment of 5.6 million Albanian francs (see a memorandum from the Bank of Albania dated 5 February 1945 in ASBI, Einaudi, 92).
15 See *Un decennio di vita della SVEA*; and Gambino, 'Le relazioni economiche fra l'Italia e l'Albania'.
16 BoE, OV 116/1, Memorandum of the Overseas and Foreign Department, 12 April 1939.
17 For information on the negotiations and the decision on the loan, see ASMAE 31–45, 'Albania', 4. The agreement for the loan was finalized on 24 June 1931.
18 ASMAE 31–45, 'Albania', 4, telegram to the Foreign Ministry of 8 July 1931.
19 ASMAE 31–45, 'Albania', 15: see the correspondence between di Soragna and the Foreign Ministry.
20 See ASMAE 31–45, 'Albania', 14.
21 See Frasca Polara, 'Il commercio estero e la politica degli scambi in Albania', p. 964.
22 See Chapter 3.
23 These included: Austria, Belgium, Bulgaria, Czechoslovakia, Germany, Egypt, Japan, Great Britain, Luxembourg, the British East Indies, Romania, the USA,

Switzerland and Hungary (Frasca Polara, 'Il commercio estero e la politica degli scambi in Albania', p. 964).

24 See Frasca Polara, 'Il commercio estero e la politica degli scambi in Albania', p. 966.

25 These events and those which follow are drawn from a memorandum of October 1932 in ASMAE 31–45, 'Albania', 14.

26 Ibid., p. 4.

27 See the report for 1933 by the Italian Legation in Tiranë in ASMAE 31–35, 'Albania', 33. Zog's attitude towards Italy during these negotiations for a customs union is viewed by modern Albanian historians as one of the sovereign's few displays of economic independence: 'At last Zogu realized his creditor had him by the throat . . . Zogu summoned up his courage and refused the Italians' proposition' (Pollo and Puto, *The History of Albania*, p. 206). It is interesting to note that the attempts at a customs union pursued by the Balkan countries during the same period, with a view to greater economic integration and in the wake of the protection of the British and French markets, ran aground. On the possible causes, see Lampe and Jackson, *Balkan Economic History*, pp. 457–458.

28 Albania's foreign policy was showing increasing signs of a desire to be free from excessive dependence on Italy, to limit its influence to what was helpful for the country, and to cultivate the friendship of France and Britain. It is in this context that we see the failure to renew the friendship pact of 1926 (see the report for 1933 by the Italian Legation in Tiranë, in ASMAE 31–45, 'Albania', 33). The following year, Zog began to decrease the number of Italian instructors in his army. The regime retorted by organizing a naval demonstration off Durrës (see Robertson, *Mussolini as Empire-Builder*, p. 79). This was the short-lived phase in which, owing partly to internal pressures, Zog conducted a more 'liberal' internal policy and adopted a more autonomous stance on the foreign front, a phase which was also marked by the replacement of Pandeli Evangjeli in government with Mehdi Frashëri, who was seen as a liberal (Pollo and Puto, *The History of Albania*, p. 209).

29 ASMAE 31–45, 'Albania', 27, telegram of 12 August 1933. The same folder contains the correspondence relating to King Zog's approaches. The Italian Minister in Albania, Koch, wrote to Rome in spring 1933, saying that Zog had been advised by the Yugoslavs and the British to approach the League of Nations in the light of pressure from the Italians regarding the repayment of the SVEA loan, which would have led to a recognition of Albania's neutrality and therefore to the opportunity to economize on the huge military expenses. In July of the same year, the Italian legations in Belgrade, Vienna, Bucharest and Prague sent word of rumours of Albania's steps towards obtaining a loan from the 'Balkan Entente' or from Yugoslavia. An unofficial attempt led by a certain Hobdari, Chairman of SITA (Società Impianti Elettrici Albania), the Albanian electrical installations company, did not fare any better. He travelled to London in April 1933 to negotiate a loan for 18 million Albanian francs, at 6.5 per cent interest, to be guaranteed by the salt marshes of Vlorë, to which SITA held the concessionary rights. However, according to the reports from the Italian Embassy in London, the Bank of England would have nothing to do with it, and the sum requested was considered by the City to be 'completely disproportionate to the credit which Albanian finances enjoy'. Moving on to Paris, Hobdari paid FF150,000 and issued bills for a further FF350,000, for the purchase of the majority share of the Crédit Français pour le Commerce

et l'Industrie, which was in turn to float bonds on the French market for FF5 million, on behalf of SITA. However, SITA's new board were unwilling to enter into the loan and the deal did not go through, but not without the immediate loss to SITA of the FF150,000 and a notice of protest on the bills issued by Hobdari. Hobdari's dealings can be found in folders 27 and 42. On the Hobdari story, and the involvement of the Bank of Italy's office in London and the Bank of England, see also BoE, OV 116/1.

30 BoE, OV 116/1, Overseas and Foreign Department memo, 12 April 1939.

31 Pollo and Puto, *The History of Albania*, p. 210.

32 See 'Agreements of 19.3.36', in ASMAE 31–45, 'Albania', 81, but see also Borgatta, 'Moneta e credito in Albania', pp. 211–212, and Royal Institute of International Affairs, *The Balkan States*, p. 142.

33 BoE, OV 116/1, Overseas Department memo, 11 December 1937.

34 BoE, OV 116/1, memo, 24 August 1943.

35 Ibid.

36 Camera di Commercio Italo-Orientale, *Il commercio estero dell'Albania e i rapporti commerciali con l'Italia* (Bari, 1934). See in particular pp. 1–5, 8 and 15–17.

37 See Gambino, 'Le relazioni economiche fra l'Italia e l'Albania', pp. 419–420.

38 Ibid., p. 421.

39 The Chamber of the Deputies had been abolished with a government's Royal Decree of 2 March 1939. The Chamber of Fasces and Corporations, a typical Fascist institution, which took its place, was later dissolved after the fall of Fascism, on 2 August 1943.

40 Part of the speech is recorded in the National Bank of Albania's report for 1938, in ASBI-Rapporti con l'Estero, 297.

41 See the 'Initial estimate of expenses and works carried out in Albania from 1925 to the present day', June 1938, in ASMAE 31–45, 'Albania', 81.

42 See ASMAE 31–45, 'Albania', 81.

43 The totals for the expenses – over the 14-year period from 1925 to 1938 – have been adjusted for inflation, in order to make them homogeneous.

44 Société des Nations, *Annuaire Statistique 1931–1932*, Geneva, 1932; *Annuaire Statistique 1938–1939*, Geneva, 1939.

45 See Borgatta, 'Moneta e credito in Albania', p. 199.

46 RDL (Royal Decree Law), 21 December 1927, no. 2325.

47 RDL, 21 July 1935, no. 1293.

48 RDL, 5 October 1936, no. 1745.

49 ASBI, Azzolini, 97, confidential note to Thaon di Revel, the Finance Minister, of 15 June 1938.

50 For more details on the reserve management policy, see Chapter 6.

Chapter 6

1 R. De Felice, *Mussolini il duce: lo Stato totalitario 1936–1940* (Turin, Einaudi, 1981), pp. 59–61. 'Men like Beneduce, or Arrigo Serpieri, or Carlo Petrocchi (the author of bold reforms of the Public Works administration, in 1922), like Pio Galletti and Tito Livio Mesina (key figures in the independent road-building agency formed in 1928) end up carrying out their own vocation as technocrats within the context of a regime which, especially within the ministries devoted to the major public services, seems to elect the "neutral" solution of a technico-administrative management of political power' (see the

paper by G. Melis, 'La "cultura dell'efficienza" nell'Amministrazione italiana dopo la prima guerra mondiale', Paper presented at the IRI conference in Caserta in honour of A. Beneduce, November 1983). I would place Alberti in this same category of individuals. See also the paper by P. Melograni, 'Alberto Beneduce: l'adesione al regime mussoliniano', given at the same conference.

2 R. Sarti, *Fascism and the Industrial Leadership in Italy 1919–1940* (Berkeley, University of California Press, 1971), p. 43.

3 De Felice, *Mussolini il duce: lo Stato totalitario*, p. 62.

4 ASMAE 19–30, 'Albania', 734, undated memorandum from Gambino.

5 Pastorelli, *Italia e Albania*, pp. 293–296.

6 In *La politica estera dell'Italia fascista*, Carocci emphasizes the heterogeneous nature of the economic and political circles which were involved in dealing with the Albanian question (p. 264).

7 For a bibliography of his output, see *Rivista italiana di scienze economiche*, January 1939, pp. 82–83.

8 Proof that Alberti was not a passive force vis-à-vis the regime can be found in an episode recorded by De Felice (*Mussolini il duce: gli anni del consenso*, p. 184). After the publication in November 1930 of an article by Alberti which was critical of the regime's economic policy, Mussolini wrote to the Prefect in Milan, suggesting that he should summon Alberti and give him an official warning to change his attitude, which supposedly could have had 'incalculably damaging consequences'. Mussolini reproved Alberti, stressing above all the fact that the criticisms were coming from a man who 'has been given important missions by the Fascist government'. (Specifically, Alberti had criticized the top management of the Credito Italiano, from which he had resigned in 1929. Possibly because of that article, Alberti left the presidency of the National Bank of Albania in early 1931. See on this point A. Roselli, *Il Governatore Vincenzo Azzolini 1931–1944* (Rome and Bari, Laterza, 2000), pp. 36–37.

9 The lawyer Giuseppe Bianchini, President of the Italian Bankers' Association, took over as President of the Bank in 1931, followed in 1935 by Senator Antonio Mosconi, who had been Finance Minister from 1928 to 1932.

10 The main source is the documents of the National Bank of Albania itself, held in ASBI, Baffi papers.

11 In 1934 a branch of the Banque d'Exportation de Belgrade opened in Tiranë; in 1937 the Albanian Agricultural Bank began trading; also in 1937 the Banco di Napoli – Albania, which was to take over the Agricultural Bank in 1939, began its activities. The Serbo-Albanian Bank, which had been among the founding banks of the Albanian Bank of Issue, operated in the border region at Shkodër, and the Bank of Athens operated in Korça and Durrës (see Borgatta, 'Moneta e credito in Albania', pp. 191 and 222 *et seq*., and Skendi, *Albania*, p. 213).

12 Instead of immediately declaring the old currency out of circulation, it was decided to reabsorb it gradually, in order to avoid the resistance and mistrust towards the new currency which private holders would probably show (Borgatta, 'Moneta e credito in Albania', p. 197).

13 A comparison between the annual figures for the 'foreign' component and those for the balance of payments shows that the two do not coincide. The divergence can be explained by the following reasons: (a) the data for the balance of payments may be 'economic' and not 'monetary'; and (b) the statistics come from different sources (the Bank of Albania and the League of Nations).

14 On this point, see the remarks on a study carried out by the League of Nations made by Paolo Baffi in 'La componente esterna della liquidità e le regole della condotta monetaria', in *Studi sulla moneta* (Milan, Giuffrè, 1965). See esp. p. 37. An excellent description of the mechanism of the gold standard is in Eichengreen, *Globalizing Capital*, ch. II.
15 See later on in this chapter for the discount rate.
16 In 'Moneta e credito in Albania', pp. 214–215.
17 G. Toniolo, *L'economia dell'Italia fascista* (Rome and Bari, Laterza, 1980), p. 189.
18 ASBI, Azzolini, 97, minutes of the Bank's board meeting of 8 October 1934.
19 On Albania's budget, see the previously quoted study by Di Nardi, 'Le finanze pubbliche dell'Albania'. This explains why, during the phase in which the flow of capital from Italy dried up, the foreign component had a heavy deflationary impact.
20 Speech for the inauguration of the Durrës branch on 9 November 1928, in *La guerra delle monete*, vol. II, pp. 305–307.
21 'Our aspiration is to bring the cost of money here to the same level as in our neighbouring Italy': from the speech by the President, Mosconi, for the inauguration of the Bank's new headquarters in Tiranë in September 1938. See ASBI, Azzolini, 97.
22 See the table below:

Real discount rate in Italy and Albania

	1928	1929	1930	1931	1932	1933	1934	1935	1936	1937	1938
Albania	5.0	13.0	20.9	6.1	26.5	30.1	18.3	–2.5	–4.3	2.5	8.2
Italy	9.7	11.6	15.9	19.2	12.0	13.3	4.6	–5.0	–7.9	–13.0	–1.9

Sources: For Italy: Toniolo, *L'economia dell'Italia fascista*, p. 190, for the years 1930–1936; Société des Nations, *Annuaire Statistique 1931–1932*, Geneva, 1932, and *Annuaire Statistique 1937–1938*, Geneva, 1938, for the other years. For Albania: See Table 6.3.

23 The view of the Communist government of Albania, as expressed in a memorandum of 1 June 1945, was that the gold basis of the monetary system was laid in the emigrants' remittances, particularly from America. This strong currency inflow, including silver and gold, was withdrawn by the Italians, against paper currency: see memo in BoE, OV 116/1. According to Carocci (in *La politica estera dell'Italia fascista*, p. 37), the main aim of the Bank of Albania was precisely that of rounding up the precious metal coins circulating in the country and substituting them for paper money. He states that it was the Italians' realization that their expansion into Albania was a mistake from an economic point of view that led them to make the economic conditions imposed on the Albanian government 'deliberately oppressive'. See also Skendi, *Albania*, p. 211.
24 Formentini, 'La Banca Nazionale d'Albania'.
25 Calmès Report, p. 21.
26 See Spinedi, 'La Banca Nazionale d'Albania', pp. 34–43. The *Korça Gazzette* of 13 September 1933, in an article quoted in a message from the Italian Legation to the Foreign Ministry, had openly made this accusation (see ASMAE 31–45, 'Albania', 14). The Minister Ugo Sola wrote from Bucharest

to the Foreign Ministry on 6 May 1936, notifying them of a new book by Dimitrie Pascu on the Bank of Albania, which contained 'many criticisms' of the institution and showed that 'it was essentially at the mercy of foreign shareholders, i.e. of Italy' (ASMAE 31–45, 'Albania', 66).

27 Undated memo, UK Representative Office, Bank of Italy, London.

28 See, for example, Martino's article, 'La Banca Nazionale d'Albania', but also the text of Professor Georges Sauser-Hall's arbitration judgement, *Arbitral Advice Pronounced in Conformity with the Agreement of Washington of 25 April 1951* (Brussels, 20 February 1953), p. 12. We will dwell further on this arbitration at a later stage.

29 In 'Moneta e credito in Albania', p. 206.

30 Ibid., p. 212.

31 Standard regression error: 8.7858 for the last six years; 10.914 over 11 years. 'Durbin-Watson statistic': 2.2469 for the last six years; 1.3643 over 11 years.

32 With a circulation, for example, of 100, the total reserve had to be 33.3 and the gold component 33.3 per cent of 33.3, i.e. 11.1.

33 Unless otherwise indicated, the data refer to the net reserves. Thus, for example, for the gold, the calculation is net of the gold circulation.

34 See Grubel, *The International Monetary System*, pp. 132–134.

35 A 'secret' memorandum from the Albania Office of the Foreign Ministry to the Minister di Revel, on 9 May 1935, in ASMAE 31–45, 'Albania', 66.

36 ASMAE 31–45, 'Albania', 27, memorandum from the Foreign Ministry of 31 December 1933. The memorandum is based upon recommendations made to the National Bank of Albania by the Governor of the Bank of Italy, Azzolini. He wanted to limit conversions to gold from foreign currency, since this currency was deposited in Italy.

37 See the statement attached to the memorandum from the Bank of Albania to Minister di Revel on 11 November 1935, in ASMAE 31–45, 'Albania', 66.

38 See memorandum quoted in note 35.

39 See note 36.

40 See again memorandum in note 35.

41 'From what I can make out', wrote the Italian Minister in Tiranë, Indelli, 'such a transaction . . . would seem to be an investment by the sovereign, motivated by the fear of a weakening in the value of the Albanian currency' (letter of 19 October 1935, in ASMAE 31–45, 'Albania', 55). In November of the same year, Zog changed 15 million lire into Albanian francs.

42 The memorandum of 29 November 1935 is in ASBI-Rapporti Estero, tape 47. The Foreign Ministry warmly supported the request from the National Bank of Albania, 'given the effects which a situation of this kind could have on Italo-Albanian relations, in which the negotiations in progress are on the whole rekindling the character of cordial cooperation which they have had in the past' (telegram to the Finance Minister of December 1935, in ASMAE 31–45, 'Albania', 66).

43 ASBI-Rapporti Estero, tape 47, letter of 5 December 1935.

44 This exchange of letters, between October and December 1936, is recorded in ASBI-Rapporti Estero, tape 47.

45 For the gold and silver prices during the period in question, see 'Gold and Silver Prices' for June/July 1925 in *The Economist.*

46 For a discussion on bimetallism, see Eichengreen, *Globalizing Capital*, pp. 9–15.

47 On this point, see Borgatta, 'Moneta e credito in Albania', p. 203.

48 ASBI, Azzolini, 97, letter of 16 May 1929.
49 ASBI, Azzolini, 97, letter of 31 May 1929.
50 In the first draft of the letter he wrote 'severe' instead of 'dubious'.
51 For a similar viewpoint, cf. P. Formentini, 'Credito e moneta in Albania', in *Rivista Bancaria*, 1930, especially pp. 736–737.
52 ASBI, Azzolini, 97, letter from Minister Tutulani of 28 May 1929.
53 ASBI, Azzolini, 97, letter of 26 June 1929.
54 ASBI, Azzolini, 97, letter of 3 July 1929.
55 The Albanian government would also be able to draw an advance (of up to 2/3) on the said sums, at the rate of 7.5 per cent. The complete text of the agreement is in ASBI, Azzolini, 97.
56 See Borgatta, 'Moneta e credito in Albania', p. 203.
57 See ASMAE 31–45, 'Albania', 55.

Chapter 7

1 From Arnaldo Mussolini's preface to the book by S. Giuliani, *Assestamento e rinascita dell'Albania* (Tipografia del Popolo d'Italia, 1929).
2 From a report by Ciano to Mussolini in May 1938, in *L'Europa verso la catastrofe* (Milan, Mondadori, 1948).
3 See G. B. Guerri, *Galeazzo Ciano* (Milan, Bompiani, 1979), ch. X, and more recently Tomes, *King Zog*, ch. 34.
4 The connection between the disappointing management of the economy and the regime's change of policy is outlined in brief but very precise terms by Mack Smith (*Mussolini's Roman Empire*). Mussolini, sensitive to the foreign press, had been particularly annoyed when he had read in *Paris Soir* that Zog was 'exploiting Italy': see Guerri, *Galeazzo Ciano*, p. 367.
5 BoE, OV 116/1, Overseas and Foreign Department memo, 12 April 1939.
6 BoE, OV 116/1, Annual Economic Report for 1938, from the British envoy, Sir Andrew Ryan, to Viscount Halifax, Foreign Secretary, 24 October 1938.
7 De Felice, *Mussolini il duce: lo Stato totalitario*, p. 478.
8 I. Kirkpatrick, *Mussolini: A Study in Power* (New York, Hawthorn Books, 1964), p. 385; P. Pastorelli, 'La politica estera fascista dalla fine del conflitto etiopico alla seconda guerra mondiale', in *L'Italia fra tedeschi e Alleati* (Bologna, Il Mulino, 1973), p. 111.
9 De Felice, *Mussolini il duce: lo Stato totalitario*, p. 543.
10 Ibid., p. 545.
11 Ibid., p. 607. 'In reality the Albanian affair had had an entirely different effect on London from the one which could originally have been expected: it had confirmed to Chamberlain and the Foreign Office that they were right in their conviction that Mussolini could not be trusted in any way' (ibid., p. 609).
12 Reported in *Il Sole* of 18 April 1939.
13 The Under-Secretariat was closed down in 1941 and from then on the development of relations between the two countries was secured by special agreements (see the Bank of Italy's Annual Report for 1941, p. 117).
14 See *Il Sole* of 18 April 1939.
15 Jacomoni was to be replaced in 1943 by General Pariani. According to Pollo and Puto (*The History of Albania*, p. 233), the latter introduced a demagogic policy of concessions, offering the Albanians, amongst other things, a review of the economic and currency agreements of 1939.
16 See the Bank of Italy's Annual Report for 1940, p. 89.

17 See *Il Sole* of 7 July 1939.
18 In the same spirit, a few months before the occupation, on the occasion of the opening of the Bank of Albania's new headquarters in Tiranë, the Director-General of the Bank of Italy, Troise, had given two statues as a gift to the headquarters, one of Julius Caesar and the other of Caesar Augustus (Agenzia Stefani, 30 October 1938).
19 See G. Balladore Pallieri, *Diritto internazionale pubblico* (Milan, Giuffrè, 1944).
20 Guerri, *Galeazzo Ciano*, p. 384.
21 See above.
22 ASBI, Azzolini, 97, confidential letter of the National Bank of Albania to Finance Minister Thaon di Revel, 15 June 1938; an anonymous additional note, but probably from the National Bank of Albania, 18 November 1938, same folder.
23 Curiously (and perhaps not by chance) the 'case-study' given as an illustration of the matter is that of an 'annuity granted by the Italian government to persons living in Albania' (an allusion to the Albanian royal court?). Whether the annuity was paid in lire or in Albanian francs, the effects of transferring the money, says the document, would be to no avail if the annuity itself were then to be used to 'acquire jewellery or other goods in Paris'. The document is also of interest because, in underlining the increasing presence of third countries in the Albanian import system, it highlights the importance of Japan as a rival to Italy. On the emergence of Japan as a commercial supplier to Albania, see Mack Smith, *Mussolini's Roman Empire*, p. 149. By 1937, the country was the fourth largest exporter to Albania after Italy, Yugoslavia and Romania. (Cf. 'Aspetti economici dell'Albania', an anonymous note in *Rivista di politica economica*, 1939, pp. 406–407).
24 ASBI, Azzolini, 97, from an anonymous source.
25 ASBI, Azzolini, 97.
26 Approved in Italy with Law no. 1046 of 6 June 1939, and in Albania with the Lieutenant General's decree on the same date as the Agreement.
27 In 1939, income from customs was around 7.7 million Albanian francs (Di Nardi, 'Le finanze pubbliche dell'Albania', p. 266).
28 See Chapter 5.
29 'Cross-rates' taken from the statistics of the League of Nations, *Annuaire Statistique 1938–1939*, Geneva, 1939.
30 An article in the *Frankfurter Zeitung* of 15 April 1939 emphasizes this aspect.
31 ASBI, Azzolini, 97.
32 The new Charter was approved at the general meeting of the Bank on 10 June 1939.
33 The texts are in ASBI.
34 More restrictive instructions for currency transactions arising from tourism were given with the order of the Bank of Albania of 20 January 1942 (see *Il Sole* of 31 January 1942).
35 This legislation is summarized in the Bank of Italy's Annual Report for 1939 (pp. 102–103).

Chapter 8

1 The Italian Peace Treaty set (in article 74, letter B) the sum of the reparations due to Albania from Italy as 5 million dollars. But there was also the question of the 'Albanian gold' (see Chapter 10).

2 In ASBI, Introna, 19. The report is certainly post-1939. Its writer introduced himself in Tiranë to Parini, who had been sent to Albania as Inspector General of the Fascist Party by Ciano in late 1939. See G. Ciano, *Diario 1939–43* (Milan, Rizzoli, 1971), p. 231.
3 See the Bank of Italy's Annual Report for 1942, pp. 108–109.
4 See Mack Smith, *Mussolini's Roman Empire*, p. 156.
5 Ibid.
6 Guarneri, *Battaglie economiche*, vol. II, p. 347.
7 Borgatta, 'Moneta e credito in Albania', p. 237.
8 Italian Centre of Studies and Publications for International Reconciliation, *What Italy Has Done for Albania* (Rome, 1946), p. 20.
9 Borgatta, 'Moneta e credito in Albania', pp. 230–231.
10 Italian Centre of Studies and Publications for International Reconciliation, *What Italy Has Done for Albania*, pp. 20–21.
11 Borgatta, 'Moneta e credito in Albania', pp. 230–231.
12 Guarneri, *Battaglie economiche*, vol. II, p. 346; the laws are of 6 July 1939.
13 Ibid., p. 347.
14 See the Bank of Italy's Annual Report for 1941, p. 115.
15 6,532 million: see Italian Centre of Studies and Publications for International Reconciliation, *What Italy Has Done for Albania*, p. 22.
16 The body created by the banking law of 1936 to supervise banks.
17 ASBI, Azzolini, 97, Azzolini to di Revel, Guarneri and Ciano, 25 April 1939; di Revel to Azzolini, 4 May 1939; Guarneri to Azzolini, 16 May 1939; Ciano to Azzolini, 4 May 1939 and 22 June 1939.
18 ASBI, Azzolini, 97, Azzolini to the National Bank of Albania, 28 July 1939.
19 R. Martino, 'Moneta, banca e istituti di credito in Albania', in *L'Italia d'oltremare*, July 1942. The Banco di Napoli – Albania, with head office in Tiranë, had branches at Gjirokastër, Korçe, Durrës, Porto Edda, Skodër, Vlorë (BoE, OV 116/1, memo of the Overseas and Foreign Department, 24 August 1943).
20 ASBI, Azzolini, 97, National Bank of Albania to Azzolini, 17 August 1939. Castronovo notes that the BNL opened its branch in Tiranë 'to handle the banking needs of the civil and military administrative services based in Albania and to support certain industrial enterprises aimed at exploiting local mineral resources'. This was in the context of 'handling transactions and special jobs on behalf of the government in the colonial dominions or in other territories which had come within Italy's sphere of influence', and it was on these operations that the BNL concentrated its work outside Italy from 1938 onwards: see V. Castronovo, *Storia di una banca. La Banca Nazionale del Lavoro e lo sviluppo economico italiano 1913–1983* (Turin, Einaudi, 1983), p. 215. On its handling of Treasury services, see the comments later in this chapter.
21 Martino, 'Moneta, banca e istituti di credito in Albania'.
22 ASBI, Azzolini, 97, memo to Azzolini, 8 May 1939.
23 ASBI-Rapporti con l'Estero, tape 47, memorandum from the Bank of Albania of 1 July 1942.
24 *Premier mémoire du gouvernement italien dans l'affaire de l'or de la Banque Nationale d'Albanie* (Rome, Ministero Affari Esteri, 1952), pp. 10–11. This is the Italian government's submission on the matter of the 'Albanian gold', presented to the arbitrator Sauser-Hall (see Chapter 10).
25 See Appendix 8 of the submission cited in the previous note.

26 There is a note of 16 November 1936 in the records of the Italian Foreign Ministry, regarding the ownership structure of SVEA: 'it appears that all the shares in SVEA are in the names of Credito Italiano, Banca Commerciale Italiana and Banco di Roma, who were the original subscribers to the share capital; in practice, however, they can all be traced back to the Istituto Nazionale per i Cambi, which appears to have already agreed to transfer them to the Royal Treasury. Therefore the shares can be assumed to be the property of the Exchequer' (ASMAE 31–45, 'Albania', 66). On the capital for SVEA, see also the account in Chapter 4.

27 This percentage climbs to approximately 11 per cent, taking into account that the face value of the funding shares was 1.25 francs, against 25 francs of the ordinary shares (see also Chapter 4).

28 For the first, see ASBI, Baffi papers. For the second, see the collection of press articles in the same archive, in particular 'Banca Nazionale d'Albania', in *Il Sole*, 18 April 1939; 'L'Assemblea della BNA', Agenzia Stefani, 7 May 1941; 'L'economia albanese dopo l'unione con l'Italia ha progredito in tutti i settori', in *La Tribuna*, 14 April 1942; 'Bilanz der Albanischen Nationalbank', in *Südost Echo*, 22 May 1942; 'L'Assemblea della BNA', in *Il Messaggero*, 9 April 1943.

29 The National Bank of Albania's investment was limited to short-term bills (no more than three months, and – from 1939 onwards – no more than six months: see the statements quoted above).

30 'Le sottoscrizioni in Albania ai buoni del Tesoro hanno raggiunto i 9 milioni di lire', *Il Messaggero*, 3 March 1940.

31 A. De Toma, 'Lo sviluppo dei prezzi in Albania dal marzo 1939 alla fine del 1940', Working paper, March 1941, in ASBI, Baffi papers.

32 By 'circulation', De Toma means the total of banknotes, token coins and cheques in circulation. The latter component may explain the percentage increase which De Toma estimates. According to the series of statistics quoted in our study (which, as we have seen, includes only banknotes and token coins under 'circulation'), the percentage increase for a slightly different period (January 1939 to December 1940) is 249 per cent (from 24.2 million in January 1939 to 84.6 million in December 1940), which is a long way off De Toma's figure. A classified memo in the Bank of England archive, dated 29 July 1943, defines the Albanian wholesale price index – not without reason – as 'a rudimentary affair', adding that, from 1940, 'our statistical blackout is complete' (BoE, OV 116/1).

33 See the Bank of Italy's Annual Report for 1942, p. 110.

34 Skendi, *Albania*, p. 205. The debasement of the currency led to a strong rise in the quotation of the 20-franc gold piece (the 'napoleon'). In January 1941 it had been quoted at 100 paper francs and in August 1943 it was over 300: see 'Appunti riservati per la Divisione finanziaria del governo militare alleato sull'attività della Banca Nazionale d'Albania', 21 June 1944, in ASBI, Einaudi, 92.

Chapter 9

1 See Borgatta, 'Moneta e credito in Albania', p. 211.

2 The two estimates (Elvepidi and Pano) are quoted from G. P. Caselli and G. Thoma, 'La storia economica albanese 1912–1950: lo stabilirsi dell'egemonia italiana e il primo tentativo di pianificazione', in *Rivista di storia economica*, 1, 2003, pp. 67–107.

3 G. Demaria, 'Il problema della politica economica albanese e lo sviluppo del reddito nazionale', in *Giornale degli economisti e annali di economia*, July–October 1940, especially pp. 399–402.
4 Ibid., p. 400.
5 H.-J. Pernack, *Probleme der wirtschaftlichen Entwicklung Albaniens*, Munich, Südosteuropa-Studien, 18, 1972, p. 95.
6 See Caselli and Thoma, 'La storia economica albanese', p. 74.
7 Banka Kombëtare e Shqipnis, 1926, p. 39.
8 Royal Institute of International Affairs, *The Balkan States*, estimate referring to 1933. Demaria takes the population to be slightly lower (1 million).
9 The report from Koch, the Italian Minister in Tiranë, to the Foreign Ministry, 8 February 1934, is of particular interest (ASMAE 31–45, 'Albania').
10 ISTAT, *Sommario di statistiche storiche dell'Italia*, p. 181.
11 ISTAT, *Sommario di statistiche storiche dell'Italia*.
12 Pernack, *Probleme der wirtschaftlichen Entwicklung Albaniens*, pp. 77 *et seq*.
13 Ibid., pp. 48 and 82.
14 Ibid., p. 84.
15 Ibid., p. 92.
16 Ibid., p. 93.
17 Skendi, *Albania*, p. 228. See also T. Favaretto and A. Masotti Cristofoli, 'Le relazioni economiche fra Italia e Albania dal secondo dopoguerra a oggi', in *Est-Ovest*, 1984, no. 2, p. 8.
18 Demaria, 'Il problema della politica economica albanese e lo sviluppo del reddito nazionale', p. 382.
19 Ibid.
20 P. Baffi, 'Stabilità monetaria e sviluppo economico in Italia, 1946–1960', in *Letture di politica monetaria e finanziaria* (Banca Popolare di Milano, 1965), p. 1207.
21 Calmès Report, p. 30.
22 P. Melograni, *Gli industriali e Mussolini* (Milan, Longanesi, 1972). Melograni also links the revaluation of the lira with this policy, whose aim must therefore have equally been to deliberately contain industrial development and the growth of the urban working class. See also A. J. Joes's biography of Mussolini, *Mussolini* (New York, Franklin Watts, 1982), pp. 278–279.
23 Mack Smith, *Mussolini's Roman Empire*.
24 On the opposition movements to Zog and the resistance movements against the Italians, see Pollo and Puto, *The History of Albania*, pp. 211–216 and 224–239.
25 J. Massei, 'Politica economica internazionale', in *Rivista internazionale di scienze sociali*, May 1940, pp. 516–517.
26 ACS, BNA-SVEA, 42, 1, SVEA to Ministry of Foreign Affairs, 25 January 1927.
27 This is a necessary but tedious itemization and any reader who wishes to skip this section will not be missing out.
28 A. Teichova, 'Industry', in M. Kaser and E. A. Radice (eds), *The Economic History of Eastern Europe 1919–1975* (Oxford, Clarendon Press, 1985), vol. I, p. 314.
29 *Un decennio di vita della SVEA*.
30 Ibid., p. 21.
31 Ibid., p. 25.
32 Ibid., p. 28.

33 The remaining 3.5 per cent concerned money for works still to be put out to tender or for reimbursing the Ministry for Public Works for studies carried out: see *Un decennio di vita della SVEA*, p. 31.
34 Ibid., p. 36.
35 F. Schipani, 'L'organizzazione economica e l'attività produttiva dell'Albania', in *Rivista di politica economica*, 1932, p. 60.
36 Alimenti, *La questione petrolifera italiana*, p. 94.
37 Ibid., pp. 95–96. See also Banca d'Italia, *L'economia italiana nel sessennio 1931–1936* (Rome, Istituto poligrafico dello Stato, 1938), part II, vol. II, p. 1933.
38 See Pastorelli, *Italia e Albania*, p. 104. SIMSA had been in Albania since 1919, when it had acquired the rights from a Franco-Ottoman company for bitumen exploitation (see E. Giansanti, 'I primi positivi risultati di una collaborazione nel campo minerario', in *L'Italia d'oltremare*, October 1942).
39 Schipani, 'L'organizzazione economica e l'attività produttiva dell'Albania', p. 59.
40 Alimenti, *La questione petrolifera italiana*, p. 94.
41 Ibid.
42 Giansanti, 'I primi positivi risultati di una collaborazione nel campo minerario'.
43 Banca d'Italia, *L'economia italiana nel sessennio 1931–1936*, p. 1647.
44 Italian Centre of Studies and Publications for International Reconciliation, *What Italy Has Done for Albania*, p. 14. The table below, taken from Skendi's Albania, gives an idea of the increase in output especially at the time of the Ethiopian war and the Second World War.

42-gallon barrels

1933	11,000	1938	752,000
1934	10,000	1939	934,000
1935	41,000	1940	1,497,000
1936	237,000	1941	1,334,000
1937	619,000	1942	1,601,000
		1943	1,100,000

45 Giansanti, 'I primi positivi risultati di una collaborazione nel campo minerario'. According to Favaretto and Masotti Cristofoli, Italy succeeded in covering its own requirements for coal, bitumen and chrome and covered around 10 per cent of its copper and oil requirements, and this was partly thanks to Albania in 1939–1940 ('Le relazioni economiche fra Italia e Albania dal secondo dopoguerra a oggi', p. 8).
46 Berend, 'Agriculture', p. 205.
47 Bank of Italy's Annual Report for 1940, p. 89.
48 Italian Centre of Studies and Publications for International Reconciliation, *What Italy Has Done for Albania*, pp. 15–16.
49 The information which follows is mainly drawn from Schipani, 'L'organizzazione economica e l'attività produttiva dell'Albania', pp. 1237 *et seq.*
50 'Aspetti economici dell'Albania', an anonymous note in *Rivista di politica economica*, 1939, p. 406.
51 Italian Centre of Studies and Publications for International Reconciliation, *What Italy Has Done for Albania*, p. 11.

52 See Chapter 2.
53 Royal Institute of International Affairs, *The Balkan States*, p. 20.
54 Berend, 'Agriculture', p. 205.
55 Borgatta, 'Moneta e credito in Albania', pp. 222–223.
56 See Chapter 5.
57 ASMAE 31–45, 'Albania', 1, report from di Soragna to Minister Grandi, 17 December 1931.
58 Pollo and Puto, *The History of Albania*, p. 206.
59 Berend, 'Agriculture', p. 205.
60 S. Basile, 'Alberghi, alberghi per l'Albania!', in *L'Italia d'oltremare*, October 1942. See also Italian Centre of Studies and Publications for International Reconciliation, *What Italy Has Done for Albania*, pp. 16–17.
61 Italian Centre of Studies and Publications for International Reconciliation, *What Italy Has Done for Albania*, p. 17. These publications and Skendi's previously quoted *Albania* can be referred to for a description of Italy's other minor industrial initiatives.

Chapter 10

1 *Premier mémoire du gouvernement italien dans l'affaire de l'or de la Banque Nationale d'Albanie*, p. 12. In view of the debt towards the Bank for International Settlements (BIS), the latter requested the restitution of 138,000 Albanian francs on 14 December 1944. Since the Bank of Albania could not meet this payment, its Rome headquarters asked the Italian Treasury to point out to the BIS that the settlement of the sum was dependent on the recovery of the gold reserve which had been removed by the Germans (see memo from Bank of Albania, 7 June 1945, ASBI, Introna, 19). The Rome headquarters, on 30 June, informed the BIS accordingly and asked for a moratorium. On 25 January 1947 the BIS was informed that even the interest on that debt, which in the meantime had climbed to around 140,000 francs, could not be accrued. The State Bank of Albania, established in Tiranë by the new revolutionary government of Albania, acquired the assets and liabilities of the old National Bank, but refused to take any position on the BIS claim, according to a BIS memo of 11 August 1947 (see documentation in BISA, 2.87, Bank of Albania, Tirana – Policy, vol. 1: 1931–2000). The outcome of the transaction is not known. For the Bank of Albania's membership of the BIS, see the Bank's Annual Report for 1944 prepared by Gambino (ASBI, Einaudi, 42).
2 Or 2,339.4 kilograms according to a memorandum from Gambino of 12 June 1945, in ASBI, Introna, 19.
3 The German troops also removed banknotes kept at the Bank of Italy (117.6 million Albanian francs) and at the Bank of Albania (2.9 million Albanian francs), which were mostly delivered to the Tiranë headquarters (see memo from the National Bank of Albania of 21 June 1944, in ASBI, Introna, 19).
4 In 55 cases, countersigned 'AN 1–55' (BoE, OV34/251).
5 Sauser-Hall, *Arbitral Advice*, p. 15 (for the full title, see note 43).
6 A lively account of the partisan war in Albania can be found in D. Smiley, *Albanian Assignment* (London, Chatto & Windus, 1984).
7 National Bank of Albania, 'Confidential Report on the Rome Operations for 1945', 30 March 1946, pp. 2–3, in ASBI, Einaudi, 92. For the political details of this phase, see Pollo and Puto, *The History of Albania*, in particular ch. X ('The Struggle against Fascism') and ch. XI ('The Way to Socialism').

8 National Bank of Albania, 'Confidential Report on the Rome Operations for 1945', p. 3.
9 Ibid., p. 5.
10 See Foreign and Commonwealth Office, *Nazi Gold: Information from the British Archives*, London, Stationery Office, 1996.
11 For the text of the declaration, see D. H. N. Johnson, 'The Case of the Monetary Gold Removed from Rome in 1943', in *The International and Comparative Law Quarterly*, January 1955, p. 97.
12 Tripartite Gold Commission, Final Report, 9 September 1998 (PRO, DG9/45).
13 This stock, made up of bars, coins and other forms, subsequently rose to 10.816 million ounces in 1974, then to 10.817 million ounces in 1996 (equivalent to approximately 337 tonnes), after further finds.
14 Tripartite Gold Commission, Final Report.
15 United States National Archives, 'Restitution of Monetary Gold: Preliminary Distribution', press statement, 17 October 1947.
16 Percentage worked out on the final calculation of the stock of available gold.
17 Tripartite Gold Commission, Final Report.
18 Sauser-Hall, *Arbitral Advice*, p. 16.
19 ASBI, Einaudi, 92, memo from Gambino to Foreign Ministry, 29 January 1945.
20 Ibid.
21 ASBI, Einaudi, 92, letter (and attached report) of 4 April 1946. In August 1944, an agreement had been signed in Bari between the Albanian Liberation Army and the Allied Command in Italy, for military equipment to be sent to the Albanian partisans. Two further agreements had followed, the first between the Albanian government and the Allied authorities (April 1945), and the second between the Albanian government and UNRRA (August 1945) for food and other aid to be sent to Albania (Skendi, *Albania*, p. 228; also Pollo and Puto, *The History of Albania*, pp. 246–247).
22 Sauser-Hall, *Arbitral Advice*, pp. 16–17.
23 Made up of: coins, 240.6 kilograms; bars, 2,214.2 kilograms; other, 124.5 kilograms; totalling 2,579.3 kilograms
(BoE, OV34/251: there is a small discrepancy of 600 grams with the figure in the text, unexplained). Note the difference between the Italian and the Albanian claims, also, in reference to the 'Tiranë gold'.
24 Sauser-Hall, *Arbitral Advice*, p. 15.
25 An OMGUS (Office of the Military Government – United States) document of 6 September 1945 concerning the recovery of Reichsbank precious metals found in the Merkers mine speaks of 2,214.2 kilograms of gold bars, which tallied precisely with the figures submitted by Albania (see note 23). It also mentions coins equivalent to 124.5 kilograms, which also corresponded to the Albanian submission to the Commission (BoE, OV34/248).
26 BoE, OV34/248.
27 See PRO, DG9/18, which gives details of all the allocations, recording their movements in and out of deposits at the Bank of England and the Federal Reserve Bank of New York.
28 Sauser-Hall, *Arbitral Advice*, p. 17. On the basis of the Treaty (article 75, para. 8), 'the Italian government shall restore to the government of the United Nation concerned the monetary gold which was taken by Italy or improperly transferred to Italy; or it shall provide the government of the United Nation

concerned with a quantity of gold equal in weight and type to the quantity which was removed or improperly transferred . . .'.

29 See further on in this chapter.

30 BoE, OV34/247, Charles Arthur Gunston (BoE) to R. A. Sutch (Treasury), 20 December 1946.

31 BoE, OV34/248, L. Bielinky (Treasury) to Gunston (BoE), 9 October 1947.

32 BoE, OV34/248, memo to Gunston (BoE), 14 October 1947; draft letter to the Treasury by Gunston, 20 October, 1947; Gunston to Bielinky (Treasury), 21 October 1947.

33 E. Hoxha, *The Anglo-American Threat to Albania: Memoirs* (Tiranë, The 8 Nentori Publishing House, 1982), p. 415.

34 See J. Halliday, *The Artful Albanian: The Memoirs of Enver Hoxha* (London, Chatto & Windus, 1986), p. 345; W. Bland and I. Price, *A Tangled Web: A History of Anglo-American Relations with Albania (1912–1955)* (London, Albanian Society, 1986), p. 247. See also BoE, 3A 150/11, memo, 18 June 1985.

35 See, for example, N. J. Costa, *Albania: A European Enigma* (New York, Columbia University Press, 1995).

36 Hoxha, *The Anglo-American Threat to Albania*, p. 418.

37 L. Gardiner, *The Eagle Spreads his Claws* (Edinburgh and London, Blackwood, 1966).

38 Ibid., p. 140.

39 BoE, OV116/2, J. E. Abbot (Treasury) to G. T. C. Campbell (FO), 22 March 1949, and Talbot de Malahide (FO) to Hughes (Treasury), 5 May 1949.

40 Sauser-Hall, *Arbitral Advice*, pp. 17–18. PRO, DG9/18.

41 The text of the agreement, signed by Henri Bonnet for France, Oliver Franks for the United Kingdom and Dean Acheson for the United States, is recorded in Sauser-Hall's *Arbitral Advice*, pp. 4–5. The effect of a decision that the gold removed from Rome belonged neither to Albania nor to Italy would not have been irrelevant, because it would have increased the amount of gold available for distribution to other beneficiaries of the gold pool.

42 Professor Tommaso Perassi, head of legal services at the Foreign Ministry, was appointed to act for Italy, with Ambassador Sola as his deputy.

43 *Arbitral Advice Pronounced in Conformity with the Agreement of Washington of 25 April 1951, between the Governments of the United States of America, the French Republic and the United Kingdom of Great Britain and Northern Ireland for the Submission to an Arbitrator of Certain Claims with respect to Gold Looted by the Germans from Rome in 1943*, Brussels, 20 February 1953.

44 Ibid., p. 25.

45 Ibid., p. 22.

46 BoE, 3A150/9, FO memo, 1 August 1979.

47 Sauser-Hall, *Arbitral Advice*, pp. 40–41.

48 Johnson, 'The Case of the Monetary Gold Removed from Rome in 1943', p. 93.

49 Ibid., pp. 95–96.

50 International Court of Justice, 'The Case of Monetary Gold Removed from Rome in 1943 (Preliminary Question)', 15 June 1954, in *I. C. J. Reports*, 1954. See also C. T. Oliver, 'The Monetary Gold Decision in Perspective', in *The American Journal of International Law*, vol. 49, 2, April 1955, pp. 216–221, and Johnson, 'The Case of the Monetary Gold Removed from Rome in 1943', pp. 101–103. The decision was not unanimous. Judge Levi Carneiro had a

dissenting opinion published along with the ruling, according to which, oddly enough, the Court did have jurisdiction in the matter of whether the Italian or British claims had priority, even though it did not have jurisdiction over the matter of the Italian claim against Albania. A commentary on the International Court's ruling is contained in the anonymous note, 'La questione dell'oro della Banca Nazionale d'Albania avanti la Corte internazionale di Giustizia', in *Rivista di diritto internazionale*, 1954, which also carries the text of the ruling.

51 Ugo Sola, Amedeo Gambino and Giovanni Rivano were the liquidators. It is interesting to note that in 1960 ex-King Zog brought proceedings against the three liquidators for the restitution of around 51 million lire which he claimed was the current value of the sum he had deposited with the Bank of Albania (see 'L'ex re di Albania cita in giudizio una banca', in *Corriere della Sera*, 13 March 1960). Zog died on 9 April 1961.

52 PRO, T312/950, FO memo, 14 November 1963; BoE, 3A150/9, FO memo, 1 August 1979. The proposal was made again in November 1960, and again was not followed up (BoE OV116/2, FO memo, 3 November 1960).

53 PRO, T312/950. The text of the Commission's decision is in a report of 21 May 1962 to the British Embassy in Brussels by the Secretary to the Commission, J. A. Watson.

54 PRO, DG9/45, Final Report of the Tripartite Commission.

55 PRO, T312/950, British Embassy in Paris to FO, 3 July 1962; Italian Embassy in London, memo, 30 January 1964.

56 BoE, OV34/249, Rootham (BoE) to Weston (Treasury), 18 January 1956. Jasper St John Rootham was an Adviser at the Bank.

57 BoE, 3A150/9, FO memo, 1 August 1979; PRO, T312/1310.

58 BoE, OV116/2, British Embassy in Brussels to FO, 17 March 1975.

59 BoE, 3A150/9, FO telegram, 5 November 1982.

60 BoE, 3A150/9, FO to British Embassy in Paris, 3 June 1983.

61 BoE, 3A150/9, FO to British Embassy in Paris, 9 May 1984.

62 BoE, 3A150/9, British Embassy in Rome to FO, 31 May 1984.

63 BoE, 3A150/9, BoE memo, 14 June 1984.

64 BoE, 3A150/9, FO to BoE, 30 July 1984; BoE 3A150/10, memo, 12 March 1985, at a BoE/FO/Treasury meeting.

65 BoE, memo, 6 March 1985; British Embassy in Paris to FO, 15 March 1985. On the subject of the interest, the BoE pointed out that, if the total dollar equivalent of the gold as valued in 1948 had been invested at the appropriate rate of interest, it would have only been worth 5.5 million dollars, as opposed to the 14.1 million of the gold revalued at 1985 prices.

66 BoE, 3A150/10, British Embassy in Paris to FO, 19 March and 20 March 1985.

67 BoE, 3A150/11, various memos and telegrams, between 6 June 1985 and 23 September 1986.

68 BoE, 3A150/11, FO to Treasury, 16 February 1988. Interestingly, the dealings between the British and Italian governments were so private that it seems the Bank of England was not aware of them. A Bank memo reads, 'Great care has been taken to keep the negotiations secret from the Italians, even though it is now thought unlikely, more than 30 years later, that they would actually press their claim' (BoE, memo, 23 May 1989).

69 FO documents.

70 Tripartite Gold Commission, Final Report, 3 September 1998 (PRO, DG9/45).
71 FO documents.
72 PRO, DG9/16, minutes of the Tripartite Commission meeting, 18 September 1996. See also House of Commons, Hansard Debates for 12 November 1996.
73 PRO, DG9/16, minutes of the Tripartite Commission meetings, 26 November 1996 and 27 February 1997.
74 Foreign and Commonwealth Office, *Nazi Gold.*
75 PRO, DG9/16, minutes of the Tripartite Commission meeting, 13 July 1998.
76 The final share of gold allocated to Italy was around 764 kilograms, equivalent to over 12 billion lire. With a law of 10 August 2000, the Italian parliament authorized a contribution of 12 billion lire to the Fund for Assistance to Victims of Persecution.

References

1 Archives

ACS	State Central Archives, Rome
ASBI	Historical Archive of the Bank of Italy, Rome
ASMAE	Historical Archive of the Ministry for Foreign Affairs, Rome
BISA	Archive of the Bank for International Settlements, Basel
BoE	Archive of the Bank of England, London
LON	United Nations Archives, Geneva
PRO	Public Record Office, Kew (London)

An ample documentation on the National Bank of Albania has been moved from the Italian Treasury Archives to ACS, but is still under reorganization. The files of the Under-Secretariat for Albanian Affairs at ASMAE are not available for consultation.

2 Books, articles and working papers

Alberti, Mario, *La guerra delle monete*, 3 vols, Como, Cavalleri, 1937

Albertini, Luigi, *The Origins of the War of 1914*, 3 vols, London, Oxford University Press, 1952–1957

Alimenti, Cesare, *La questione petrolifera italiana*, Turin, Einaudi, 1937

Amoroso, Luigi, Il contributo italiano allo sviluppo economico dell'Albania negli ultimi quindici anni, in *Rivista italiana di scienze economiche*, April 1939

Baffi, Paolo, La componente esterna della liquidità e le regole della condotta monetaria, in *Studi sulla moneta*, Milan, Giuffrè, 1965

—— Stabilità monetaria e sviluppo economico in Italia, 1946–1960, in *Letture di politica monetaria e finanziaria*, Banca Popolare di Milano, 1965

'Balcanicus', L'opera economica e finanziaria dell'Italia in Albania, in *Sud*, May–June 1927

Balladore Pallieri, Giorgio, *Diritto internazionale pubblico*, Milan, Giuffrè, 1944

Banca d'Italia, *L'economia italiana nel sessennio 1931–1936*, Rome, Istituto poligrafico dello Stato, 1938

Banca d'Italia, Relazioni annuali, various years

Basile, Sandra, Alberghi, alberghi per l'Albania!, in *L'Italia d'oltremare*, October 1942

Berend, Ivan T., Balkan Economic Development, in *The Economic History Review*, May 1984

—— Agriculture, in M. Kaser and E. A. Radice (eds), *The Economic History of Eastern Europe 1919–1975*, 3 vols, Oxford, Clarendon Press, 1985
Bland, William and Price, Ian, *A Tangled Web: A History of Anglo-American Relations with Albania (1912–1955)*, London, Albanian Society, 1986
Boldrini, Marcello, Sull'antropologia e la demografia degli albanesi, in *Principii di economia albanese*, Padua, Cedam, 1940
Bonomi, Ivanoe, *La politica italiana da Porta Pia a Vittorio Veneto*, Turin, Einaudi, 1944
Borgatta, Gino, Moneta e credito in Albania, in *Principii di economia albanese*, Padua, Cedam, 1940
Bosworth, Richard, The Albanian Forests of Signor Giacomo Vismara: A Case Study of Italian Economic Imperialism during the Foreign Ministry of Antonino Di San Giuliano, in *Historical Journal*, XVIII, 1975
—— *Italy and the Approach of the First World War*, London, Macmillan, 1983
Burgwin, H. James, *Il revisionismo fascista*, Milan, Feltrinelli, 1979
Camera di Commercio Italo-Orientale, *L'Albania economica*, Bari, SET, 1928
—— *Il commercio estero dell'Albania e i rapporti commerciali con l'Italia*, Bari, 1934
Carocci, Giampietro, *La politica estera dell'Italia fascista*, Bari, Laterza, 1969
—— Appunti sull'imperialismo fascista degli anni 20, in *Il regime fascista*, Bologna, Il Mulino, 1974
Caselli, Gian Paolo and Thoma, Grid, La storia economica albanese 1912–1950: lo stabilirsi dell'egemonia italiana e il primo tentativo di pianificazione, in *Rivista di storia economica*, 1, 2003
Cassels, Alan, *Mussolini's Early Diplomacy*, Princeton, NJ, Princeton University Press, 1971
Castronovo, Valerio, *Storia di una banca. La Banca Nazionale del Lavoro e lo sviluppo economico italiano 1913–1983*, Turin, Einaudi, 1983
Chekrezi, Constantine, *Albania Past and Present*, New York, Macmillan, 1919
Ciano, Galeazzo, *L'Europa verso la catastrofe*, Milan, Mondadori, 1948
—— *Diario 1939–43*, Milan, Rizzoli, 1971
Cipolla, Carlo Maria, *Le avventure della lira*, Milan, Comunità, 1958
Costa, Nicholas J., *Albania: A European Enigma*, New York, Columbia University Press, 1995
De Felice, Renzo, Alcune osservazioni sulla politica estera mussoliniana, in *Il Regime fascista*, Bologna, Il Mulino, 1974
—— *Mussolini il duce: gli anni del consenso 1929–1936*, Turin, Einaudi, 1974
—— *Mussolini il duce: lo Stato totalitario 1936–1940*, Turin, Einaudi, 1981
Demaria, Giovanni, Il problema della politica economica albanese e lo sviluppo del reddito nazionale, in *Giornale degli economisti e annali di economia*, July–October 1940
De Toma, A., Lo sviluppo dei prezzi in Albania dal marzo 1939 alla fine del 1940, Working paper, March 1941, in ASBI, Baffi papers
Di Nardi, Giuseppe, Le finanze pubbliche dell'Albania, in *Principii di economia albanese*, Padua, Cedam, 1940
Di Nolfo, Ennio, *Mussolini e la politica estera italiana 1919–1933*, Padua, Cedam, 1960
Donosti, Mario, *Mussolini e l'Europa: la politica estera fascista*, Rome, Leonardo, 1945
Durham, Edith, *Albania and the Albanians*, ed. B. Destani, London, Centre for Albanian Studies, 2001

Eichengreen, Barry, *Globalizing Capital: A History of the International Monetary System*, Princeton, NJ, Princeton University Press, 1996
Favaretto, T. and Masotti Cristofoli, A., Le relazioni economiche fra Italia e Albania dal secondo dopoguerra a oggi, in *Est-Ovest*, 1984, no. 2
Fishta, Iljaz and Toci, Veniamin, *Ekonomia e Shqipërisë në vitet e para të ndërtimit socialist, 1944–1948*, Tiranë, Akd. e Shkencave e RPS të Shqipërisë, 1984
Foreign and Commonwealth Office, *Nazi Gold: Information from the British Archives*, London, Stationery Office, 1996
Formentini, Paride, La Banca Nazionale d'Albania e il riordinamento monetario albanese, in *Rivista Bancaria*, 1927
—— Credito e moneta in Albania, in *Rivista Bancaria*, 1930
Frasca Polara, Paolo, Il commercio estero e la politica degli scambi in Albania, in *Rivista di politica economica*, 1932
Gambino, Amedeo, Le relazioni economiche fra l'Italia e l'Albania, in *Rivista internazionale di scienze sociali*, 1940
Gardiner, Leslie, *The Eagle Spreads his Claws*, Edinburgh and London, Blackwood, 1966
Giansanti, Enrico, I primi positivi risultati di una collaborazione nel campo minerario, in *L'Italia d'oltremare*, October 1942
Giolitti, Giovanni, *Memorie della mia vita*, Milan, Garzanti, 1945
Giuliani, Sandro, *Assestamento e rinascita dell'Albania*, Tipografia del Popolo d'Italia, 1929
Grubel, Harry G., *The International Monetary System: Efficiency and Practical Alternatives*, Harmondsworth, Penguin, 1969
Guarneri, Felice, *Battaglie economiche*, 2 vols, Milan, Garzanti, 1953
Guerri, Giordano Bruno, *Galeazzo Ciano*, Milan, Bompiani, 1979
Gulinelli, Adolfo, L'Albania e il suo riordinamento monetario, in *Giornale degli Economisti e Rivista di Statistica*, September 1927
—— L'azione italiana in Albania, in *Rivista di politica economica*, VII–VIII, 1927
Halliday, Jon, *The Artful Albanian: The Memoirs of Enver Hoxha*, London, Chatto & Windus, 1986
Harrod, Roy, *Money*, London, Macmillan, 1969
Homer, Sidney and Sylla, Richard, *A History of Interest Rates*, New Brunswick and London, Rutgers University Press, 1991
Hoxha, Enver, *The Anglo-American Threat to Albania: Memoirs*, Tiranë, The 8 Nentori Publishing House, 1982
International Court of Justice, The Case of Monetary Gold Removed from Rome in 1943 (Preliminary Question), in *I. C. J. Reports*, 1954
ISTAT, *Sommario di statistiche storiche dell'Italia 1861–1975*, Rome, 1976
Italian Centre of Studies and Publications for International Reconciliation, *What Italy Has Done for Albania*, Rome, 1946
Jacomoni di San Savino, Francesco, *La politica dell'Italia in Albania*, Bologna, Cappelli, 1965
Joes, Anthony, *Mussolini*, New York, Franklin Watts, 1982
Johnson, D. H. N., The Case of the Monetary Gold Removed from Rome in 1943, in *International and Comparative Law Quarterly*, January 1955
Kaser, Michael, Economic Continuities in Albania's Turbulent History, in *Europe–Asia Studies*, vol. 53, 4, 2001
Kirkpatrick, Ivone A., *Mussolini: A Study in Power*, New York, Hawthorn Books, 1964

La Marca, Nicola, *Italia e Balcani fra le due guerre. Saggio di una ricerca sui tentativi italiani di espansione economica nel Sud Est europeo fra le due guerre*, Rome, Bulzoni, 1979

Lampe, John R. and Jackson, Marvin R., *Balkan Economic History, 1550–1950: From Imperial Borderlands to Developing Nations*, Bloomington, Indiana University Press, 1982

Lenti, Libero, Gli scambi internazionali dell'Albania, in *Principii di economia albanese*, Padua, Cedam, 1940

Lessona, Alessandro, *Memorie*, Florence, Sansoni, 1958

Lyttelton, Adrian, *The Seizure of Power: Fascism in Italy 1919–1929*, London, Weidenfeld & Nicolson, 1973

McCartney, Maxwell H. H. and Cremona, Paul, *Italy's Foreign and Colonial Policy*, London, Oxford University Press, 1928

Mack Smith, Denis, *Mussolini's Roman Empire*, Harmondsworth, Penguin, 1977

Martino, Riccardo, La Banca Nazionale d'Albania, in *L'Italia d'oltremare*, August 1942

—— Moneta, banca e istituti di credito in Albania, in *L'Italia d'oltremare*, August 1942

Maserati, Ennio, L'Albania nella politica estera italiana degli anni 1896–1901, in *Clio*, January–June 1977

Massei, Jacopo, Politica economica internazionale, in *Rivista internazionale di scienze sociali*, May 1940

Mazzetti, Massimo, L'Italia e la crisi albanese del marzo-maggio 1913, in *Storia Contemporanea*, June 1973

Melis, G., La 'cultura dell'efficienza' nell'Amministrazione italiana dopo la prima guerra mondiale, Paper presented at the IRI conference in Caserta in honour of A. Beneduce, November 1983

Melograni, Piero, *Gli industriali e Mussolini*, Milan, Longanesi, 1972

—— Alberto Beneduce: l'adesione al regime mussoliniano, Paper presented at the IRI conference in Caserta in honour of A. Beneduce, November 1983

Morozzo della Rocca, Roberto, *Nazione e religione in Albania (1920–1944)*, Bologna, Il Mulino, 1990

—— *Albania. Le radici della crisi*, Milan, Guerini e Associati, 1997

Myrdal, Jan and Kessle, Gun, *Albania Defiant*, New York and London, Monthly Review Press, 1976

National Bank of Albania, Relazioni annuali, various years

Nobili Massuero, Ferdinando, La rinascita economica dell'Albania, in *Rivista di politica economica*, 1927

Oliver, Covey T., The Monetary Gold Decision in Perspective, in *The American Journal of International Law*, vol. 49, 2, April 1955

Pastorelli, Pietro, *Italia e Albania 1924–1927. Origini diplomatiche del Trattato di Tirana del 22 novembre 1927*, Florence, Biblioteca della Rivista di studi politici internazionali, 1967

—— *L'Albania nella politica estera italiana, 1914–1920*, Naples, Jovene, 1970

—— La politica estera fascista dalla fine del conflitto etiopico alla seconda guerra mondiale, in *L'Italia fra tedeschi e Alleati*, Bologna, Il Mulino, 1973

Pernack, Hans-Joachim, *Probleme der wirtschaftlichen Entwicklung Albaniens*, Munich, Südosteuropa-Studien, 18, 1972

Pirelli, Alberto, *Taccuini, 1922–1943*, Bologna, Il Mulino, 1984

Pollo, Stefanaq and Puto, Arben, *The History of Albania, from Its Origins to the Present Day*, London, Routledge & Kegan Paul, 1981

Robertson, Esmonde M., *Mussolini as Empire-Builder*, New York, St Martin's Press, 1977
Romano, Sergio, *Giuseppe Volpi: industria e finanza fra Giolitti e Mussolini*, Milan, Bompiani, 1979
Roselli, Alessandro, *Il Governatore Vincenzo Azzolini 1931–1944*, Rome and Bari, Laterza, 2000
Royal Institute of International Affairs, *The Balkan States*, London, Oxford University Press, 1936
—— *The Problem of International Investment*, London, Oxford University Press, 1937
Rumi, Giorgio, Revisionismo fascista ed espansione coloniale, in *Il regime fascista*, Bologna, Il Mulino, 1974
Salvemini, Gaetano, *Mussolini diplomatico*, Bari, Laterza, 1952
Sarti, Roland, *Fascism and the Industrial Leadership in Italy 1919–1940*, Berkeley, University of California Press, 1971
Sauser-Hall, Georges, *Arbitral Advice Pronounced in Conformity with the Agreement of Washington of 25 April 1951*, Brussels, 20 February 1953
Sayers, Richard S., *The Bank of England 1891–1944*, 3 vols, Cambridge, Cambridge University Press, 1976
Schipani, Filippo, L'organizzazione economica e l'attività produttiva dell'Albania, in *Rivista di politica economica*, 1932
Sédillot, René, *Toutes les monnaies du monde*, Paris, Recueil Sirey, 1955
Seton-Watson, Christopher, *Italy from Liberalism to Fascism 1870–1925*, London, Methuen, 1967
Skendi, Stavro, *Albania*, New York, Praeger, 1956
—— *The Albanian National Awakening 1878–1912*, Princeton, NJ, Princeton University Press, 1967
Smiley, David, *Albanian Assignment*, London, Chatto & Windus, 1984
Société des Nations, Commission Economique et Financière, Comité Financier, *La Situation Economique et Financière de l'Albanie, Rapport présenté par le professeur Albert Calmès (Luxembourg) à la suite de la mission d'études en Albanie* [Calmès Report], Geneva, September 1922
Société des Nations, Premier rapport du Conseiller financier après du gouvernement albanais, *Journal Officiel*, January 1924
—— *Annuaire Statistique*, Geneva, 1928, 1932, 1934, 1937, 1938, 1939, 1945
—— *Balances des paiements*, Geneva, 1932, 1933, 1935
Spinedi, Francesco, La Banca Nazionale d'Albania nel mercato finanziario mondiale, in *Rassegna monetaria*, 1936, nn. 7–8
Sulliotti, Italo, *In Albania. Sei mesi di regno*, Milan, Treves, 1914
Swire, Joseph, *Albania: The Rise of a Kingdom*, London, Williams & Norgate, 1929 (the quotations are taken from the reprint by Arno Press and *New York Times*, 1971)
Tajani, Filippo, Le comunicazioni albanesi, in *Principii di economia albanese*, Padua, Cedam, 1940
Teichova, Alice, Industry, in M. Kaser and E. A. Radice (eds), *The Economic History of Eastern Europe 1919–1975*, 3 vols, Oxford, Clarendon Press, 1985
Tomes, Jason, *King Zog: Self-made Monarch of Albania*, Stroud, Sutton Publishing, 2003
Toniolo, Gianni, *L'economia dell'Italia fascista*, Rome and Bari, Laterza, 1980
United Nations, *National Accounts Main Aggregates*, unstats.un.org

Vickers, Miranda, *The Albanians: A Modern History*, London and New York, I. B. Tauris, 1995
Volpe, Gioacchino, *Formazione storica dell'Albania*, Rome, Reale Accademia d'Italia, 1939
—— *L'Italia moderna*, Florence, Sansoni, 1949
Webster, Richard A., *Industrial Imperialism in Italy, 1908–1915*, Berkeley, University of California Press, 1975
Zamboni, Giovanni, *Mussolini Expansionpolitik auf dem Balkan*, Hamburg, H. Buske, 1970

The Albanian Lek, in *International Currency Review*, July 1977
Aspetti economici dell'Albania, in *Rivista di politica economica*, 1939
Banka Kombëtare e Shqipnis, 1926
Un decennio di vita della SVEA, Rome, La Libreria dello Stato, 1936
The Kingdom of Albania, New York, Italian Library of Information, 1939
Premier et deuxième mémoire du gouvernement italien dans l'affaire de l'or de la Banque Nationale d'Albanie, Rome, Ministero Affari Esteri, 1952
La questione dell'oro della Banca Nazionale d'Albania avanti la Corte internazionale di Giustizia, in *Rivista di diritto internazionale*, 1954
Situazione economica dell'Albania, Report presented to the International Chamber of Commerce, Stockholm, 1927

3 Newspapers, magazines and news agencies

Agenzia Stefani
Corriere della Sera
The Economist
Frankfurter Zeitung
Il Messaggero
Il Sole
Südost Echo
La Tribuna

Index